ISBN 978-0-331-21379-9
PIBN 11029098

THE LOWER-CANADA WATCHMAN.

Pro Patria.

Kingston, U. C.

1829.

James Macfarlane, Printer.

DEDICATED,

Without either solicitation or permission,

TO

George, Earl of Dalhousie,

LATE GOVERNOR-IN-CHIEF

OF

BRITISH NORTH AMERICA,

NOW

Commander of the Forces

IN

INDIA;

AS A MARK OF THE AUTHOR'S RESPECT FOR STERN UNYIELDING PATRIOTISM, STRICT FIDELITY TO PUBLICK TRUST, AND THE GENUINE GENEROSITY OF A BRAVE SOLDIER.

of that Constitution which is a counterpart of the noblest production of the mind of man. *How* I have performed this task is not for me to determine. But I assure all CANADA, that there is not an individual within her bounds who is more ardently attached to her interests, or more zealously devoted to her rights and liberties. I have no motive for being otherwise disposed. I have broke in upon private engagements, and disturbed the repose and even tenor of domestick life for the sake of my Country. To the best of my abilities, I have warned that country of its danger ; and it only remains for me to pray for its welfare.

I admit that, in doing so, I have made use of strong language on various occasions, and towards several individuals. But how is insolence to be checked, and public crimes punished, but through the medium of persons? Like the assassin and the highway robber, they are themselves alone to blame who have become obnoxious to publick censure. If *I* have assumed to myself the scales or the sword of justice, it is because my country has called me to an office as yet unoccupied by an abler man. Therefore, the sentences which I have given, are not the decisions of a frenzied imagination, nor of an arbitrary and vindictive heart; but the plain dictates of reason, and the imperative voice of the law. I am, or, at least, ought not to be, no more obnoxious to odium or personal malignity, than the ermined Judge who proaenneea doom on the most abandoned malefactor. I have not gone in search of victims to offended justice. They have voluntarily presented themselves before me at the bar of publick responsibility.

I am not a stranger to the cant which has of late become so fashionable with respect to strong language; but nothing, be it ever so popular, will ever drive me out of my course, if it interfere with the principles of true honor or the salvation of my country. I have accordingly used the language which I conceived most applicable to the nature of the work; and I feel no compunction for having done so.

Should the CRITICKS deign to notice this humble production, I beg leave candidly to inform them, that though I respect their ingenuity, I entertain but little dread of their ill nature. I have declared towards the conclusion of the volume, that I wrote neither for fame nor profit. I therefore hold myself amenable to no tribunal whatever, save the judgment-seat of patriotism and true love of British liberty and justice. This is the only tribunal that I shall ever respect as a public writer; and to none else shall I ever bow with submission.

Upon the whole, I am not without my hopes but this work will produce some good effects, even in a country where there is but little public opinion, and where the influence of the press itself is but feeble and instable. I shall therefore conclude in the words of JUNIUS:—" When Kings and Ministers are forgotten, when the force and direction of personal satire is no longer understood, and

1st June, 1829.

THE LOWER CANADA WATCHMAN.

No. I.

However slightly the circumstances attending the dissolution of the late Provincial Parliament may have been viewed, and whatever degree of importance may have been attached to the cause of that dissolution, and the unparalleled situation of this Province in general, it was impossible to look forward to the meeting of a new Parliament otherwise than with expectations of the deepest and most fervent interest. In truth, the history of this Province, fertile as it has been of incidents calculated to rouse the feelings and excite the prejudices of a mixed and unharmonizing population, never presented a period which can be compared to the present, either as to the magnitude of the prize at stake, or the dangers which beset either its attainment or final abandonment. It was, therefore, with feelings of no ordinary satisfaction that we beheld even the most indifferent to public affairs looking forth with an eye of eager anxiety to the twelfth of November, the day appointed by his Excellency the Governor in Chief for meeting the Provincial Parliament. If the result has unhappily been found to disappoint the real friends of the Country, there still remains behind the pleasing consolation, that, in a government like ours, the native inherent powers of the constitution are sufficiently sound and healthful to withstand whatever attacks may be made upon them either from foreign force or internal corruption.

The style and form of opening our Provincial Parliaments I must be familiar to every one; but as it is our intention to preserve some record of the one which has just been congregated, and to make such remarks now and hereafter as its proceedings may justify, and the situation of the country may require, we shall give a concise but correct detail of the proceedings attending the opening of the first, and we fear the *last*, session of the Thirteenth Provincial Parliament of Lower Canada.

The 2)th of Nov. being the day appointed for this purpose, the Governor in Chief went down in state to the Legislative Council Chamber, and being seated on the Throne, the gentleman Usher of the Black Rod was ordered to desire the attendance of the house of Assembly; and that house being come up, the honorable Speaker of the Legislative Council informed them, that he was commanded by his Excellency to say, that he did not think it fit to declare the cause of summoning this Provincial Parliament until there should be a Speaker of the House of Assembly; and that it was, therefore, his Excelloney's pleasure, that they should repair to the place where their sittings were usually held, and there make choice of a fit person to be their Speaker, and to present the person who should be so chosen to his Excellency in that house. the next day at 2 o'clock, for his approbation: At the time appointed, his Excellency again went down to the Legislative Council Chamber, and being seated on the Throne, and the Members of the Assembly being in attendance below the Bar, Louis Joseph Papineau, Speaker elect, announced that the choice of the Assembly had fallen upon him. The usual terms of this annunciation we believe to be as follows:

" *May it please your Excellency*,

"In obedience to your Excellency's commands, the house of Assembly of the Province of Lower Canada, have proceeded to the election of a Speaker, and I am the person upon whom has fallen the honour of their choice.

"The extent and importance of the duties attached to that exalted station being far above my powers, and my zeal, however ardent, not sufficiently compensating for my incapacity, I *most respectfully implore the excuse and commands of your Excellency*."

On Mr. Papineau's pronouncing this harangue, the hon. Speaker of the Legislative Council answered as follows:

Mr. Papineau, and gentlemen of the Assembly,

"*I am commanded* by his Excellency the Governor in Chief to inform you that his Excellency doth not approve the choice which the Assembly have made of a Speaker, and in his Majesty's name his Excellency doth accordingly now disallow and discharge the said choice.

"And it is his Excellency's pleasure that you gentlemen of the Assembly do forthwith again repair to the place where the sittings of the Assembly are usually held, and there make choice of another person to be your Speaker—and that you present the person who shall be so chosen to his Excellency in this House on Friday next at 2 o'clock for his approbation.

"And I am further directed by his Excellency to inform you, that as soon as a Speaker of the Assembly has been chosen with the approbation of the Crown, his Excellency will lay before the Provincial Parliament certain communications upon the present state of this Province, which by his Majesty's express command he has been directed to make known to them."

Though this is the first instance in this Province, and, with the exception of one in Nova Scotia in 1806,* the first in British *America*, as at present constituted, of the exercise of this particular prerogative of the Crown; yet, neither the Country, nor the house of Assembly, nor Mr. Papineau himself, beheld such an event either unanticipated or with surprise. It is true that, with reference to the long subsisting and daily increasing Legislative difficulties of this Province—the public misery and domestic heartburnings in which it has for years been involved—the necessity which has now become absolute of adopting some effectual plan for preserving the integrity of the Province—and the general hope entertained that the deliberations of

* See Appendix No. I.

the new Assembly would lead to some-final adjustment of our present most unnatural and destructive dilemma, induced many well-disposed persons to think, that with whatever justice the prerogative of negative upon the Speaker of the house of Assembly might be exercised in referrence to Mr. Papineau, in the event of his being elected, the rudeness of the man himself, and the vain and insolent folly of his friends in the Assembly, might once more be passed over in silence as the effervescence of over-acted party zeal, in order to come as speedily as possible to some point of adjustment of our protracted difficulties. But there are others, and we candidly confess ourselves to be one of the number, who, witnessing with disgust aud abhorrence that tissue of loathsome defamation, vulgar abuse, mean insolence, daring libel, seditious menace, and blackguard scurrility, with which the Government of this Province, and especially the distinguished individual who represents his Majesty in it, have been incessantly assailed for some time back, by a party and a set of low unprincipled scribblers, of whom Mr. Papineau has become the head leader, and organ, came, without hesitation to the conclusion, that, not only would the dignity of Majesty itself be compromised, but the very source of honour sullied, and of justice corrupted, if one of those legal checks, so wisely prescribed by the constitution, were not at the proper time put in force against an individual when exalted to a situation which brought him in immediate contact with the objects of his abuse and slander. It was, therefore, with the most unfeigned and heart-cheering satisfaction that this respectable and stable majority of all that is sound and healthful in the political constitution of the country, beheld the exercise of a prerogative which, however much it may be despised, contemned and rejected by those whose ambition it curbs, or whose insolence it destroys, is one of the most sacred and unimpaired of all the rights and privileges entrusted by the Constitution to the King's prudence and discretion. The thanks of the country are due to his Excellency for the manly and decisive manner in which he exercised the prerogative in question, and for that calm tone of dignity and self-possession with which he placed himself between the Crown and one of the mast bloated and destructive inroads upon government and the constitution that ever was devised in a British Colony. We have no doubt but the approbetiou of the Imperial Government and of the Mother Country at large, by whom the rights of King and people are better understood and more liberally interpreted than by a certain class of persons in this Province, waits so honest and faithful a public servant.

As to the Speaker elect, it is very evident, that, however much he may have endeavoured on this trying occasion to quell the tumultuous emotions which arose in his soul, and to conceal from himself the despicable and degrading figure which he cut in the eye of his country, he felt the full force of his fallen condition. The scene was indeed a most humbling one; and such as no man of honor, virtue, or true patriotism, would ever wish to be placed in. But perhaps we do not say too much when we assert, that it was an element congenial to the sentiments and disposition of Mr. Papineau. This much is certain, if we may judge from his past conduct, in which we have never been able to discover any thing bordering on what is either great or dignified, that the more he embroils himself with the constituted authorities of the country, and the deeper he involves himself in the vain and fruitless attempt to elevate himself by the degradation of his betters, the more his self-complacency gets the better of his judgment, and the lower he sinks in the opinion of those who can form a proper estimate of the dignity of human nature. There he stood, however, under the contemptuous but well-meritted ban of his Sovereign, a scathed and miserable monument of indiscretions and follies, if not of political crimes which, for the honour of our country and mankind, we would fain conceal, but which, for the sake of truth and justice, it is our duty and intention to make as public as the rising and setting of the sun. For the present, however, we shall content ourselves with the enumeration of such of them as we conceive to have been a well-grounded reason for denying to him the approbation of his Majesty as Speaker of the house of Assembly during the present Parliament.

We shall say nothing of Mr. Papineau's anti-British prejudices—of his natural and avowed antipathy to British customs, manners, language, laws and government; neither shall we trace him into those dark and retired circles where his influence is most felt, and his fiat more readily obeyed. His public acts are sufficient for our present purpose. Is there then any man in the country who does not know, that Mr. Papineau, inheriting from a long line of ancestry, which he himself and his ready scribes and flattering satellites throughout the country describe as having been *noble*, but which no individual living can trace beyond the limits of Dr. Johnson's forefathers, which, notwithstanding all his learning, he admitted he could not do beyond his grandfather, all the prejudices and antipathies natural to so obscure an origin, has many years since formed and put himself at the head of a party whose sole object it is to create such a distinction between his Majesty's old and new subjects in this Province, as will pave the way, if not to their ultimate separation, at least to such a state of things as will place in the hands of the party in question the entire management and administration of public affairs? With this disgraceful project before his eyes, which could scarcely excite the ambition of a Canibal Gaffra Chief, he has never ceased, since he has become a public character, to pour forth, by means of declamation, as tumid as it is insidious and irrational, the most dangerous doctrines that can possibly be listened to in a Province like this, composed, as it unfortunately is, of a population much divided in political opinions, and the majority of which is in a high and alarming degree inflamable when the brand of commotion is applied by a hand whose community of birth, language, and manners, is tantamount to the imperative voice of legal authority. Few countries, however peaceful and happy, but are cursed and disgraced by characters of this description; but in no country that we know of is the evil likely to produce such destructive and desolating consequences as in Lower Canada, if not checked and absolutely put down in proper time. Generally speaking, the Demagogues of Europe act on their own insolated responsibility until their projects are ripe for action, and derive no other authority from law or other public institutions than is the birthright of every member of the community. In this Province, however, the case is very different. Here, from the peculiar construction of society, our Demagogues, and they are neither few nor small, are also our Legislators! Our chief Demagogue has been Speaker of the house of Assembly for six saccessive Parliaments! It is thus that the poor Canadians are deceived.—Their simplicity and ignorance are so great, that they believe Mr. Papineau and his bandits to be acting under public authority, and with the express approbation of a constitutional government.—None need be told how propitious and advantageous such a state of things must be for carrying on the machinations of the party opposed to government and headed by Mr. Papineau; nor how dextrous these gentlemen are on all occasions, in availing themselves of it. Even the journals of the house of Assembly bear witness to the insolence of this party, and of Mr. Papineau in particular, in defaming and libelling the most necessary and legal acts of government; and it is equally his disgrace that the walls of Parliament have re-echoed times without number declamation the most personally abusive of the noble and exalted individual who at present administers the government of the Province. Many proofs might be given in support of this assertion; but we deem it sufficient at present to refer the reader back to some debates which took place in the house of Assembly in the Session of 1825, when the Governor in Chief was in England, and with regard to whom expressions are said to have been made use of which would disgrace the lowest pot-house in Quebec. The resolutions passed last year in the Assembly, with respect to *supplies* and *despatches*, bear ample testimony to the contempt with which Mr. Papineau and his gang have ever been disposed to treat the constitutional communications emanating from the present head of the Provincial government.

Out of Parliament, the conduct of Mr. Papineau has been equally glaring and unconstitutional. No sooner was the last Parliament prorogued, than he published a *Manifesto*, breathing not only revenge and defiance to the Governor in Chief personally, but teeming with a tissue of the grossest prevarication and the foulest abuse that ever fell from the tongue or the pen of any individual of the least pretensions to education or genteel society. In that well known production, published in the face of all the laws of decency, and every principle of a constitutional government like ours, and rendered eternally infamous by the well-applied castigation of our friend, a fellow labourer, Delta, Mr. Papineau not only charges his Excellency with altering what was *false*, in his proroguing speech, but the King himself, and the imperial government, with having confirmed and sanctioned an act granting supplies in 1825, which they had been actually disallowed and disapproved of *in Council!*

But there are a few more items in our account against Mr. Papineau. Fearing, as he had just cause to do, that his own *Manifesto* would not have the effect of rousing what his Chief Scribe at Montreal calls the "*slumbering energies of the country,*" he prepared a number of resolutions, disapproving of the prorogation of the late Parliament and the general conduct of the Governor in Chief, which he circulated to his numerous emissaries throughout the province; begging of them not to lose a moment in calling public meetings to adopt these ready made declarations of his own and his party's purity, to the utter disgrace of the *Governor*—not the government. In a few places, where the time and the vanity of the people exceeded their good sense, this brand of discord took effect; but to the honour of the people in general, and the consternation of Mr. Papineau, *this method* of embroiling the country in an open rupture with the government that protected its rights and independence, did not succeed. For a time Mr. Papineau was left to his own resources; and, in justice to his zeal and activity in the cause of anarchy, it must be admitted, that he made the best possible use of them. His address and speeches to the electors of Montreal may be placed in competition with the most chaste and eloquent productions of Hunt and Gobbet, for awakening the people to a senso of their degradation under the present system of things, and in inducing them to throw aside that respect, attachment, and gratitude, which they owe to the government under which they live, and, we have no hesitation to add, live contented and happily too, in despite of Mr. Papineau and his loathsome popular harangues. In any other country but this, the *Husting harangues* of this man would degrade the individual who uttered them far beneath those wonders of eloquence which we so frequently find congregated amidst the haunts of the weaving and cobbling politicians of the manufacturing towns of England. They did not contain a single patriotic sentiment, nor one passage worthy of rehearsal by the lowest and most ignorant blockhead that stood gaping at their utterance, if we except, and except them we must, in such an inquiry as the present, these sublime passages which heaped such a depth of odium and disgrace on the admininistrator of the provincial government. As to the address of thanks, it is one of the most unique things we have ever perased. There it stands before us as copied into the Canadian *Courant*, confirmatory, to use its own words, of "*the sentence of condemnation which has been already passed by the whole country from end to end against the claim of the Executive*;" and the disgrace equally of the author and those to whom it is addressed.

One charge more, and we have done for the present with such of Mr. Speaker's elect delinquencies as legally debar him from being the organ of communication with his Majesty's representative in either or any branch of the legislative body. There are three newspapers published in Montreal, which we scorn to name, as they are utterly beneath even the most contemptuous regard. It is the sole business of these journals to belch forth every species of abuse and defamation that words are capable of conveying against his Excellency the Governor in Chief of this province, in his public as well as in his private conduct and character. As a proof of their outrageous and insolent conduct, the authors of one and all of them have been lately presented by the Grand Jury of the District which they contaminate with their scandalous vulgarity for libels upon the most sacred institutions of civil society. Mr. Papineau is the chief patron and supporter of all those journals! Need we say any more?

Who now, we boldly ask, will dare to blame the Governor in Chief for refusing to convoy his Majesty's approbation of the choice made by the Aessembly of Mr. Papinenu as their Speaker? If there be any such, let them take their stand with Mr. Papineau and his colleagues, for it is high time that the people of this Province should rank themselves for or against the constitution, that the good may be distinguished from the bad, that the loyal may be known from the disloyal, and true Britons, known from their enemies.

It is evident that tho members of the house of Assembly, upon the refusal of the Governor to sanction the man of their election as prolocutor, departed to their own apartment under feelings of high and unusual irritation, and of this we desire no better proof than the tumultuous and disorderly manner in which they conducted their proceedings on arriving at their usual arena of debate. Their exit from the Legislative Council Chamber might not inaptly be compared to a pack of tarriers just unkenneled with their leashes ready to be slipped for the purpose of beginning the sports of the day, but who had been in an unauspicious moment countermanded by their Lord, and sent back to their den howling with rage and disappointment. And there we leave them for the present, intending, before we proceed to the investigation of their ulterior conduct, to consider the basis upon which the prerogative of the crown was founded and exercised upon the present occasion.

Before doing so, however, we may be permitted to state, as a piece of antiquarian lore, that authors are not agreed either as to the period when the Speaker first appeared in the house of Commons, or the individual who first filled that important and distinguished situation. This office, like the constitution itself, dawned upon mankind amidst those clouds of feudal barbarism which still hung heavily over England even towards the middle of the thirteenth century; and when, like the Astronomy of the Chaldeans, though there might be many to study and admire, there was no hand to record so invaluable a privilege. It is peremptorily stated in the Parliamentary history, that Sir Peter de le Mare, Knight of the Shire of Herefordshire, who was chosen Speaker in the first Parliament of Richard II. is the first Speaker on record. Yet, upon the authority of the 51st of Edward III. 1376, a year before his death and the accession of his grandson, Richard II. it appears, that Sir Thomas Hungerford, is mentioned on the last day of the Parliament as being Speaker of the house of Commons: The words of the Roll are, 'Qi *avoit les Paroles pur les Communes d' Engleterre en cest Parlement*." In the discussion of this point, it seems, however, to be forgotten, that in presenting a petition to Edward III. to remove from his person the celebrated *Alics Pierce*, the favorite of his dotage, and others, Sir Peter de la Mare appeared as

Speaker of the Commons; and though it is asserted that he was not Speaker, "*but a considerable Knight of Herefordshire, both for prudence and* eloquence," yet it seems unaccountable how he should undertake the duties of Speaker on so delicate an occasion without having been legally inducted in the office. Be this as it may upon the death of the Black Prince, the favourites were recalled to court, and poor Sir Peter was imprisoned for a twelve month for the discharge of the Speaker's duty.

The first instance on record of the exercise of that branch of the royal prerogative which empowers the King to dissallow the choice of Speaker of the house of Commons, took place in 1450, and in the reign of Henry VI. Sir John Popham was chosen Speaker, but his excuse was accepted by the King, and he was discharged in these words:—"Rex ipsum suam excusationem admisit, et ipsum de occupatione predicta exoneravit."* On the same *day* the Commons presented William Tresham, Esq. *for the same purpose*, who was allowed. On the 22d of Feb. 1592, Sir Edward Coke, in his disabling speech, says, "*this is only as yet a nomination and no election, until your Majesty giveth allowance and approbation.*"

On the 6th of March, 1678, the Commons

* See Appendix No. II. which contains in ample detail a host of precedents from such authorities as it would be more than Quixotick to attempt to combat.

chose Sir Edward Seymour, Speaker; but on his being presented to the King,—Charles II. on the 7th, the Lord Chancellor, by his Majesty's command, disapproves of him, and directs them to proceed to another choice.

It appears from *Hatsell*, who records these precedents, that Seymour knew, that it had been determined at a Council the night previous to the meeting of the Parliament, to accept of his excuse, on account of some dispute he had at the time with Lord Danby, *a mere minister of the Crown, and* in no *shape representing the King*, purposely avoided making any, in order to puzzle the Lord Chancellor in refusing him. However, it is certain, that notwithstanding this stratagem, that his election was disapproved of, and that he was excused, as above stated, by the Lord Chancellor from performing the duties of Speaker. The account which the historian *Rapin* gives of the whole of this matter is worthy of being transcribed and perused at length.

"The Parliament," says he, "began with a warm dispute between the King and the Commons, about the choice of a Speaker.—The Commons chose Mr. * Edward Seymour, the King, who knew Seymour, was a particular enemy of the Earl of Danby, refused his approbation, and ordered the Commons to proceed to a new choice. The House was extremely displeased with this re-

---

* He is designed *Sir* elsewhere. He was Treasurer of the Navy at this time.

fusal, alleging, *that it was never known that a person should be excepted against, and no reason at all given, and that the thing itself of presenting a speaker to the King was but a bare compliment*—The King, on his side, insisted on the approbation or refusal of the Speaker when presented to him, as a branch of the prerogative. During a six day's dispute the Commons made several representations to the King, to which he gave very short answers. At last, as the Commons would not desist from what they thought their right, the King went to the Parliament, and prorogued it from the 13th to the 15th; that is, for one day's interval between the two Sessions. The Parliament meeting on the 15th, the King ordered the Commons to proceed to the choice of a Speaker. Then, to avoid a revival of the disputo, they chose *Mr. William Gregory*, Sergeant at Law, who was approved by the King." †

It thus seems to be the undoubted and inherent prerogative of the crown, that, in all cases, and under all circumstances, no Speaker can legally act as such until his election, or rather his "*nomination*," as Coke terms it, be approved and confirmed by the King.—Our great constitutional lawyer, *Blackstone*, speaks concisely but decidedly on this point: *The Speaker of the House of Commons*," says he, vol. 1. p. 181, " is CHOSEN *by the House, but* MUST *be approved by the King*."

But the question at present at issue is, whether this prerogative extends to the King's

Representatives in the Colonies, without being specially and in express terms conferred by letters patent or by law? So far as regards these Provinces, the constitution of which is modelled with great care and precision on that of the Mother Country, the best and safest answer that can be given to this question is, that if His Majesty's representative cannot exercise this particular prerogative in common with those which stand on a similar basis, so neither can our Houses of Assembly make choice of a Speaker. The constitutional act, though it authorises the Governor to appoint the Speaker of the Legislative Council, is nevertheless silent as to the right of the Assembly to make choice of its own Speaker. It may, indeed, be presumed, from the *twenty-seventh* section of that act, that the Assembly are entitled to have a Speaker; but his powers are thereby wholly confined, like that of his colleague of the Legislative Council, to the casting vote in case of an equality of voices. If, therefore, the Assembly have a right, without the *express* authority of the constitution to elect a Speaker, surely the Governor, as the representative of the King, has an equal right to exercise every legal prerogative of the Crown, the one in question as well as all the rest. The one privilege is contingent upon the other; nor can the one in our system of Government, exist without the other. In a word, if the Assembly have a right to elect a Speaker, the Governor has an equal right to confirm or reject their *nomination* as he may think most conducive to his own dignity, and the interests of the country.

That this special prerogative *has* been extended to, and actually exercised in the British Colonies, there cannot be a doubt in the mind of any one who has read their history. The Nova-Scotia case before referred to, ought to carry great weight along with it. There is, however, a more remarkabe, and, perhaps, a stronger case now lying before us, the particulars of which we shall state in a few words. A short time after the accession of Geo. I. to the Crown of Great Britain, he appointed Colonel Shute, a highly respectable officer, who had served under the Duke of Marlborough, to the Government of New-England. The conduct of Colonel Shute was highly meritorious; but, as has almost uniformly been the case with every Governor coming to the Colonies, he failed in gaining the cordial co-operation of the Legislature; and the Assembly gave him so much trouble, that he was at last forced to carry oyer to England a complaint against them; a constitutional practice which we could wish were practiced more frequently in our own times. Mr. *Cook*, the agent for the Representatives complained of, admitted the charges to be true, *except* the second and fourth, which consisted of "*Refusing the* Governor's NEGATIVE of the Speaker," and "adjourning themselves for more than two days at a time." With respect to these two articles not acknowledged, an *explanatory charter* was made out in the 12th of Geo.

II. which contains the following clause—"Whereas, in their Charter nothing is directed *concerning a Speaker* of the House of Representatives, and of their adjourning themselves, it is hereby ordered, that the Governor or Commander in *Chief shall have a* NEGATIVE *in the election of the Speaker*; and the House of Representatives may adjourn themselves not exceeding two days at a time."

But we find that we must postpone the further consideration of this very important question till our next.

No. II.

The main object of our last was to establish, by precedents, usage, and history, the uninterrupted existence till this day of one of the most ancient prerogatives of the Crown—the power of confirming or rejecting the individual nominated by the House of Commons as its Speaker; and, by consequence, the right of the King's Representative not only in this, but in every other British Province in the enjoyment of a representative government, to exercise similar prerogatives. This important constitutional point established, our purpose at present is to enquire, not *whether*—for that can never be made a question in the mind of any one who has studied the British Constitution for an hour—but how deeply and dangerously the majority of the House of Assembly of this Province have involved themselves in an attempt to abrogate a prerogative, which, although the factious spirit of party may have sometimes repelled and questioned it, has never been abrogated in that country and government from which we not only have received our political existence, but profess to borrow every constitutional maxim necessary to the preservation of so popular, but so permanent a species of government. In order, however, to avoid all recurrence in future to a right established on so firm, and, we hope, so lasting a basis, and which no man will ever dare to question except he who is ready to combat every principle of good government, we deem it necessary to put down in this place such additional proofs and precedents of the existence of the prerogative in question, as the industry of our contemporaries and our own researches have placed at our command. We shall then discuss the matter fully armed; and think that by bringing the facts and reasoning of the one side into visible, direct, full, and decisive conflict with the other, we shall be able to withdraw from the contest with all the laurels that can be won in such a field of controversy.

We have already given at length RAPIN's account of the circumstances which attended the election and rejection as Speaker, of Seymour, in 1678. HUME's account of them is equally interesting, and no less worthy of perusal:

But the King soon found that, notwithstanding this precaution, notwithstanding his concurrence of the prosecution of the Popish plot, notwithstanding the zeal which he expressed, and even at this time exercised against the Catholics, he had nowise obtained the confidence of his Parliament.

"The refractory humour of the Lower House appeared in the very first step which they took upon their assembling. It had ever been usual for the commons in the selection of their Speaker to consult the inclinations of their Sovereign, and even the long Parliament in 1641 had not thought proper to depart from so established a custom. The King now desired that the choice should fall on Sir Thomas Meres; but Seymour, Speaker to the last Parliament, was instantly called to the Chair, by a vota which seemed unanimous. The King, when Seymour was presented to him for his approbation, rejected him and ordered the Commons to proceed to a new choice. A great flame was excited. The Commons maintained that the King's approbation was merely a matter of form, and that he could not, without giving a reason, reject the Speaker chosen. The King, that, since he had the power of rejecting, he might, if he pleased, keep the reason in his own breast. As the question had never been before started, it might seem difficult to find principles upon which it could be decided. By way of compromise it was agreed to set aside both candidates. Gregory, a Lawyer, was chosen, and the election was ratified by the King. It has ever since been understood that the choice of the Speaker lies in the House, but that the King retains the power of rejecting any person disagreeable to him." —*Pocket Edition, Vol. IX., p. 233.*

The *Notes* subjoined to this text are very important :—" In 1566 the Speaker said to Queen Elizabeth, that *without her allowance* the election of the House was of no significance.—*D'Ewes' Journal*, p. 97. In the Parliament of 1592—93, the Speaker, who was Sir Edward Coke, advances a like position.---*D'Ewes*, p. 459. *Townshend*, p. 35. So that this pretension of the Commons"—that is, of persisting in their choice of Speaker—"seems to have been somewhat new; like many other powers and privileges." Bolingbroke, writing of these times, accounts in a manner for the usurpations of the Commons in Seymour's case, by saying of the Commons---"that they lost their temper on some particular occasions must not be denied. They were men, and therefore frail."

We copy the following cases from the Quebec *Mercury* and the *Montreal Gazette, by Authority*.

Woodeson says, (vol. 1. p. 57,) "The Commons cannot sit without a Speaker after their first meeting," and this is also laid down in the 4th Institutes, pp. 7 and 8.

In the mode of appointing the Speaker, some change has taken place since the revolution, but the leading principle that the Royal approval is necessary to give effect to the choice of the Commons, has never been disputed.

The manner of electing the Speaker is explained by Whitelock, vol. 1. p. 224.

"Then the Commons repayre to their house, and usually some of the members before acquainted with the King's mind doth nominate one among them to be chosen for their Speaker whereon there is seldom contradiction. Coke saith (4 Inst. p. 8) that after their choice the King may refuse him, and that the course is, for avoiding expense of time and contest, as in the Conge d'Elire of a Bishop, that the King doth name a discreet and learned man whom the Commons elect; he adds that the Speaker is so necessary that the House of Commons cannot sit without him."---*Whitelock*, vol. 1. p. 224.

"In 1778---79, on the meeting of the then new Parliament, Charles Wolfran Cornwall, Esq. was proposed by Lord North as Speaker, in preference to Sir Fletcher Norton (afterwards the first Lord Grantley,) who had filled that office during the preceding Parliament, and Lord North gave as one of the reasons for this extraordinary step, that it would be useless to elect Sir Fletcher, inasmuch as he was personally obnoxious to the Sovereign, and that this feeling would operate as a cause for his rejection and disallowance. The event is familiar to every one acquainted with the Parliamentary annals of that period, and is therefore unnecessary for us to lengthen our remarks with the cause of the objection to Sir Fletcher. In consequence of this intimation from the Minister and perhaps for other motives, Mr. Cornwall was chosen, and afterwards allowed."

We are indebted to the *Quebec Official Gazette*, for the following important information. The Nova-Scotia case alluded to, in conjunction with the New England one detailed in our last, forms a remarkable connecting link between the mother country and the Colonies in regard to this royal prorogative.

"Just one hundred years ago, Speaker

Onslow, when he was elected by the Commons to that Chair which he filled for 33 years with unequalled ability, and in which, says Hatsell, the distinguishing feature of his conduct was 'a regard and veneration for the British Constitution as it was declared and established at the revolution,' this eminent Parliamentary authority thus addressed his Sovereign, 'Happy is it, Sir, for your Commons, that your *Majesty's disapprobation* will give them an opportunity to reconsider what they have done. I am therefore to implore your Majesty to *command your Commons* to do what they can very easily perform, *to make choice of another person* more proper for them to present to your Majesty.'

"In Nova-Scotia, in the year 1806, a Speaker chosen by the Assembly was disapproved by the then Lieutenant Governor; the Assembly proceeded to another election and chose the other candidate who had been before unsuccessful, but who was more acceptable to the Governor, and was accordingly approved. The only notice which the Assembly thought it proper to take of this rejection, was in the following paragraph of their address in answer to the Speech: While we lament that your Excellency has been pleased to exercise a branch of His Majesty's prorogative long unused in Great Britain, and without precedent in this Province, we beg leave to assure your Excellency that we shall not fail to cultivate a good understanding," &c. &c.*

---

* See again Appendix No. 1.

It now becomes our painful but necessary duty to detail the conduct and question the right of the House of Assembly in refusing to acknowledge the exercise on the part of the Crown of this prerogative, established, as we have seen it has been, on the same basis and by the same authority as the most sacred privileges claimed by the Assembly itself.

When the Assembly returned to the Chamber of its deliberations, in obedience, to the directions of the Governor in Chief, the Speaker *elect*, contrary to all precedents, especially the remarkable one of Sir Edward Seymour, who did not assume the chair, and as if that were necessary to fill to the brim the cup of his hostile feelings, insolence and malignity towards the King's representative, to whom, for once at least, he was compelled to succumb, took, without any hesitation, the chair, and caused the mace to be laid on the table. Nor could the voice of the constitution, declared by several members of the House in a manner that might force conviction upon any understanding but his own, prevail upon him to retire from it, until he had intimated to the House the terms in which his election as Speaker was disapproved of by the Governor in Chief; thus rendering himself in the eyes and the ears of his country the herald of his own degradation and downfall. No man possessed of a spark of modesty, or the least notion of that respect cultivated by every man of honour and virtue towards the constituted authorities of his country could ever have assumed a station fit only for brass or marble. But Mr. Papineau differs from other men on a variety of subjects; but on none more than that great and useful maxim of private and public society, which enjoins a respect for others by a diffident respect of ourselves. Sir Edward Seymour's example might, in this instance at least, be followed to great, creditable, and lasting advantage.

We stated in our last that the debate which took place on the return of the Assembly to its own place of sittings, so far as regarded the majority, was tumultuary and unconstitutional. This has since been denied; but the denial came from a source unworthy of a moment's hearing, when the united voice of our contemporaries and of many respcotable individuals present, loudly and emphatically declare otherwise. It is, therefore, unworthy of being detailed at length in this place, though, in the sequel, some of the principles laid down in it may be adverted to, in order to be confuted. We shall here content ourselves with what may be termed the *official* results of this debate; and the first before us is the resolutions proposed to the House by *Mr. Cuvillier*—resolutions which, from the information we have received, and many concurring circumstances, we have no hesitation to assert, were prepared at Montreal long previous to that and the other member's simoltaneous embarkation for Quebec, in the full anticipation of *Mr. Papineau's* rejection as peaker elect, by the Governor in Chief. These resolutions will long be had in remembrance, no less on account of the studied strain of insult in which they are couched with respect to the King's representative, than for the daring novelty, gross ignorance, presumptive insolence, and menacing unconstitutional principles which, from end to end pervade the whole.

"Resolved :—

"1° That it is necessary for the discharge of the duties imposed upon this House, viz : to give its advice to His Majesty in the enactment of Laws for the peace, welfare, and good government of the Province, conformably to the Act of the British Parliament under which it is constituted and assembled, that the Speaker be a person of its free choice independently of the will and pleasure of the person entrusted by His Majesty with the administration of the local Government for the time being.

"2° That Louis Joseph Papineau, one of the Members of this House, who has served as Speaker in six successive Parliaments, has been duly chosen by this House to be its Speaker in the present Parliament.

"3° That the act of the British Parliament under which this House is constituted and assembled, does not require the approval of such person so chosen as Speaker by the person administering the Government of this Province in the name of His Majesty.

"4° That the presenting of the person so elected as Speaker to the King's Representative for approval is founded on usage only, and that such approval is and has always been a matter of course.

"5° That this House doth persist in its choice, and that the said Louis Joseph Papineau, Esq. ought to be and is its Speaker."

These Resolutions, after an interval of adjournment, having been sanctioned and agreed to by a *majority of thirty-nine* to *four*, the following address to His Excellency, copied from that which the Commons presented to the King in Seymour's case, in 1678, was voted, and a committee appointed to wait on His Excellency to learn when he would be pleased to receive it.

"May it please your Excellency,

"We, His Majesty's dutiful and loyal subjects, the Assembly of Lower Canada, in Provincial Parliament assembled, having taken into our most serious consideration the communication made to us by the Speaker of the Legislative Council, by order of your Excellency, respecting our choice of a Speaker, humbly request your Excellency to be fully assured that we sincerely respect the rights of His Majesty and his Royal prerogative, which we acknowledge to be annexed to His Imperial Crown for the benefit and protection of his people. We are fully assured that your Excellency could intend nothing which could destroy or diminish our constitutional privileges, without which we cannot fulfil our important duties towards his Majesty and his people of this Province, and in this persuasion we in all humility submit to your Excellency that it is the incontestible right of the Commons of this Province to have the free election of one of their members to be their Speaker, and perform the duty of their House; that the speaker so elected and afterwards presented to the King's Representative, according to usage, ought always by uniform practice to be continued as Speaker, and fulfil his office as such, unless he be therefrom excused from corporeal infirmity, alleged by himself or on his behalf in full Provincial Parliament, that, according to that usage, Louis Joseph Papineau, Esq. has been duly elected, and chosen in consideration of his great ability and fitness, of which we have had experience during several Parliaments, and has been by us presented to your Excellency as a person worthy our confidence, and who we conceived would be agreeable to your Excellency; for which reasons we humbly hope that your Excellency, after having considered the old precedents, would be pleased to remain satisfied with our proceedings and not deprive us of the services of the said Louis Joseph Papineau as our Speaker, but, that your Excellency would be pleased to give us a favorable answer, such as His Majesty and His royal predecessors have ever given to their faithful Commons in such case, in order that we may be enabled to proceed without further delay to the dispatch of the important and arduous affairs for which we are convoked in which we hope to give convincing proofs of our affection for the King's service, and of our solicitude for the peace and welfare of the Province."

The firm and constitutional determination of his Excellency in refusing to recognize either the House of Assembly or their messengers until the House should be legally constituted by the appointment of a Speaker approved by the Crown, and his subsequent prorogation of the Parliament, rather than be longer menaced and insulted by a desperate and enraged party, whose characteristic it has ever been to hear none in power but themselves, closed this remarkable scene; a scene which, for headlong fury and determined violation of a fundamental principle of the constitution, is unparalleled in the history of every British colony, save those which have shaken off the supremacy of the Mother country. We scarcely know one principle of the constitution where an assault would be attended with more alarming consequences than the one which has thus been assailed, if not resolutely defended and repulsed as it has been on the present occasion. If this point were once taken by force or tamely surrendered, the whole fabrick would fall to the ground. If his Excellency had given way at this point, there is scarcely another point within the whole compass of the edifice committed to his care at which he could make a stand. The peculiar construction of our constitution very frequently renders its defence a task requiring no ordinary powers of intellect and presence of mind. But its tacticks are fortunately for us very simple. They consist only of a steady and undeviating adherence to the rules laid down, and a resolute determination on the part of those entrusted with its maintenance, King as well as people, never to yield any single one of its known and practised rights without the unanimous consent of all interested. Now, to follow out the simile, when a certain system of defence has been successfully practised for a series of years, and has been found to secure us against encroachments of whatsoever nature, whether of popular excesses on the one hand, or of sovereign despotism on the other, does it not consist with reason, with fortitude, and, above all, with true patriotism, that the same system should be persevered in, either until it has been found useless, or until another and a better one has been adopted by the unanimous consent of all concerned? Shall we then blame the individual, or the set of individuals, who, bound by authority and law to follow the plans laid down before them, refuse to sanction the schemes of the first bold usurper who takes it into his head to violate the first principles of our social compact? In one word, is it to be endured, that either the King's Representative or the House of Assembly, no matter from what motives, may establish for themselves at every meeting of the Legislature, a new system of procedure neither sanctioned by our constitution, nor practised in that country by which we not only affect, but are bound to be guided in every thing that concerns our public welfare? As for the King's Representative, we think that we are quite safe in asserting, that he has never hitherto overstepped the bounds of any one of those rights and prerogatives with which he is entrusted, and may with equal safety express our confidence, that he never shall be found to do so. We regret that we cannot say as much for the House of Assembly.—We have not exactly arrived at that point of the present enquiry at which we have determined to investigate such parts of their conduct as have been deemed unconstitutional; but if we may judge of the future by the past, the sooner their career of usurpation shall have been arrested, the happier and the better for the country. Of late their progress in iniquity has indeed experienced a few checks; but the misfortune is, that these checks, though they may serve to ward off from time to time the impending blow; and prevent the citadel from being sacked by the enemy, are, nevertheless, but the partial sallies of a brave and resolute Governor calculated only to preserve his charge from destruction until the arrival of a more potent force from the Mother country. Nor need we fear that this assistance will be long in arriving. The general misfortunes of the Province demand it; and the people call aloud for assistance, and a termination to a state of politcal anarchy which must end in their ruin, if not, once for all, destroyed.—Meanwhile, let us proceed to a more minute examination of the question now at issue, which is one equally interesting to Government and people. We find, however, that we must postpone this investigation till our next number; the present having swelled into a prolixity which we did not anticipate.

No. III.

It is of the last importance in all constitutional discussions or political disputes, that preper notions be entertained not only of the subject matter of debate, but the source whence it sprung, and the consequences to which it may lead; otherwise, the combatants will eternally be floundering in a path that will never bring them to a proper understanding or amicable adjustment of their differences. It is true, indeed, that it is seldom we find political disputants travelling on the same road towards the attainment of their objects: some take a short and more direct way, while others imagine thet a circuitous, though the longest, is always the surest route to the end in view. But there ought, and there ever must be a starting point; and it is principally on this that the fairness of the race and the value of the prize will depend. If there be no legitimate starting point, there can be no legal winning one; and the parties must return to their original stations, with no other advantage than a little experience of the folly of setting out in the dark without a sufficient knowledge of their ground, and an expenditure of some puffing and blowing from fatigue, the consequence of over exertion. Had the House of Assembly been as well aware as they probably are by this time, of the egregious presumption and folly of embarking in a crusade against the prerogatives of the Crown, without either a star or compass to guide them on their dangerous voyage, it is reasonable to think they never would have launched in such a tumultuary manner, and have placed at their head an individual who had already exhibited such glaring proofs of his incapacity to discharge with credit to himself, or profit to his country, the important duties of so high and distinguished a station.—They never would have placed at their head an individual who, instead of being a mediator, became a partisan in the contest—who, instead of assisting with might and main to guide the vessel of the state into some safe heaven or commodious barbour, lent all the powers and faculties of his mind to lead her out of the proper course into the irresistible current of popular commotion, there to drift with the tide, and be finally sunk or shattered to pieces amidst the rocks and quicksands of overwhelming anarchy; who, instead of being the bearer of the fair flag of truce and peace, hoisted the banner of exterminatory hostilities, and, to use the forcible language of Mr. A. Stuart—language, to which we regret to say little justice was done in the reports of our contemporaries who had the word "War" imprinted on his forehead; and who, to complete the climax, instead of being the amiable herald of peace and tranquility, flung far asunder the portals of

Janus that the whole country might* enter and arm for the approaching contest. The Assembly, however, like all other beings, whose ambitious projects render them obnoxious to the dictates of reason, convinced themselves in their fury, that might was right; and, accordingly, set out on their career of foolish and usurping errantry, without knowing whence they started, or whither they were going. It will therefore be our business in this chapter to concentrate all parties on the ground of their original existence as a constitutional body, being the only means of ascertaining how far they have deviated from the courses laid down on that chart which they are all so willing to recognize as the rule of their conduct, and the basis of our political superstructure. For this end we shall take a cursory glance of the royal prerogative, as settled at the revolution of 1688, an era to which no political writer can possibly object, whatever his principles or aims may be. We shall then inquire shortly how far the constitution of Canada is modelled on that of Great Britain, as settled at the era alluded to, and by that means ascertain how far the Province has deviated from or adhered to the practice of the metropolitan state, taking principally as our text the resolutions proposed by *Mr. Cavillier*, and passed by the majority of the Assembly.

By the word *prerogative*, says Blackstone,

---

* See Appendix No. 3.

we usually understand that special pro-eminence, which the King hath over and above all other persons, and out of the ordinary course of the common law. It signifies, in its etymology, (from *prae* and *rogo*) something that is *required* or *demanded* before, or in preference to, all others. And hence it follows, that it must be in its nature singular and eccentrical; that it can only be applied to those rights and capacities which the King enjoys alone, in contradistinction to others, and not to those which he enjoys *in common* with any of his subjects: for if any one prerogative of the Crown could be held in common with the subject, it would cease to be prerogative any longer. One of the principal bulwarks of the British Constitution was the limitation of the King's prerogative by bounds so certain and notorious, that it is impossible he should over exceed them, without the consent of the people, on the one hand; or without, on the other, a violation of that original contract, which in all states impliedly, and in ours most expressly, subsists between the prince and the subject. The great end of the revolution which placed William and Mary upon the throne, was the reparation and final establishment of this bulwark, which had fallen into almost irreparable decay by the tyrannical encroachments of the Stuart's. When the new monarch ascended the throne, he found himself in possession of ample, but well defined prerogatives; so ample, that they contained every power consistent with the splendour, dignity, and authority of the regal functions, and so well defined, that nothing but the most unwarrantable pretensions to despotic power on the part of the Sovereign, or the most unjustifiable usurpations on the part of the people, could lead to a violation of them. We shall not at present speak of them in their utmost bounds, but confine ourselves to a general allusion to them in their political or legislative character. The King can convoke, adjourn, prorogue, and dissolve Parliament at his pleasure. He is a constituent part of the supreme legislative power; and, as such, has the prerogative of *rejecting* such provisions in parliament as he may judge improper to be passed. He is the fountain of justice and general conservator of the peace of the kingdom. He is the fountain of honour of office and of privilege. He possesses the right of choosing his own council, and of nominating all the great officers of the state. In the exercise of these prerogatives, the King is irresistible and absolute, according to the forms of the constitution; "for otherwise," adds Blackstone, "the power of the Crown would indeed be but a name and a shadow, insufficient for the ends of government, if, where its *jurisdiction is clearly established and allowed*, any man, or body *of men*, were permitted to disobey it, in the ordinary course of law."

The customs and usages of Parliament, previous to the revolution, must have been too well known and too generally practised to lead us to suppose, that if they contained any thing prejudicial to the interests, or at variance, with the rights of the people or their representatives, they should not at that eventful period, which presented the fairest opportunity that ever occurred for doing themselves justice, be retrenched or totally cancelled. Yet, in the *thirteen* memorable conditions made by the Lords Spiritual and Temporal, and Commons with the Prince and Princess of Orange, not one is to be found declaratory of the rights and privileges of Parliament, *as a parliament*, except the ninth, which declares, "*That the freedom of speech, and debates, or proceedings in Parliament, ought not to be impeached or questioned in any court or place out of Parliament.*" It is, therefore, very evident, that if all the other privileges peculiar to the commons, such as the freedom from arrest, the right to arrest, and punish such as impeached or questioned their proceedings and the nomination and final appointment of Speaker, were inherent in their own body without any reference whatever to the crown, such inherent rights and privileges would be declared and insisted on in the Bill of Rights, along with the assertion of all their other ancient rights and liberties. This, however, they did not do; and whether it is to their wisdom or their folly that we are indebted for the perpetuation of a prerogative as ancient as their own constitutional existence, it is not for us or even a branch of the legislature, to impugn it until duly abrogated by the *united* legislative authority of the state. The new monarch, to use the words of Smollett, retained the old regal power over parliament in its full extent; and, so far as the particular prerogative in question is concerned, has handed it down to his successors unimpaired and unimpeached. There cannot be a stronger proof of the intention, if not the determination, of parliament to continue the old customs, with respect to the source and exercise of its privileges, than what took place at the revolution. When the convention parliament met and chose its Speakers—the Marquis of Halifax by the Peers, and Mr. Henry Powle by the Commons—there was no authority in the Kingdom to confirm such elections; the source of all public offices and employments having ceased to flow in consequence of the desertion of the ill-fated James, the last monarch of the ill-fated Stuarts. But the instant that the convention was converted into a parliament, or, at all events, as soon as the new parliament met, the old customs and usages of parliament were resorted to, though William was no great stickler for prerogative, provided the means were furnished for carrying into effect his warlike and foreign projects. As usual, the Speaker of the House of Lords was appointed by the King; and he of the Commons, though nominated by that body, could not act until confirmed by the same authority. The Commons by the mouth of their Speaker thus approved of, demanded their ancient privileges; and, upon comparing the proceedings of parliament at each new meeting after the revolution with those prior to it, it was found that no alteration or innovation whatever had been made upon them.

It is, therefore, highly foolish, stupid and absurd, to assert, that the current of these usages, which has flown in one uninterrupted channel from the revolution down to the present time, gathering additional force and strength in its course, can be diverted at the pleasure of any one branch of the legislature without the consent of the whole. These usages now form part and parcel of the constitution. They are as deeply ingrafted on the King's prerogative as the right to call together, prorogue, and dissolve parliament itself. No power can annul them except the united voice of parliament in all its constituent parts. The Commons will not, and dare not attempt it on their own strength; and we all knew, that though the Commons have the right to maintain, they have no power to alter or destroy the constitution. Besides, the Speaker of the Commons, with regard to whose nomination and confirmation our present inquiries are principally directed, is a magisterial and judicial officer; possessing power not only over certain rights and liberties belonging to the members of the body over whom he presides, but also over the persons and liberties of his Majesty's subjects in general. Can the *Commons* endow him with such extensive authority? No; they possess it not themselves: it is not inherent in them. The constitution restricts their powers to *legislation* only; and it is one of the first and greatest and best maxims of that constitution, that the legislative and judicial powers cannot be united without the destruction of the whole fabric. They cannot even assemble without being summoned by the King; for they are not, like him, a self-existing power in the State. They cannot clothe themselves with the smallest vestige of executive authority; and, without the consent of such executive authority, how can it be supposed that the mere election of their speaker can confer upon him *judicial* powers scarcely inferior to those of our highest courts of justice? The idea is absurd! Such powers can only flow from that common fountain of justice whence all jurisdiction over persons and property proceeds; and the Commons might as well take it into their heads to appoint the Lord High Chancellor of England, as appoint their own Speaker without the consent and approbation of the King. If the authority of the Speaker were restricted to the mere overseeing of the internal proceedings of the House; to the reading of messages; to the maintenance of order and decency in debates; to the putting of questions from the chair; to the preservation of silence; to the rehearsal of precedents; and to pronouncing the casting vote in case of an equality of voices, the thing might do very well; and neither King nor people, we are sure, would be much inclined to disturb him in the exercise of his dry and monotonous duties, nor interest themselves more in his nomination than they are accustomed to do in the appointment of the chairman of a committee for inquiring into the best means for improving turnpike roads. But when we find him, in the full plenitude of his *judicial* powers, exercising a lordship and jurisdiction as extensive as the kingdom itself, issuing his warrant for taking into custody some scribbler or popular speechifier—who has been unguarded enough to commit a breach upon the privileges of the house, and pronounce doom depriving him of his liberty during several months, it is high time to look into the authority whence such potent power proceeds; for, however imperious force may be, no Briton is bound to submit to power without law. We have already said that such judicial powers are not indigenous to to the Commons. Indeed they have never laid claim to them as such. How could they? They have hitherto had the good sense to know, that without the sanction of the supreme executive magistrate, from whom all judicial power emanates, no privilege of this description could be inherent in a popular eccentrical body, whose very existence depends upon the nod of that distinguished personage. They, therefore seek it where alone they can obtain it—at the foot of the throne. Whether as a been or as a matter of right, they always claim it, and dare not act upon it, nor even anticipate its assumption, until conferrred upon them.—Can we then suppose for a moment that such an enlightened body as the Commons of Great Britain and

Ireland have ever been, would condescend to implore and intreat from his Majesty, as they continued to do at the commencement of every parliament, the privilege of acting in any judicial capacity, if such privilege had been co-existent with parliament, and that they had the right of exercising and enforcing it at their own will and by their own sole authority independent of any other constituent part of the supreme legislative power? What simpletons they must be if they possess powers and privileges inherent in themselves, and have not the courage to enforce them without bending the knee to any other authority on earth! What has become of the daring of Old England! What has become of the spirit that extorted MAGNA CHARTA at the point of the sword! Has the blood that overflowed the nation in defence of law, justice and liberty, been spilt in vain! What has become of the bold but mistaken zeal that brought a monarch to the block in defence of liberty! What has become of the Hampdens, the Russels, the Sidneys, the Chathams, the Pitts, the Foxes, and the Burkes, that have shed their blood and spent their lives to preserve our liberties and constitution! Have they already been forgotten; or were they the mere phantoms of the brain that passed in shadowy pageants before our feverish imaginations! Could *such* events and *such* men pass into oblivion and not leave one solitary token behind them of their disapproval of the custom of seeking the Commons' Speaker, and privileges from the Crown, if such were contrary to their rights, and at variance with all the known principles of the constitution! Could *such* men crouch for a *boon* when there existed a *right*? Was it for *them* to *ask* what they had already been in possession of? Could *such* men stoop and cringe and fawn at the footstool of the Bel and Nebo of undefined prerogative, and beg from the crown rights and privileges inherent in the reprosentatives of England? Surely that man is not in possession of his faculties, who can for a moment believe, that if the House of Commons have a right to the full and free exercise of the extensive privileges which they now enjoy, and to the election of the Speaker without the intervention of the Sovereign, they would not long before now lay claim to them, and maintain them with as fearless and dauntless a brow as ever they spoke or fought in the cause of rational freedom. It is therefore most vain, most presumptuous to imagine that they can at pleasure assume rights which were never reserved to them before; that they can now establish in themselves precedents and principles which were neither set up nor sanctioned at the revolution. But even if they did, such is the nature of the regal prerogative as now limited and bounded, that the wheels of government must cease to revolve, and the whole machine of legislation cease to operato, until such a claim should be finally set to rest, either by the positive refusal of the Crown to sanction it, or the united voice of the legislature admitting and confirming it. In short, matters must remain as they are, until altered by the consent of *all* the constituent parts of the legislature. It is not the individual pretensions of the Crown or of the Commons than can alter the constitution. They may and they have at times destroyed it, each in their turn; but it is impossible that they can either amend or remodel it without the consenting voice of the whole.

As to the right of the Crown to exert a regal faculty which has lain dormant for years because no corresponding event has occurred to demand its exercise, nothing can be more absurd than to deny the actual existence of such a faculty and power. There is a very material difference between a state of torpidity and activity; but surely that fool does not live who will say, that a torpid animal has ceased to exist because it has ceased to move---that it has ceased to feel because its pulse can scarcely be felt, or because the heavings of its bosom are not visible. Approach it in its lair; watch it narrowly and minutely, and you will easily discover all the symptoms of existence. Probe it, and it may awaken and turn upon you, and, if strong enough, perhaps overwhelm you. It was once attempted to be proved by the emissaries of despotism, that because a parliament had not been summoned for ten or a dozen of years, the right to do so had been lost by the Crown. Shortly afterwards this whim, for it was nothing else, went entirely out of fashion, and one directly the reverse came into vogue, namely, that parliament once assembled could sit as long as it pleased. The consequence was that anarchy ensued; and there was neither peace, justice nor liberty in the land until the proper authorities agreed among themselves upon certain rules and principles which should for the future guide them in the administration of public affairs. It was not stipulated that, if any of these rules should fall into disuee it should immediately become obsolete and of no effect, but on the contrary declared that they should forever continue in force as the law of the land until altered by the undivided consent of the same national authority. Let us not therefore suppose, that because the King has not since the revolution refused to confirm the Speaker nominated by the Commons, his *right* to do so has ceased. No doctrine could be more dangerous; no doctrine could be more fatal to the mutual rights of Sovereign and people; for there are rights and privileges on both sides which have not been enforced for upwards of a century, and these we could easily enumerate were they not too obvious to be beyond the view of the most careless looker-on. There is one, however, which is so much in point that we cannot forbear alluding to it. It is a standing rule of the House of Commons, that no report can be published of its proceedings without a breach of its privileges; and with the exception of one remarkable instance not many years ago, we do not remember the enforcement of this rule for upwards of half a century. Now, will any one say, that the right to exercise this privilege is not now as strongly implanted in the Commons as it was the day after its enactment ? The Right Honorable Speaker would look rather surly and indignant were you to tell him anything to the contrary, and perhaps desire the Sergeant at arms to take you into custody, however much he might be inclined, to disseminate useful political information and manly British eloquence : The Speaker therefore and the nation at large must pardon us, if we expect the same concessions from them with respect to that branch of the prerogative of the Crown which preserves, though not exercised a negative upon the Speaker of the Commons.

This brings us down to the consideration of the prerogative and privileges inherent by analogy in our provincial constitution and their application ; but this we must postpone till another opportunity.

No. IV.

Having thus, by reasonable arguments and inevitable deduction, established the important truth, that, by the constitution of the mother country, no branch of the royal prerogative is established on a firmer basis than that which allows a negative in the appointment of Speaker of the House of Commons, we now proceed to trace the analogy which subsists, or, at least, ought to subsist, in the free constitution of this Province, in common with all our other colonial possessions, whether what has been termed provincial establishments, proprietary governments, or charter governments.

No one need be told the general form of government established throughout the British Colonies. It is in all of them borrowed from that of Great Britain. It is impossible that it should be otherwise; for all the power that exists among them, either judicial or legislative, is bestowed upon them by the King and Parliament, whose prerogatives and Privileges they may indeed imitate, but cannot overstep, as declared by the statute 7 and 8 William III. c. 22, and, so far as regards this Province, by the second section of the constitutional act of 1791. But whatever may be said of the want of *prospective* prudence and policy which characterized the

f

extension of a free representative government to this Province, in none of the Colonies have the general outlines and most prominent features of the British Constitution been so closely imitated as in the Canadas. Whatever powers and prerogatives are enjoyed by the King in the metropolitan state, he possesses in this Province; and he is as much King of Canada as he is of Great Britain and Ireland. He can come into the Province whenever he pleases, and exercise all the sovereign functions belonging to the Imperial Crown, civil and military, as well as ecclesiastical. He may summon and convoke, prorogue and dissolve, the Provincial Parliament at pleasure. He can reject such Legislative provisions as he judges improper to be passed. He can delegate his judicial powers to whomsoever he pleases; and appoint such civil and military officers as he may think proper. He may confer such honours and dignities as he may deem advisable. He may pardon what offences he pleases; and, in a word, may, as already said, exercise all the sovereign powers of Constitutional King of the British Empira. Nay, more, he can appoint whomsoever he pleases to perform all these regal functions as fully and freely as he could do himself; and therefore, though not personally present, ought always to be considered as the spring and regulator of every royal transaction. Such are the rights, powers, and prerogatives of His Majesty in this Province.

With respect to the other branches of our

Legislative Government—the Legislative Council and the House of Assembly—their powers are confined by the Constitution to giving advice and consent to His Majesty in making "*Laws for the peace, welfare, and good government,*" of the Province; such laws not being repugnant to that act, or the Constitution of the Mother Country. If, however, in the performance of these express declaratory powers, the two lower branches of the Provincial Legislature found it necessary, for the maintenance of their dignity and authority, to imitate the proceedings and assume the privileges of the corresponding branches of the supreme Imperial Legislature, that could only be done by following the same plan which had been immemorially adopted by the object of their imitation. We have already seen what that plan is. All their privileges with the exception of those claimed and maintained by the Bill of Rights, are only obtained by humble verbal petition to the throne, without which procedure they can neither be assumed nor exercised; for no power is self-existent by our constitution except that of the Crown. Accordingly, when the Legislature of this Province was organized, in virtue of the powers conferred by the constitutional act, both Houses, but the House of Assembly in particolor, proceeded without hesitation or delay to consider the best means of securing to themselves the rights and privileges enjoyed by the Parliament of England. In so doing they had the good sense to perceive, that, as the Constitution had been entirely silent in relation to such matters, their views could only be accomplished by following throughout the example laid down in the mother country; and to assume *brevi manu* any privileges resembling those of the Commons, without being legally conferred and confirmed, would be usurping at once an authority which the constitution could not possibly recognize or sanction. The deliberations and proceedings of the Legislature, with respect to the Speaker of the House of Assembly, in the first session of the first Provincial Parliament, is worthy of being noted, both as matter of interesting historical detail, and as the best criterion by which the extraordinary propositions laid down in the resolutions of Mr. Cuvillier can be canvassed and judged of.

"Quebec, *Monday*, the 17th Dec. 1792.

"Shortly after, a Message was delivered by Mr. William Bouthillier, Gentleman Usher of the Black Rod, viz.

"*Gentlemen*,

"The Lieutenant Governor commands this Honorable House to attend His Excellency immediately in the Legislative Council house."

"Accordingly, the House went up to attend His Excellency in the Legislative Council House, where he was pleased to deliver the following speech.

"*Gentlemen of the House of Assembly*,

"Parliamentary usage, and the proper conduct of the business you are about to undertake, making it necessary that you should have a Speaker, it is my pleasure that you return to your House, and make choice of a fit person to fill that office, who you will present FOR MY APPROBATION on Thursday next at twelve of the clock, when I shall declare the cause of convening this Assembly."

"Tuesday, 20th December, 1792.

"Mr. Speaker elect having taken the chair, proposed as questions to the House, and on which he wished to take advice of the House, (to wit:)

"That the Speaker being presented at the Bar, he should say, (among other observations.)

"My incapacity being as evident as my zeal is ardent, to see that so important a duty as that of the first Speaker of the Commons House of Assembly of the Representatives of Lower Canada be fulfilled, I most respectfully implore the excuse and command of your Excellency, in the name of our Sovereign Lord the King."

IF THE ELECTION OF SPEAKER IS APPROVED OF, he may say,

"I most humbly claim, in the name of the same Assembly, the freedom of Speech, and generally, all the like privileges and liberties as are enjoyed by the Commons of Great Britain our mother country;" &c. &c.

In conformity with these claims, sanctioned by the Governor in the name and behalf of His Majesty, and the actual exercise of some of them during the next session of the Provincial Parliament, the House of Assembly resolved, "*That in all unprovided cases, resort shall be had to the rules, usages, and forms of the Parliament of* Great *Britain, which shall be followed* until *the House shall think fit* to *make a* rule or rules *applicable* do *such* unprovided cases." And accordingly, we find, that ever since the commencement of the constitution, both the prerogatives of the Crown and the privileges of Parliament have been maintained and exercised in this Province on the same footing that they are established in the mother country, till the House of Assembly, in the last session, thought it proper to deny the prerogative at the same time that they persisted in the exercise of their own privileges; thus annihilating rights and powers which, if permitted to exist at all, can only be exercised mutually and reciprocally. But it is time to advert to what Mr. Cuvillier and the other GENS TOGATA of the Assembly say upon the subject. We shall take up their Resolutions *seriatim*; and their first decree runs thus:

"*Resolved*, 1. *That it* is *necessary for the* discharge *of the* duties *imposed* upon *this House; viz. to give its* advice to *His Majesty in the* enactment *of laws for the* peace, *welfare, and good government of the Province, conformably to the Act of the British Parliament, under which it is constituted and assembled, that its Speaker be a person of its free choice, independently of the will and pleasure of the* person entrusted *by His Majesty, with the administration of the local* government *for the time being*."

We scorn to comment on the disrespectful terms in which this resolution is express-

ved. Those who can treat the representative of his Britannick Majesty in this Province as a "PERSON," without title or dignity, are themselves unfit to be treated like gentlemen; far less like wise and prudent legislators, sincerely desirous of their country's welfare by those salutary means prescribed by the constitution. No wonder if men unacquainted with the ordinary rules of decency and good manners, should also be strangers to the maxims of the British constitution. But if it be true, as it is here for the first time asserted, that his Majesty's representative, or rather the King himself, whose prerogatives are now called in question, has no voice in the constitutional appointment of the Speaker of the House of Assembly, the choice of whom is independent of the "*will and pleasure*" of the Crown, then it is equally true, that every House of Assembly, from the first which met on the 17th of December, 1792, till that notable one which met on the 20th Nov. 1827, has been unfaithful to its duties as representatives of the people, and compromised its own rights and privileges in a manner most disgraceful to any branch of a constitutional Legislature. If the principles laid down in the foregoing resolution be well founded, the various Houses of Assembly of this Province have not acted like men of honor, worth, and independence, but like craven hearted cowards and traitors. They have, one and all of them, betrayed their trust, and, unlike true Britons, become the passive slaves and minions of a power which held no controul over them, and of whose "*will and pleasure,*" so far at least as regarded the choice of Speaker, they were entirely free and independent. But it is the particular good fortune of this Province as of mankind in general, that knowledge is progressive, and that though the clouds of barbarous ignorance have hung long, dense, and heavily, over our forefathers, the sun of the British constitution has at last penetrated through the intellectual gloom, and swept from the atmosphere every vestige of our pristine obscurity. The first short session of the thirteenth Provincial Parliament will form as memorable an era in constitutional as the discovery of the new world did in civil history; and the resolutions now under consideration will forever be the MAGNA CHARTA of Canadian privileges. As for Mr. Cuvillier and his coadjutors, theirs will be the high and enviable distinction of having consigned to eternal oblivion the constitutional ignorance and stupidity of all their predecessors, and of pronouncing over it one of the finest specimens of funereal orations that ever was uttered in the world. This being the case, it only remains to lament the folly and ignorance of all preceding Houses of Assembly, especially the first, for having so far compromised their rights as to receive their privileges, but in partitular their Speaker, from the hands of another, when there existed sufficient authority in themselves to assume and maintain them. Why, when desired to present their Speaker FOR HIS

MAJESTY'S APPROBATION, did not the *first* House of Assembly tell the "PERSON" then "entrusted by His Majesty with the administration of the local government," that its Speaker was a person of its own free choice "*Independently*" of his "WILL AND PLEASURE?" Why did they not THEN anticipate the glories of 1827? But why, Oh! why did they hint in their deliberations at the bare possibility *of the rejection* of their Speaker by recording those ominous words, "IF THE ELECTION OF THE SPEAKER IS APPROVED OF?" Why, moreover, when that approval happily took place, did the Speaker "*Most humbly claim in the name of the same Assembly, the freedom of speech, and generally all the like privileges and liberties as are enjoyed by the Commons of Great Britain, our mother country?*" Why did all the succeeding Assemblies follow the same course? Why, if their general privileges and the election of their Speaker existed in their own right "*Independently*" of the Crown, did they thus become a party and the chief actors in a mere theatrical pantomime that could only entail disgrace upon their proceedings, and load their own memories with the contempt of future ages? But, to the praise and honor of the *first* House of Assembly, be it seriously spoken, they understood the constitution which brought them together, and its relation to its Imperial model, as well, if not much better, than any Assembly by whom they have been succeeded. Finding that the Constitutional Act contained no provision with regard to the rights, privileges, immunities, and usages, necessary in the preservation of the dignity and authority of a free representative Parliament, but rather that these were permitted to spring up as a concomitant plant of the new Constitution, as they had before done in the mother country, they nurtured it with the greatest possible care and attention, and procured shelter for it where alone they could find it—in the wide-spreading branches of constitutional prerogative. They did not imagine, like our modern theorists, that, as a matter of course, all these privileges were inherent in themselves without the sanction of higher authority, or that they could innovate at pleasure the forms and proceedings so long practiced in the mother country. The enjoyment of the right was enough for them, without the dangerous power of destroying it in whole or in part. They were happy to embrace it as they found it, and to exercise it as had been done to such advantage before them. In particular, they looked upon their Speaker as an officer of the Crown as well as their Cheirman; deriving considerable emoluments, dignity, and honour, from the Crown; and, therefore, as much in the choice and approbation of the Crown as in their own. At all events they sought his confirmation from the Crown, and received it; and, if we may judge from their temper and talents, as well as their proceedings, would have admitted his rejection as a right which they had neither the inclination nor the power to controvert. Their successors must be judged by the same rule; and it is equally to the honour and the disgrace of the Province, that it is almost the same individuals who have denied the just prerogatives of the Crown, and, by their general unconstitutional conduct, plunged a happy and loyal people in troubles which their children's children may not live to see appeased.

Resolved, 2. *That Louis Joseph Papineau, Esq. one of the Members of this House, who has served as Speaker in six successive Parliaments, has been duly chosen by this House to be its Speaker in the present Parliament.*

Our only object in inserting this resolution is to introduce Mr. Papineau as one who not long ago thought differently than himself and his colleagues do on the present occasion with respect to the legal election of Speaker, and to prove that the boasted experience of "six successive Parliaments" has failed to mature his judgement on *one* subject at least. All Canada remembers the proposal made in the Imperial Parliament to unite the Provinces of Upper and Lower Canada, and the stir which the intelligence created in this country, as well among those who were favorable as unfavorable to what, we must not conceal was at that time, but is still more so *now*, a most desirable measure. It may also be remembered, that Mr. Papineau, being a noted orator and Statesman, was one of the delegates whom the anti-union fraternity sent to England to plead for them. The Provincial Parliament being about to meet in the mean time, it became necessary for him to intimate his absence from the Speaker's chair. This he did by addressing a letter to the Clerk of the House of Assembly, in which, contrary to all usage and precedent, he took occasion to express his sentiments on *two* topics which, in all probability, will be equally memorable in this Province. The one related to the contemplated union, and the other had reference to the appointment of Speaker of the House of Assembly. The first of these not being under discussion at present, all we deem it necessary to say is, that had *we* been the " PERSON entrusted by His Majesty with the administration of the local government," the man who had so unnecessarily libelled the Imperial Government and Parliament, should never afterwards be allowed to place himself in the Speaker's Chair. As to the second point, we shall extract Mr. Papineau's own words; and think they will not only speak but cry aloud for themselves :—" *It is* not, there*fore*, to avoid *fulfil*ling *the* duti*es of th*at *h*onora*ble* station *with which it has* pleas*e*d *his Excellency the Governor-in-Chief and the House of Assembly to honor me, and in the exercise of which their constant kindness has supplied my insufficiency, that I absent myself,*" &c. &c.* If, we will simply ask, *His Excellency the Governor-in-chief* had, in 1823, a co-efficient or co-equal voice in the nomina-

* Vide Journals of the House of Assembly for 1823.

tion of Speaker of the House of Assembly, as here admitted by Mr. Papineau himself, by what authority—in virtue of what law has his right and prerogative been lost in 1827? How can the Speaker of 1827, to use the words of the resolution, be "*duly chosen*" *without* the approbation of the Governor, which is asserted to be a mere piece of tawdry form, if that approbation was necessary in 1823; or if the Speaker had EVEN been appointed by the united voices of the *Governor* and *Assembly*? The inconsistency of some men is astonishing!

"*Resolved, 3. That the Act of the British Parliament under which the House is constituted and assembled, does not require the approval of such person so chosen as Speaker, by the person administering the Government of this Province in the name of His Majesty.*"

This we hold to be the most important resolution of the whole series, because it appeals to the highest and last resort. "Hast thou appealed unto Cæsar? Unto Cæsar shalt thou go." It is very true that the Act of the British Parliament under which the House is constituted and assembled, does not REQUIRE the approval of such person so chosen as Speaker; but does it DENY the right of such approval? If not, the proposition is null and void; and the House of Assembly, in demanding the approbation of the Governor, acknowledge the right of rejection as well as approval. They affirm the former to be unconstitutional; if so, we affirm the presentation for approval to be equally so ; and moreover, that every time the House of Assembly have exercised what they term their liberties and privileges, they have acted unconstitutionally, and without the authority of a single section, clause, expression, or word, in " the Act of the British Parliament under which the House is constituted and assembled." Whence, then, the authority of those Parliamentary rights and privileges which the House of Assembly has daily exercised since the commencement of the constitution, and of which they seem so singularly tenacious? For our own part we can discover none, except the inherent powers and prerogatives of the Crown.—Here they are asked and here they are conferred. Yet the Assembly deny to the Crown, *the source of all their own privileges*, the corresponding prerogatives ; without the enjoyment of which the Crown would want that constitutional check and balance which are so necessary to controul the undue exercise of these privileges. The Assembly, like hungry mendicants, are ready to receive all the privileges that they can possibly exercise; but when you tell them that a corresponding prerogative has been kept in reserve, they suddenly turn upon you, and answer, " such things must not be ; we indeed are entitled to our privileges, notwithstanding the constitution is silent on the subject ; but the Crown cannot lawfully retain or exercise any prerogative, especially the negative in the choice of our Speaker ; for " the Act of the British Parliament under which the

House is constituted and assembled, does not require it!" No, as already observed, it does not *require* it; but at the same time that it does not *deny* it, does it *require* that the House of Assembly, who are but a branch of an inferior and subordinate legislature, should possess all the privileges of the Supreme Legislature? No, it does not. The King can exercise his lawful prerogatives in any part of the Empire and so may the commons their privileges; But when the King chooses by himself or by commission to exercise those prerogatives in Canada, where is the power that can controul him? If the commons of England have not the jurisdiction, surely the commons of Lower Canada cannot pretend to it. The King and Parliament is the only power on earth that can limit and restrict the royal prerogatives. Not having done so in Canada, whether they relate to the Speaker or to any other question, they may and ought to be exercised whenever occasion may require it. Seeing that no privileges whatever are conferred on the House of Assembly by the Constitutional Act; and that consequently all the privileges that they enjoy are derived from the Crown, would they annihilate every prerogative except that which confers these privileges?—Yet this is what in practice they have attempted to do. Never did this or any other country witness so parricidious an act of policy. No mind but a frantic one could entertain; no arm but that of a democrat could strike the blow.

We have said that the House of Assembly have on various occasions exercised privileges similar to those enjoyed immemoriably by the Commons of England: and we have seen that such privileges have not been derived from the constitutional act, but from the Crown, which alone had the right of giving them away in the absence of all legislative enactments. If we can prove this, we can on very just grounds and with a very bold countenance ask, how dare the assembly apply a rule to the prerogative of the Crown which they refuse to adopt with respect to their own privileges? During the second session of the first parliament a member of the house having been arrested for debt on the eve of embarkation for Europe, complained of a breach of privilege in a letter to the Speaker, who, strange to say, was himself the professional man who had sued out the writ. The terms of the complaint are so remarkably applicable to the general strain of our argument, that we cannot help using its own words, which are, "That on opening the FIRST session, he (the Speaker) in the name of the house, had claimed such privileges and liberties as are enjoyed by the commons of Great Britain, and the LIEUTENANT GOVERNOR, in his answer, had recognized the enjoyment of all just rights and privileges." It was voted, "that the member had been arrested in direct violation of the rights and privileges of the house; and that the SPEAKER, as the Attorney, the creditor and the Sheriff were severally guilty of a breach of privilege;" and these persons apologised accordingly at the bar. During the second and third parliaments Charles Baptiste Bouc was twice expelled by a vote of the House of Assembly in consequence of being convicted of a conspiracy to defraud one of His Majesty's subjects of various sums of money; which, being a great stretch of privilege, could not be carried into effect without the sanction of an act of the legislature, which was accordingly introduced and passed. In the second session of the fourth parliament, a Montreal newspaper having published some toasts given at a public dinner at that place, reflecting on a party in the Assembly, the chairman of the dinner and the printer of the paper were voted guilty of a high breach of the privileges of the House, and ordered to be taken into custody. In the same session, it was resolved, "That Thomas Carey, Editor of the newspaper entitled 'The Quebec Mercury,' for undertaking in his paper of yesterday, to give an account of the proceedings of this house, to be taken into custody of the sergeant at arms attending this house." On the 20th February, 1808, it was resolved, "That Ezekiel Hart, Esquire, professing the Jewish religion, cannot take a seat nor vote in this house." In the same session it was also resolved, "That to send for a member of that house, when in his place, attendant on the duties thereof, and on his withdrawing in consequence into an apartment thereof, or appendage thereto appertaining, to serve upon him a summons, or other civil process, is a breach of the privileges of this house," and "That John Johnson, a Bailiff for the Court of King's Bench, for such breach of the privileges of this house, be taken into custody by the sergeant at arms, and that Mr. Speaker do issue his warrant accordingly." The fith provincial parliament was dissolved in consequence of the Assembly having attempted, by a mere vote, to disfranchise certain classes of His Majesty's subjects. "The House of Assembly," said Sir J. H. Craig, in dissolving the sixth Provincial Parliament, "the House of Assembly has taken upon themselves without the participation of the other branches of the Legislature, to pass a vote that a Judge of His Majesty's Court of King's Bench, cannot sit nor vote in their House." In 1812–13, the Assembly commanded the attendance at their bar of the Officers of the Legislative Council, without leave being previously asked for the purpose. In 1814, the Governor in Chief, Sir George Prevost, having thought it inexpedient "to suspend the Chief Justice of the Province and the Chief Justice of the District of Montreal, from their offices, upon an address to that effect from one branch of the Legislature alone, founded on articles of accusation on which the Legislative Council had not been consulted, and in which they had not concurred," the House resolved, "That His Excellency the Governor in Chief, by his said answer to the address of this House, has violated the constitutional rights and privileges of this House." To conclude, in 1823, the printers and publishers of the Canadian Times were voted guilty of a breach of the privileges of the House, and ordered to be taken into custody for merely saying that the *composition* of the *majority* of the House was *anti-British* ; a term than which nothing could be more applicable.

Now, without going into further particulars, what can be more inconsistent, perverse and factious, than the late attempt to deny to the Crown the exercise of one of those just and lawful prerogatives which is almost annually practised in the mother country, and which has also been practised in this Province ever since the commencement of the constitution, while such extensive rights and privileges have been claimed and exercised by the Assembly itself? Is not this setting up for law the sole *dictum* of the House of Assembly; and telling the King, " Sire, you must not, and cannot, by the constitution, exercise in this Province any branch of the prerogatives enjoyed in the mother country, EXCEPT conferring upon us our usual privileges; which privileges we *may* and *can* enjoy, even to the denial of your Majesty's authority, whenever we think it proper!" If such an act is not a direct attempt on the part of the Assembly to destroy the just balance of the constitution, we know not what is; and scarcely remember any thing resembling it, except that memorable vote of the Commons of England, in 1648 " that whatever is enacted or declared for law by the Commons in Parliament assembled, hath the force of law; and all the people of this nation are concluded thereby, although the consent and concurrence of the King or House of Peers be not had thereto." To do themselves justice, and be consistent, the House of Assembly ought to have continued the parallel and made it good. But, poor maniacs! though they had the audacity to *attempt* the destruction of the constitution, they wanted the courage to carry their desires into execution. Like most innovators, it may be presumed they entertained the ambitiou, but dared not adopt the means. That very wise saying of Cato becomes, therefore, very applicable: "*Nae tu stultus homuncio es, qui malis veniam precari quam non peccare.*

"*Resolved,* 4. *That the presenting of the person so elected as Speaker to the King's representative for approval, is founded on usage only, and that such* approval *is, and* hath *always been, a matter of* course."

"Resolved, 5. *That* this House *doth persist in its* choice, *and* that *the said* Louis Joseph *Papineau, Esq.* ought to *be and is its Speaker.*"

Our observations on the other Resolutions having embraced these two last ones, it will only be necessary to remark, that even if the "approval *is founded on* USAGE *only,*" the right would be equally good, until the united voice of Parliament had declared otherwise. But what is usage? Is it not the basis of our whole system of government? Is it not the foundation of all our laws and all our rights? Is it not the palladium of the

British Parliament, and the corner stone of our Courts of Justice? Whence the most sacred pillar of the whole edifice—*trial by Jury*? Yet, the House of Assembly of Lower Canada, set their own will up in opposition to usage, and declare their own votes as superior to the wisdom and practise of centuries!*

We thus conclude our observations on the pretensions of the House of Assembly in regard to the appointment of their Speaker.—We are aware that we have not done the subject that justice which its importance merits. But feeble as we are, we trust we have said enough to convince every reasonable man that truth and justice are on our side, while nothing but folly and falsehood characterize the other. We shall now turn our attention to other topics of paramount importance. That the country is in danger need not be concealed: it would be childish. It therefore becomes every loyal subject to do all in his power to preserve unimpaired the ancient rights and liberties of Britons. We are not indeed in open warfare with foreign enemies; but we are in rupture with a foe equally dangerous, *foreign* laws, manners, principles, and sentiments. If, in acting our part in this warfare, we should at any time make use of energetick language, we entreat those to whom it may apply to believe that we mean nothing *personally* hostile. Personallities we despise and abhor; but should

---

*See Appendix No. IV.

any individual fall under our weapon when brandished only in self-defence, the intruder, and not us, can alone be to blame. To conclude, we are not, like Mr. Papineau and his gang, warriors *ad internecio*; but will lay down our arms the moment the enemy leaves our borders. In the mean time, the inscription of our banner is PRO PATRIA, and blighted be the patriotism that does not adept and follow it.

No. V.

To Louis Joseph Papineau, Esq.

SIR,

Seeing that the most unwarrantable and unprecedented proceedings have attended the opening of the present session of the Provincial Parliament, I cannot refrain, whatever may be the consequences to myself or to others, from raising my voice, single and feeble though it be, in reprobation—express and fearless reprobation—of such preccedings. It covers me with shame and confuston, that a country like this, where the freedom and practice of the British Constitution are enjoyed in their fullest extent, should, in the first place, by conduct which has been on all hands declared unconstitutional, subject itself to a state of anarchy and confusion almost without example in Colonial history; and, in the second place, with the view of retrieving what had been so recklessly and thoughtlessly lost, expose itself to such animadversions as are only applicable to deeds of corruption and breaches of trust. How sincerely do I regret that such *language* as this should ever have been applicable to this portion of his Majesty's dominions, fostered as it has been by every civil and religious indulgence. Would to God, in the words of that honest man and brave soldier, SIR JAMES KEMPT, that "an *oblivion of all past jealousies and dissensions,"* may be the result of the present session of the Provincial Parliament. But however much so great and enviable a blessing is to be desired by all, I will thus early most candidly declare, that I shall be the last man in the country who shall seek my end, or accept any boon that may have been obtained through illegal or unconstitutional means. I blush for my country: I blush for the good people of this Province: But more especially do I blush for their Representatives, when I reflect, that, in no Constitutional measure that has ever engaged their attention, has that wisdom or forethought been employed which was necessary to carry it to a finally *happy issue.* I blush for my country: I blush for the good people of this Province: But more especially do I blush for their Representatives, when I reflect, that even when controuled by constitutional authority, mellowed by indulgence, or tempered by experience, they have never been able to regain one false step without plunging deeper into another. Finally, I blush for my country: I blush for the good people of this Province: But more especially do I blush for their Representatives, when I reflect, that, at no period of our history, have these characteristicks been more conspicuous than during the proceedings attending the meeting of the present Session of the Provincial Parliament.

To treat of those proceedings is the sole object of this communication; and as you, Sir, have ever been, and still are, the pivot on which almost the whole machinery of our late Legislative differences turn, I cannot conceive to whom I can more properly address my observations than to yourself, unfortunately branded and distinguished as you thus have been. In doing so, I do assure you, that I shall have little to do either with theory or theoretical deductions. I shall set down nothing but simple and recorded facts; and whatever conclusions may be drawn from them can only be attributed to the necessary consequences of such facts, and not to the ingenuity or imagination of any individual whatever. Shall I extend the right hand of fellowship to the man who has injured me, except, instead of grasping it violently from my side, or seizing it clandestinely from behind my back, he beg it by those forms instituted by society? Is stolen property to be stolen again in order to restore it to the owner? Is it not rather to be recovered by the rules prescribed by law, and by those alone? By what rule is traduced or tarnished honour to be retrieved? By traducing or tarnishing that of the traducer? By no means. But by the law of honour alone, which, while it prescribes forms to regain that which has been already lost, in the most ample and satisfactory way, will never sanction a *new* breach upon the rights of another, merely to gratify the passion or the revenge of the sufferer. "*Let all things be done in order*," was a notable maxim of one of the greatest orators of antiquity. And, indeed, nothing can possibly be more fatal and ruinous to the rules and institutions, as well of private as of public life—as well of civil as of religious bodies—than an attempt to break through them with impunity, and the unmanly and indecent assumption of power by undue and illegal means. But to the point.

No man can be ignorant of the circumstances which attended the meeting and prorogueing of the parliament called for the despatch of business on the 20th of November, 1827. Of these, however, it becomes necessary for my present purpose to recapitulate some; and I shall do so very briefly. His Majesty's Representative being seated on the throne, the Black Rod was ordered to summon the House of Assembly into His Excellency's presence. That body being come up, they were informed, in the usual terms, that His Excellency did not think it fit to declare the cause of summoning this Parliament, until *there should be a Speaker of the House of Assembly.*" Accordingly, the Assembly were ordered to repair to their usual place of sittings, and there to make choice of a Speaker, and present him next day for the approbation of His Excellency. This was done; and you Louis Joseph Papineau, being presented as Speaker elect, and making the usual and prescribed excuse, that excuse was sustained by the Speaker of the Legislative Council in the following words:

"*Mr. Papineau, and*
Gentlemen of the Assembly,

"I am commanded by His Excellency the

Governor-in-Chief to inform you, that His Excellency doth not approve the choice which the Assembly have made of a Speaker, and in His Majesty's name His Excellency doth accordingly now disallow and discharge the said choice.

"And it is His Excellency's pleasure that you, Gentlemen of the Assembly, do forthwith AGAIN REPAIR to the place where the sittings of the Assembly are usually held, and there make choice of ANOTHER PERSON to be your Speaker—and that you present the person who shall be so chosen to His Excellency in this House on Friday next at two o'clock, for his approbation."

But this command, which was the last command of His Majesty to the House of Assembly until the appearance of the Black Rod on the 21st inst. was DISOBEYED. Instead of proceeding to the election of "ANOTHER PERSON," you, Sir, and the majority of the Assembly, proceeded to declare the FIRST election legal; and the following memorable Resolutions are the Decree by which you pronounced it legal:

"*Resolved, 1. That it is necessary for the discharge of the duties imposed upon this house, viz. to give its advice to His Majesty, in the enactment of laws for the peace, welfare and good government of the Province, conformably to the Act of the British Parliament, under which it is constituted and assembled, that its Speaker be a person of its free choice, independently of the will and pleasure of the person entrusted by His Majesty with the administra-*

tion of the local government for the time being.

"2. *That* Louis *Joseph Papineau, Esq. one of the* Members *of this* House, *who has served as Speaker in six* successive Parliaments, *has been duly chosen by this House to be its Speaker in the present Parliament.*

"3. *That the Act of the British* Parliament, *under which this house is constituted and* assembled, *does not require the approval of such* person so *chosen as* Speaker *by the person* administering *the* government *of this Province in the* name *of* His *Majesty.*

"4. *That the* presenting *of the* person *so elected as Speaker, to the King's Representative for approval is founded on usage only, and that such approval is and hath always been a matter of course.*

"5. *That this house doth persist in its choice, and that the said* Louis *Joseph Papineau, Esq.* ought *to be and is the* Speaker."

I will abstain from any remarks upon these Resolutions, because I have already proved that they were violent, illegal, and unconstitutional, in the highest degree. I only rehearse them to enable me to prove in fewer words and in clearer terms than I could otherwise have done, these two important prepositions: 1st That the commands of His Majesty to elect "another person," different, *in all respects*, from you, were NOT obeyed, contrary to your statement to the present Governor on the 21st inst. and, 2dly, That the honour and integrity of the House of Assembly, of which you are now Speaker, have been compromised; their faith broken, and their Journals falsified!

1. When, in obedience to the commands of His [present] Excellency, you and the House of Assembly went up to the Legislative Council Chamber, it was there intimated to you that His Excellency did not see fit to declare the causes for which he had summoned that Provincial Parliament, until there should be a Speaker "duly elected and approved." Your reply, sir, is no less extraordinary now than it will be memorable hereafter:—

"*May it please Your Excellency*,

"In obedience to His Majesty's Commaude, the House of Assembly has proceeded to the election of a Speaker, and I am the person upon whome their choice has fallen. I respectfully PRAY that it may please your Excellency to give your approbation to their choice!"

Here you say, sir, that it was "in obedience to His Majesty's commands" the House proceeded to the election of a Speaker, and that their choice had fallen upon you. I respect your station very much, sir, but I respect the honour of my country, and the rights of the people still more. I regret, therefore, to be under the necessity of contradicting you in the plainest and flattest terms. I say, that in obedience to His Majesty's commands—the last commands which you received previous to the present meeting of Parliament—you DID NOT, in the terms of these commands, and in obedience to them,

" again repair to the place where the sittings of the Assembly are usually held, and there make choice of another person to be Speaker;" *your election*, Mr. Papineau, having been disapproved of in these words "*I am* commanded *by His Excellency the* Governor *in Chief to inform you that His Excellency* doth not approve *the choice which the Assembly have made of a Speaker; and in* His Majesty's name, *His Excellency doth accordingly now* disallow *and* discharge *the said choice*." On the contrary, you passed the Resolutions above recited, and the House "persisted in its choice" of you as Speaker!

Sir, these are brief, but most damning facts! and the country calls aloud on you to gainsay them, if you can. They not only convict *you*, now a public officer of the state and of the Government, of having, at the meeting of the present session, gone up to the presence of *your* Sovereign's *Representative* with a *most false and erroneous statement in your mouth*; but stamp the House of Assembly itself with a character neither enviable in itself, nor suitable to the honour and respectability of the Province.

2. I come now to consider with equal brevity my *second proposition, namely*, *That the honour and dignity of the House of Assembly, of which you are now Speaker, have been compromised; their faith broken, and their Journals falsified.*

After stating, in the words which I have already recited, that the choice of the Assembyl had fallen upon you, "*you* respect*fully* *pray, that it might please His Excellency to give his approbation to their choice!"* When you prayed after this form and manner, did it ever occur to you that you were establishing a formulary for the perpetual damnation of the Resolutions of 1827; consecrated by a great majority of votes in the Assembly, and already carefully deposited in the archives of the Provincial Parliament? Whether it did or did not, this is a fact, that by such *prayer* and proceedings in the face of these memorable Resolutions, you have, not tacitly nor constructively, but in reality, compromised the honour and dignity of the Assembly; broken its faith, and falsified its Journals. What *now* becomes of these famous Resolutions, so clamorously called for, and so eagerly voted! What *now* becomes of the vote, That for the discharge of the duties imposed upon the House, it was necessary that its Speaker be a person of its free choice, *independently* of the will and pleasure of His Majesty: That Louis Joseph Papineau had been DULY chosen as Speaker: That the act of the British Parliament, under which the Assembly was constituted, DID NOT require the APPROVAL of the Speaker by His Majesty or his Representative: That the presenting of the person elected as Speaker to the King's Representative for approval, was founded on usage only; and that such approval was, and had always been, *a matter of course*; and, That *you, sir, without such approbation*, ought to be, and was Speaker? What, I ask, sir, becomes of all this? And, moreover, what becomes of the "competency" of the House, as urged by *Mr. Blanchet*, without such approbation? What now becomes of the "common sense" of that learned gentleman; and what do his "sound sense", and his "good sense" say to the new liturgy of the praying-to-be-approved-of-Speaker? What has become of *Mr. Bourdages'* "*despatch of public business*," which he affirmed to be competent without the usual approval of the Speaker? But, above all, what has become of *Mr. Vallieres'* "*life*." Has it been "*forfeited*" or not? for he declared, in his place, that he would as soon lose his life as forego his privileges. These, sir, have *now*, indeed, become very important questions for you and your friends in the Assembly to ponder upon, and to answer, if you will. *My* object will have been attained by the mere recital of them; because I am convinced, that every man of sense or discretion who peruses them, will unite his suffrages with mine, and declare the whole conduct of yourself and the present Assembly on the subject of Speaker, no less a gross insult on the dignity of the Crown, than a stigma on the publick character of the Province.

From what I have *now* said, and I am not at present disposed to touch upon any other topick, it appears perfectly evident, that you, sir, and the body which you lead, or, to speak, more properly, which you serve, have completely abandoned Constitutional principles for interested and time-serving systems; these systems like the Indian philosophy, having neither foundation nor rule of action, except the caprice, the passion and the heedless ambition of a few theorists and demagogues. You have entirely and for ever forfeited your character as a legislative body; for you have not only broken faith with the country, but trampled on your own Resolutions. Can you be trusted for the future? Do you suppose you can always thus act? Do you suppose you can thus perpetually go on, drawing upon the approbation and confidence of your constituents, and then, the moment your object is accomplished, plot and carry into execution some new measure of self-degradation—some new scheme for involving the Province in party-feuds, and yourselves into an exterminatory state of warfare with all the other public bodies of the State. Believe me, sirs, this game, in which there is neither chance nor fair-play for all parties, will not last long. Your constituents are far wiser, dexterous and cleverer men than you give them credit for. They will not always be unfortunate without knowing the cause. They will not always be thwarted in the public measures which you prescribe for their solicitation, and not inquire both into your right to dictate to them, and your prudence to guide them. "Experience teaches fools" says the proverb; and, with respect to this Province, it *now* seems very likely, that the experience of the past will ensure more wisdom for the future. On the present subject—I mean that of Speaker and the co-relative prerogative of the Crown—you screwed them up almost to a pitch of desperation, with the confidence in which you addressed them of the righteousness of your measures. To convince them that it was impossible for *you* to be wrong, you told them—and some of them absolutely believed it—that in the last exercise of the prerogative, the late Governor in Chief was "MAD!" But what will they say when you inform them, that all you said, all you did, and all you preached on this subject was to no purpose; and that instead of following it out, and abiding like men and legislators to your "RESOLUTIONS" through good and evil report, you totally abandoned them in a manner too dastardly to be repeated; leaving their constitutional legality, as well as merits and demerits, to be discussed only in the winter's evening *Chteriss* of the *habitants*? Will they not, when they rightly consider all this, be apt to say, that it was you yourselves who were really "MAD" and not the King's Representative. And will they not add, that, if you found yourselves in reality to be wrong, it would have looked much better, and sounded more constitutionally wise in the ears of every sensible man, had you publicly and boldly repealed and abrogated your celebrated *Cuilleur* "Resolutions" admitted your error, and promised better for the future, instead of the craven part you have acted; shrinking from any reference to your past conduct; and choosing rather to slur and veil it over with an egregious mis-statement than candidly declaring before God and your country that you had abandoned the claim which you had set up to the appointment of Speaker without the approbation of the Crown. Not only did you abandon, and for ever, the point at issue; but you patiently and meekly submitted to an innovation (I will not say an unjustifiable or unconstitutional one) of the forms in which you are usually permitted to elect your Speaker; the words "Until there be a Speaker of the Assembly duly elected and approved" being substituted for the old expressions "Until there should be a Speaker of the House of Assembly." You are thus, your constituents will tell you, when they next meet you, doubly chained—voluntarily chained by your *own acts*, as well as constitutionally by the prerogative of the Crown. This particular prerogative with respect to the Speaker, they will naturally add, you especially despised, disregarded and contemned; but we now see it rivetted round your necks tighter, faster, stronger, and heavier than ever. Can we longer endure such treatment? Can we endure to be embroiled in feuds and quarrels respecting our rights with our Sovereign and his Representatives merely to countenance you in your ambitious struggle for powers that do not of right belong to either of us, and then be told, as our only excuse and palliation, that you were in error! We shall be on our guard for the future; and depend upon it Gentlemen Representatives, that when you next quarrel with the powers of the State, but especially with the King's lawful proragative, you shall find us neither by your side, nor dragged on to our own destruction by the chariot wheels of your mistaken and ill-founded ambition. You have deceived us once more; but it shall be the last time. *We shall have* no more *Punic Houses of Assembly to rule over us!*

Whilst thus discharging a most painful, but important and necessary duty to my country, by exposing the delinquencies of you, sir, and your friends in the Assembly, and a duty which I trust I shall never again be called upon to perform, I cannot refrain from expressing my admiration of the manner in which *Sir James Kempt* discharged his duty to his King and country in opening the present Session of Parliament. He has been accused of *compramiring*; but this I positively deny. *He* could have no personal or political objections to you, sir, as Speaker. You told him, that in *obedience* to *His Majesty's commands* the Assembly had proceeded to the election of a Speaker, and that their choice had fallen upon you. You prayed *for his approbation.* He took you at your word, and he granted your request. It was not for His Excellency to inquire whether you had spoken truth or falsehood. He found you in the situation of every other Speaker at the opening of Parliament, with the prescribed address upon your lips; and it was not for him then and there—at the commencement of a Session which I trust will ever prove important to the interests of the Province—

to read lectures either on moral philosophy or consistency of public conduct. The country is deeply indebted to His Excellency for having thus once more afforded us an opportunity of putting the wisdom and patriotism of our Representatives to the test: and whatever may be the result—and let us cherish the best hopes---our gratitude and thanks to *His Excellency* will be equally unalloyed.

I am Sir,

Yours, &c.

T. L. C. W.

29th Nov. 1828.

No. VI.

Meeting of the Provincial Parliament—Message—Resolutions—Declaration of Independence—&c.

Notwithstanding the irregularity and breach of constitutional trust which we have already pointed out as characterizing the commencement of the present session of our Provincial Parliament, we *did* hope, once a sitting had been actually effected, that some advantage to the country might ultimately be the result; at all events, we flattered ourselves with the expectation, that some progress would have been made towards an adjustment of those differences which have so long injured the interests and disgraced the character of the Province. Indeed such an issue was not only to be expected, but almost confidently relied upon, from the gracious and conciliating manner of the speech from the throne, which, above and beyond all things, enjoined "An oblivion of all past jealousies and dissensions." But we hoped, and flattered ourselves in vain. We ought to have recollected; that no distemper is so inveterate as national jealousy, party prejudice, and factions ambition: that nothing can take a deeper and firmer hold of the heart and the understanding, than self-conceived power cherished by ignorance: and

that no advice, no precept, no maxim, however wisely conceived, or faithfully urged, can ever make a proper impression on the fool, the bigot, or the enthusiast. It is, therefore, with grief and dismay that we look onwards. The vista of the future seems dark and obscure to our sight; for we can now perceive no object, discern no point, on which to fix those hopes and anticipations for our country which late events taught us to cherish. We can descry nothing but the dark and jarring elements of perpetual strife. To speak more plainly, the spirit and genius of the House of Assembly is too turbulent to be tamed by fair words and wholesome advice. Agitators and disturbers of the public peace, like them, are not easily appeased or conciliated. Despising the boon of good will, they must have the concession of fear. We must yield to menace, and give because we dare not refuse. After having for the last ten years warred against every thing sacred to *true* British affection: after having paralyzed the strong and legitimate arm of government by fears unworthy of men and pretensions unworthy of legislators: after having usurped powers which solely belong to the executive: after having completely stopped the whole machine of our Provincial government: after having poured out their complaints at the foot of the throne, and in the presence and hearing of the supreme Legislature of the Empire, after seeing these complaint maturely weighed and considered: and after receiving the clear and impartial answers & decisions of the greatest & gravest authorities of the State, who could do otherwise than hope---who could do otherwise than believe, that an end would immediately be put to the political feuds and dissensions which have so long retarded the prosperity of the Province; and that the Assembly, instead of again renewing the disgraceful contest, would be the first to retire to that legitimate ground of cordial peace and good will which should ever characterise a free and happy people. But alas! the olive branch was held out in vain. It has been not only rejected and trampled under foot, but the torch of discord has been raised in its place midst the shrieks and howlings of a furious and discontented party, proclaiming "*everlasting warfare*," in place of "*an oblivion of all past jealousies and dissensions.*"

It now becomes, of necessity, our painful task to recapitulate how this has been done. We shall add such observations as must appear obvious to the understanding of every man in the country who is not blind to its true and most important interests. We may be alone in these observations. But we care not. We have a deep stake in the prosperity of the Province. We have a reverence for her institutions, modelled as they are, or, at least, were intended to be, on those of the parent State; and should consider ourselves as the most abject and worthless of parasites if we did not raise our voice against the course which is now about to be pursued for the destruction of all that is dear to a Briton's feelings. In the mean time, we must warn the Province against entertaining any expectations of the present session of the Assembly. When the core and the stem of the tree are unsound and rotten, can the fruit be good or plentiful? It is difficult to stop the career commenced in inquiry. It may terminate in virtue; but the issue must ever be precarious; and our hopes always feeble.

The first bad feature in the character of the present Assembly which we shall point out, is, the manner in which the address, in answer to the speech from the throne, was proposed and got up. That there was a deviation from, and an innovation upon, the established rules of the House, all must admit; but no one can justify. It was usual, in conformity to the practice of the House of Commons, to refer the speech to a committee. On the present occasion, when new forms of procedure, new rules, and new maxims are so much in vogue, a committee of a few members would not do—could not do; having entirely forfeited the esteem and respect of the Assembly. There must be a committee of the "*whole house.*" It is a pity the whole country, and the whole world, could not be added! The ostensible reason assigned for this innovation and deviation, was, that "*it would afford to all the members of the House an opportunity of expressing their sentiments, and of furnishing the grounds or foundation for the Address.*" But this was not the real reason; and if it had been so, it would afford but a flimsy and execrable excuse for deviating from a rule established at the commencement of the Constitution: for every member of the House had the same right when the report of the committee would be brought up. The real reason was this, that Mr. Bourdages and his circle had matters in cogitation which they were *afraid*, to use their own words, to trust to a committee. They could depend, they said, upon a *majority* of the "*whole house*;" but as, in the appointment of a committee, respect must necessarily be paid to an appearance *of impartiality*; and as, consequently, individuals of the *true stamp*, might be named members, deemed it an easier affair to fight one battle than two, which they must inevitably do, had a committee been appointed, and any one or more reasonable and enlightened men made members of it. Mr. Bourdages, therefore, came up to his place with the Resolutions preparatory to the address cut and dry in his pocket, where they had been snugly deposited the preceding night to the no small satisfaction of himself and those in the secret of his intentions to insult as well as to innovate. As to the *matter* of the Address itself, it is certainly worthy of the manner; and this is the first instance in the annals of the country of a legislative body, either metropolitan or provincial, having introduced matter into an address which did not correspond with the subject of the speech. What can possibly exhibit in a more glaring light the spirit which pervades the Assembly!

What can more distinctly point out their want of true gentlemanly respect and feeling in form, and want of principle in action! And what, in short, could be more shockingly insulting to His Majesty than the long and extraneous tirade introduced into the Address against His Majesty's late administration in this Province. Did His Majesty over disavow or disapprove of that administration? Did His Majesty recall the head of that administration *because* he disapproved of it? Quite the contrary; and of this the Journals of the present Assembly *already* bear ample testimony. But even had His Majesty done this, and declared so to his "*faithful Commons*" of Lower Canada, was it fit, was it respectful, was it decent, in answer to a speech from the throne, breathing conciliation throughout, and enriched with a vein of the purest spirit of paternal affection and good-will, thus to cast reflections on His Majesty's administration in this Province! Was it constitutional to interlard and beslubber a State document of mere form and compliment with complaints of imaginary grievances, while other opportunities and other means remained behind for conveying such unwelcome sentiments to the foot of the throne! Was every channel shut against complaint but the address! Nay, was it loyal thus at once to declare to *His Majesty's Representative*, that although he took it upon himself to enjoin "*An oblivion of all past jealousies and dissensions*, it was by no means *their* intention to do so while a vestige of them dwelt upon their remembrance: and in order to convince him they were in earnest, that they had embraced the *very first* opportunity of stating a fact so clear to them? The gross ignorance and presumption of a legislative body that could stand up and act such a part as this, is amazing. They suppose, we presume, that there is not on the face of the whole earth, any power—feeling—interest—passion—prejudice or sentiment to be considered but what belongs to themselves. We sincerely wish them joy of the flattering idea; but we regret, at the same time, that there are various other powers on the earth, whom, as we respect more, we shall consult the oftoner.

As to the *tirade* itself introduced into the Address so unnecessarily, extraneously, and indecently, it is truly *unique*, and, to all intents and purposes, like every other thing that is great and wonderful, forms a class by itself. We know not, however, whether it is not intended more as a panegyrick upon the past conduct of the Assembly themselves, than as a reflection upon *Majesty*; for they have ever been famous for the bombastick egotism and adulation with which they overwhelmed themselves. But be that as it may, we scarcely ever met with a more striking specimen of petty, shallow, powerless, feeble, declamation—of puny, puerile, low scurrilous "sound, and fury signifying nothing." It falls greatly below the common-place tawdry, insane, rhapsodies of the tools, emmisaries, demagogues, and idolators of the Assembly out of doors. It is as worthy of the authors as of their cause. But however contemptible it may be in itself—and that it is contemptible who will deny?—it forms part of the address of the House of Assembly of Lower Canada to His Majesty's Representative; and, as such, exhibits in rich and luxuriant profusion both the characteristics of the party whence it emanated, and the ultimate object of their mistaken ambition. It will, therefore, in conjunction with other notable instances of the mad fervour of the Assembly, be of use in directing our attention to their present wayward path; and to which we would also seriously recommend the observation of all our loyal and constitutional readers. No one can pass by the observations of the minority on this question without being struck with their singular justice and propriety. Well might Mr. Stuart challenge the risible fortitude of the gravest individual, upon witnessing the style and matter of the extraneous meteor introduced into the Address; and, upon Mr. Vallieres' justification of the bombastick fervour of the language made use of, well might he add, "that those who wrote fervidly were apt to write foolishly." Never was any apothegm more faithfully realised than this one, for never before were such folly and loathsome insanity introduced into a state document; never did an intended compliment to Majesty carry in its train such insulting malignity; and never was the path to the throne strewed with such filth, impurity, and reptile slime. We know not how we should have borne to be of the same party with those who acted thus. It is bad enough, God knows, to be of the same species.

But we approach matter of still graver importance—matter in which the dearest and best interests not only of the Province, but of the Empire at large are involved. We allude, as may be readily perceived, to the Message sent down by His Excellency and the Resolutions voted by the Assembly in answer to it. His Excellency, rightly considering the great anxiety that existed in the Province for a declaration of His Majesty's sentiments with respect to our present condition, and the importance of an early discussion of them by the Legislature, with the view of alleviating the miseries of the country, lost no time in making these sentiments public the moment that the preliminary business of the session could admit of it; and the thanks of the people are due to His Excellency for his promptness in acceding to their wishes.

The Message is, indeed, a document which ought to be studied by every individual in the country. It is a direct emanation from His Majesty; and is a free, clear, and candid expression of his sentiments with respect to the various questions of importance which have so long agitated, and retarded the prosperity of this Province. It is, at the same time, the result of the frequent and mature deliberations of His Majesty, surrounded by all his legal and constitutional advisers. It is the only authentic record in existence of the real, unbiased opinion of that august council on the public state of affairs in this country; and of consequence, becomes to the people of this Province, as well as to its legislature, their only rule of conduct and guide—their only polar-star in leading to a definitive adjustment of all our past disputes and differences. There are some persons who will be guided by no authority however exalted—who will be swayed by no rule of conduct, however prudent and wise—except the dictates of their own vain and inflated imaginations. But with such persons, we would warn the loyal and the good of this Province to hold no communion; for they—the true and the loyal---are as good judges of the rights of free-men as the loudest declaimer and most brawling demagogue amongst their opponents. Let the honest and true, therefore, think and feel, that the document in question is a direct appeal by His Majesty to their loyalty and good sense. It does not flatter our vanity, nor draw upon our imagination: neither does it yield one point with the view of cajoling us into a ready compliance with another. It sets forth the rights and privileges of all parties; maintaining with a firm and manly grasp those belonging to one side, and pointing, with a candid generosity worthy of its source, to the course which ought to be pursued by the other, in order to attain that cordial peace and permanent happiness which all seem to desire. It is not the manifesto of any party or faction.

It is neither the Creed nor the decalogue of an administration : nor is it the Circular of a proud unyielding minister, ready to trample on right and justice for the attainment of his own ends. *But it is the voice of the law itself*, uttered by the Crown and its ministers, as the organs of the Constitution and government of the Empire---it is in truth the law of the Empire, the dictates and principles of an Act of the Imperial Parliament, which neither the Crown itself nor any other *individual* power in the state can controul or alter. Knowing it to be such, it is our duty, without hesitation or delay, to receive it in the spirit of enlightened men and loyal subjects ; ready to obey the law when the law speaks, and willing to yield when it is neither our right nor to our advantage to contend.

It is not our intention at present, to particularize the general principles and positions laid down in the Message. We shall restrict our observations to that part of it alone wherein a judgment and decision is pronounced on the Financial Question---the great question which has given birth to all those difficulties by which we are at present surrounded and menaced. Our observations will also necessarily embrace the Resolutions voted by the House of Assembly in reference to this question.

The position laid down in the Message is very simple and easy to be understood. His Majesty after stating his conviction that the Provincial Legislature will cheerfully acquiesce in every effort to reconcile past differences, looks forward with the hope, peculiar to his great mind and generous disposition, to a period when no other subject will engage or engross the attention of the legislature, but "*the best methods of advancing the prosperity and developing the resources of the extensive and valuable territories comprised within His Majesty's Canadian provinces.*" With this view, and the view of "obviating all future misunderstanding," His Majesty referring to the "serious attention" which he has bestowed on the discussions which have taken place in the province, "*respecting the appropriation of the revenue,*" sets forth "*in what manner these questions may be finally adjusted with a due* regard to *the prerogatives of the Crown as well as* to *their*(the Legislature's) Constitutional *privileges, and to the general welfare of his faithful subjects in Lower Canada.*" His Majesty then states, "that the Statutes passed in the 14th and 31st years of the reign of his late Majesty, have imposed upon the Lords Commissioners of His Majesty's Treasury the duty of appropriating the produce of the revenue granted to his Majesty by the first of these Statutes, and that whilst the Law shall continue unaltered by the same authority by which it was framed, *His Majesty is not* authorized *to place the Revenue under the controul of* the Legislature *of the* province.

"The proceeds of the Revenue arising from the Act of the Imperial Parliament, 14. Geo. III, together with the sum appropriated by the Provincial Statute, 35. Geo. III, and the duties levied under the Provincial Statutes 41. Geo. III c. 13 & 14, may be limited for the current year at the sum of £34,700.

"The produce of the casual and territorial revenue of the Crown and of fines and forfeitures may be estimated for the same period at the sum of £3400.

"These several sums making together the sum of £38,400, constitute the whole estimated revenue arising in this Province, which the Law has placed at the disposal of the Crown.

"*His Majesty has* been pleased to direct that *from* this collective revenue *of* £38,100 *the salary of the officer* administering *the government of the Province and the* salaries *of the judges should be defrayed.*"

What can be more concise—more explicit---more candid. But what renders this communication of threefold value to the loyal inhabitants of this Province is, its great and remarkable consistency—its singular, its exact uniformity with every despatch, communication and declaration that has ever been made to the Provincial Legislature on the subject of the financial question. This is no new or timeserving doctrine. It has not been got up to please a minister or a party—to keep the one in office, or screen the other from publick obloquy. *It is the dictates and principles of our constitution.* It has its foundation in acts of the Imperial and Provincial Parliaments; its interpretation in the solemn opinion of the highest legal authority of the

State; and its execution in the orders and instructions of His Majesty; and these orders and instructions ever were, and we hope, ever will be, acted upon, to use the words of the Message, "Whilst the law shall continue unaltered by the same authority by which it was framed."

Unhappily for the country, however, the House of Assembly think, or at least says otherwise. Blinded by a sottish and brutal ignorance worthy of the darkest ages and most barbarous people that ever inhabited the face of the earth; and goaded by an ambition which can only be satiated by the complete and uncontrolled possession of all the powers of government, this body denominating themselves a Legislative body, and the Representatives of a free and enlightened people—contradict His Majesty, the law, and the Imperial Parliament, and contend that the control and appropriation of these provincial funds belong to them—*and them alone!* To establish their unjustifiable position they have travelled over and over again all the rounds of the statute-book; they have denied the plainest and clearest letter of the law; they have rejected the most evident principles of the constitution: they have distorted facts: they have raked up the very kennels of oblivion for the remains of all those unnatural abortions which the stupidest of legislators—the most unprincipled of lawyers—or the most ignorant of politicians may have begotten in their wildest and most fantastick reveries; they have spurned the advice and recommendation of Majesty itself; they have disbelieved and discredited the despatches of the minister; they have often and often insulted the King's representative while communicating these despatches: they have resolved and voted—disputed and wrangled—printed and published—brawled and brayed—howled and hissed—kicked and cuffed, until at last they gained their real object by raising such an uproar and ferment in the country, that nothing can ever extinguish but the strongest and most decisive measures that can possibly be executed in a free and independent state. External appearances, must, however, be preserved a little longer; and perceiving that matters were not quite ripe for the blow which they meditated, they put off the event till a more convenient season, and in the meantime amused the country, the people, and the government with another *mock appeal* to the throne, but the decision of which they neither intended to acknowledge nor obey. In proof of this we have only to refer to their own resolutions in answer to the Message.

The present House of Assembly have a manner, as well as matter in all their proceedings, that is peculiar to themselves.—They are men of mode as well as of action. The ancient method of going about business and performing their work they despise.—The "*march of intellect*" has made extraordinary progress and wrought marvels amongst them. Innovations have been made on the most simple operations.

An axe for the future, must not be taken by the handle but by the edge of the weapon itself. A saw must be grasped by the steel, and the wood severed with the frame. Every fashionable table must be furnished with the shovel and tongs instead of knives and forks. The tail of every beau's coat must be worn upwards; and every fashionable lady who has any regard for her reputation, must wear rings on her toes instead of her fingers, and in her nose instead of her ears. Not less ridiculous, certainly, are the innovations already introduced, and about to be introduced into the proceedings of our House of Assembly. Whenever a member wishes to carry a favourite measure, or to pass what he may conceive to be a most excellent law, he has nothing to do but simply perform the necessary operation in his own mind on some given preceding night—write down his law or his resolutions—carry them in a corner of his pocket up to the Assembly—stand up bare-pated in his place---read them—and presto, the business is done! The ears of the sage and patriotick gentleman is immediately and clamorously assailed by the "OUIS"—Anglice "YEAS"—of almost every individual in the house. It is quite unnecessary for the learned gentleman to give himself any trouble with preliminary explanation of the nature and object of his measure. The mere recital of his resolutions is quite enough. Men's minds are now more sensitive and penetrating than before. They intuitively perceive an object without the old-fashioned aid of any explanation or reasoning whatever.---Oratory has now become too old-fashioned a commodity to be thrown away in our publick deliberative assemblies for nothing; and one short resolution is worth twenty long speeches. So no doubt, thought Mr. Neilson ---at least, so he acted when, on the fifth of the present month of December, in the your of our Lord, 1828, he submitted his famous resolutions in reply to His Excellency's Message.

This gentleman, knowing from long and successful experience, the mute and passive disposition of his fellow-representatives, drew his resolutions from his pocket, and with a confidence worthy of his knowledge, silently presented them to the house. Wrapping himself carelessly up in the mantle of what Mr. Stuart happily denominated a "predetermined majority," he condescended merely to solicit the concurrence of the house as a matter of course! It ought to be well observed and long remembered, that among the fifty individuals who constitute the House of Assembly of Lower Canada, there were only six who spoke on one of the most momentous questions that ever occurred in the deliberations of a Colonial legislature; this question being in reality, however much it may be attempted to be disguised---whether this province is longer to endure the legislative supremacy of the Mother Country? Three of those six, be it observed, were on either side of the debate. As to the rest, Baluam's Ass was a prince among orators---a very Demosthenes, a Cicero, a Chatham, a Burke---in comparison with them ; for the honest brute spoke most rationally and to the question when knocked on the head, an experiment, which we are sure, might frequently be essayed to no purpose in the Assembly. These silent gentlemen---these mute automatons---came there to act, not to prate, to vote, not to speechify. It is not at all requisite that they should be well-informed as to the proceedings of the house. They are sent there by three hundred thousand electors who can neither read nor write ; and they are fully satisfied that one speaker or leader for every hundred thousand is a fair and just representation. What an excellent commentery on Mr. Huskisson's story of the Crosses to the petitions of grievances ! The truth is, and it is high time the truth should be known---that there are not six members on the major side of the house who can discourse for ten seconds with any rational portion of judgment on the simplest question of our constitutional laws ; and we will bet a rump and dozen, that there are not twelve men in the whole house who can tell the difference between a monarchical and democratick government, or between the British constitution and that of the United States of America ! Yet these are the individuals who, not only arrogating to themselves the wisdom and discretion of an enlightened legislative body, but the possession and control of all the executive powers of government, have reduced this province to a state of anarchy.

and boldly persist, by their insane ignorance, in rejecting every measure calculated to restore the peace of the province and save the people from impending ruin. Let no man tell us that all this is more declamation. We utterly scorn the mean alternative. Our observations are founded on truth---self-evident and undeniable truth; and that they are so, we have only to refer to the sentiments and opinions set forth in the resolutions under consideration.

The first of these Resolutions states; "*that the House derived the greatest satisfaction from the gracious expression of His Majesty's beneficent views towards this province,*" yet, as if sorry and ashamed that any complimentary expressions, even to their Sovereign, should have passed their lips, the majority of the house, in the second resolution, hasten to declare that they have "Never*theless* observed *with great* concern, *that it may be inferred from that* part *of the Message which* relates *to the appropriation of the revenue, that the* pretension *put forth at the* commencement *of the late Administration,* to *the* disposal *of a large* portion *of the revenue of this province may be persisted in.*"

This is extraordinary language, both as to style and sentiment, to be held forth to a constitutional Sovereign, who has, and who can have, no other object, to use his own words, but the "Welfare of his faithful Canadian Subjects;" and whose present communication to the legislature of this province is founded not only on the general constitution of the Empire, but on solemn acts both of the Imperial and Provincial Parliaments.— The *style*, however, we pass over with that silent scorn and indignation becoming the loyal subjects of one of the greatest and best of Sovereigns, thanking our stars, we have been reared in the conviction, that the sternest of publick duties is not incompatible at once with decent manners, and the language of sobriety and respect. As to the sentiments, having somewhat to say to them, and being convinced that the example of history is the best possible mode of instruction, if not of conviction also, we shall here enter into a brief historical detail of the *Permanent Revenue* of the province. By this means we hope to be able to say, with unerring certainty, on which side the "*pretension*" really and truly lies.

When Great Britain conquered Canada— plucked it from the tyrannical and despotick grasp of old France---rescued the Fathers of the House of Assembly from feudal bondage and slavery---and restored them to the freedom and independence of the British Constitution, it was found that certain duties imposed upon the importation and exportation of merchandize were the principal means existing for the support of the government of the colony. These finances, which perhaps did not exceed seven or eight thousand pounds sterling per annum, were at the entire disposal and administration of the Intendant, an officer in the French government who, by his commission, was authorized to exercise, fully and freely, all those powers of appropriation

yes

and control which at present constitute the primary ambition of the Assembly. The powers of the Intendant, indeed, were such as we should not like to see engrossed by any one individual branch of our government, free and mixed as it is. He not only enjoyed the right of collecting and disposing, but of levying and imposing it also in any manner most suitable to his wishes and inclinations, not to the circumstances and good-will of the People, who, until the conquest, were considered as more military slaves and feudal *vileyns*, without a voice in the government or influence in the state. As soon as the definitive treaty of Paris had been signed, the British government appointed a "Receiver-General, and collector* of the royal patrimony rents, revenues, farms, taxes, tythes, duties, imports, profits and casualties, arising within the province of Quebec," with power to "apply the monies which should come into his hands of the said duties and revenues in the first place for and towards defraying the necessary expense of Government, and the necessary charge of managing the revenue under his care; remitting home by good bills of exchange the surpluses of the monies which from time to time should remain in his hands after payment of those expenses, in order that the same might be applied to the reimbursing the publick here, (in Great Brit-

---

* Thomas Mills, Esq. was the first appointed to this office, and his commission is dated the 10th of July, 1765.

ain,) the monies that had been necessarily advanced for that purpose, by reason that the aforesaid duties and taxes had not been levied within the two years last past." In this way the above duties continued to be levied, collected and appropriated or applied till the year 1774, when the celebrated act, 14th Geo. III. cap. 88., was passed by the Imperial Parliament. This act is entituled "*An act to establish a fund towards further defraying the charges of the administration of justice, and support of the civil government within the province of Quebec in America.*"— By this act all the duties which were imposed on goods imported into, or exported from this province under the authority of His Most Christian Majesty, were discontinued from and after the 5th day of April, 1775; and in lieu thereof the several rates and duties therein mentioned, were ordered "to be raised, levied, collected, and paid unto His Majesty, his heirs and successors for and upon the respective goods herein-after mentioned, which shall be imported and brought into any part of the said province over and above all the other duties now payable in the said province by any act or acts of parliament." It was then enacted "That all the monies that shall arise by the said duties (except the necessary charges of raising, collecting, levying, recovering, answering, paying and accounting for the same) shall be paid by the collector of His Majesty's customs into the hands of His Majesty's Receiver-General in the said province for the time being, and shall be applied in the first place in making a more certain and adequate provision towards defraying the expenses of the Civil Administration of Justice and of the support of the Civil Government of the said province; and that the Lord Treasurer or Commissioners of His Majesty's Treasury or any two or three of them for the time being, shall be, and is or are hereby impowered from time to time by any warrant or warrants under his or their hand or hands to cause such money to be applied out of the said produce of the said duties towards defraying the said expenses; and that the residue of the said duties shall remain and be reserved in the hands of the said Receiver-General, for the future disposition of Parliament."

By this law the Lords Commissioners of His Majesty's Treasury became fully invested with the uncontrolable power of applying or appropriating the duties imposed in virtue of its enactments towards defraying the expences of the administration of justice, and of the support of the civil Government of the Province, so far as the amount of these duties would admit of such appropriation.--- But these Commissioners have always delegated their authority to the Governors of the Province, all of whom, in the execution of such authority, and in obedience to the concurring commands and instructions of His Majesty, have always appropriated the revenues in question for the purposes described in the act itself, without being subjected to the controul of any authority whatever in the

Province. Indeed, until the passing of the Constitutional act, in 1791, there existed no power or authority in the Province which had the right to call into question these appropriations; and even then, as will presently be seen, the new constitutional bodies created by that act neither arrogated to themselves, as some of them have since done, nor received from Parliament any the smallest right to interfere with the delegated powers of the Lords Commissioners of the Treasury. In 1795, however, four years after the passing of the Constitutional act, it was discovered, that the permanent revenue created, as above, by the act of 1774, was inadequate to the purposes for which it had been raised; and the provincial legislature of that day not wishing like the present, that the arms of the government should be shortened, or any of their powers dissolved, passed an act of which this is the title:---"An act for granting to His Majesty an additional and new duties on certain goods, wares, and merchandizes, and for appropriating the same towards further defraying the charges of the administration of Justice, and support of the civil government within this Province, and for other purposes therein mentioned." The sum consigned annually into the hands of His Majesty by this act, was *five thousand pounds sterling*; and its authors, imitating the words and intentions of its imperial prototype of 1774, ordained, that "the due application of all such monies pursuant to the directions of this act, shall be accounted for to His Majesty, his heirs, and successors, through the lords commissioners of His Majesty's Treasury, in such manner and form as His Majesty, his heirs and successors shall direct."

It will here be observed, that the Legislature of 1795, so far from claiming the "*inherent right*" of appropriating the revenue created by the imperial act of 1774, added, by a free and voluntary enactment of their own, a considerable sum *to it*, to be applied and accounted for in the same manner as the orginal act of the Supreme Legislature : thus ---not tacitly, nor constructively, but openly and spontaneously---declaring their own incapacity to interfere with the rights of their Sovereign. Is it possible to adduce stronger or more conclusive evidence of the absurdity and injustice of the claims of the present Assembly, than this abstinence from executive intervention on the part of their predecessors of 1795 ? The assembly of that time were in possession of every legal and constitutional right that can possibly be kenjoyed now ; and surely we cannot thin so meanly of them as to believe, that if they really possessed any authority over the Crown revenues, they were destitute of sufficient courage to claim and exercise it. The act of 1774 was then as much in force as it is now ; and the provisions of the subsequent constitutional act of 1791, were then as extensive and as well understood as they are now. His Majesty was therefore left in the peaceable enjoyment and disposal of his revenue, which he augmented still further by the casual and territorial revenue of the Crown, and fines and forfeitures; making together, as stated in the Message of the 29th of November last, the sum of £38,100. This far, then, it is pretty clear, that the "pretension put forth to the disposal of a large portion of the revenue of this Province," was not the act of the "LATE ADMINISTRATION."

Towards the year 1810, another spirit and more dangerous principles were infused into the House of Assembly by the introduction of new members, pretending to wiser heads and more courageous hearts than any of their predecessors. These gentlemen, instigated by a long-cherished conviction that no barrier remained between them and the entire possession of *all* the powers of government, as well executive as legislative, except the right to control and apply the *whole* public revenue of the Province, prevailed upon the House of Assembly to make an offer to the King of "*the necessary sums for defraying the civil expenses of the government of this Province.*" This step having been taken of a sudden by a dark and intriguing majority of the Assembly, without any motion or suggestion of the Crown, or the concurrence of the Legislative Council, its unconstitutional aspect was perceived by all men, while but few were able to penetrate into the ulterior and real objects of this majority. His Excellency Sir James Henry Craig was one of these few; and the answer of this stern but constitutional Governor to the Assembly, when they approached him with their novel offer, can never be sufficiently admired. His Excellency firmly and candidly told them, that their offer was not constitutional, inasmuch as the usage of the Imperial Parliament forbade all steps on the part of the people towards grants of money which were not recommended by the Crown; and that, although by the same parliamentary usage, all grants originated in the Lower House, yet they were ineffectual without the concurrence of the Upper House. For these reasons His Excellency conceived the address brought up by the Assembly to be unprecedented, IMPERFECT IN FORM, and being merely founded on the resolutions of that House, without the sanction or concurrence of the Legislative Council, must be ineffectual. His Excellency thought it right, however, to apprize His Majesty of their present proceedings and offer, however imperfect in form and unconstitutional in matter. Considering the views of the Assembly, it may be easily imagined that this answer acted upon them somewhat similar to the effects of a first discovery upon the nocturnal deliberations of a band of assassins or resurrection-men. The plot was evidently discovered, and the first step taken towards its accomplishment utterly destroyed. They thought the road to the sole and complete controul of the public revenue, and by consequence, to all the powers of government, entirely open. The guardian of the public welfare, who met them so sternly in the path and pushed them back to their original ground, was therefore, and forever declared a public enemy; and no wonder if the administration of Governor Craig was afterwards one of unprecedented aggression and turbulence on the part of the House of Assembly. Had the Assembly at this time imposed upon themselves the burthen of any *balance* that might be necessary for the support of the civil government and administration of justice *in aid of the permanent funds already at the disposal of government* the offer would have looked and sounded better, however unconstitutionally made; and would have proved that the Assembly both studied and understood the true interests of their country. But to have come thus up with an offer to defray the *whole* expenses of the government, in hope that His Majesty and Parliament would at once forego their pre-existing rights and revenue, exhibited them in the character of the greatest asses and blockheads that ever existed. However, that man must be either exceedingly simple and stupid, or exceedingly wicked and hypocritical, who never exhibits symptoms of mortified ambition; and we accordingly find, that the leaders of the Assembly have ever since become at once more openly loud and clamorously urgent in their demands, whether they relate to the finances of the Province, or other questions of constitutional government. In the meantime, down till 1818, the permanent revenue continued to be applied by the Crown as usual; and the claims of the Assembly to that revenue continued unmooted for eight years longer, during which, neither was any step taken by Government to encourage their pretensions.

On the 7th of January, 1818, the Legislature met. Sir John Cospe Sherbrooke, was Governor. In the opening Speech *His Excellency* informed the Assembly, that he was commanded to call upon them "to vote the sums necessary for the ordinary annual expenditure of the Province." When, in pursuance of these commands, the estimates for the civil list were sent down to the Assembly, the purport of the word "necessary" here made use of, became more obvious. The estimates amounted to £73,646 8 9. From this sum, however, there were deducted £33,383, being the average for the last three years of the amount of the funds alread provided by law for the support of the administration of justice and the civil government. The balance of £40,263 8 9 was consequently left to be provided for by the Assembly. Ovserve that they were not called upon to provide for the £73,646 8 9 the whole and entire sum necessary for the civil list, but for the £40,263, 8 9; the difference being already provided for by acts of the Imperial and Provincial Parliament, namely, the 14 Geo. III, cap. 83. and the P. S. 35 Geo. III. cap. 9. with neither of which the Assembly had now nothing to do, either directly with themselves, or indirectly with the funds created in virtue of their authority. And to do the Assembly justice, they for once, at least, understood the matter in this light. Their *vote* on the occasion, though unconstitutional in point of form, not having the concurrence of the Legislative Council, is a memorable record of the fact. It states, "that the House having taken into consideration His Excellency's recommendation on the subject of the expences of the Civil Government of this Province, for the year 1818, have voted a sum, *not exceeding* £40,263 8 9 currency, towards defraying the espanco of the Civil Government of this Province, for the year 1818, exclusive of the sum already appropriated by law; but that the peculiar circumstances which have prevented the House from receiving at an earlier moment the estimate of the civil list revenue and public accounts; and the advanced state of the Session not admitting the passing of a bill of appropriation for the purpose, they pray His Excellency will be pleased to order, that the said sum, not exceeding £40,263 8 9 currency, be taken out of the unappropriated monies which, are now, or hereafter may be in the hands of the Receiver General of this Province, for the purposes aforesaid; and assuring His Excellency, that this House will make good the same at the next session of the Provincial Parliament." The act passed next session to fulfil this engagement, directed the above supply "to be charged against the unappropriated monies in the hands of the Receiver General of this Province, which may have been raised, levied and collected under and by virtue of any act or acts of the Legislature of this Province."

Thus far the House of Assembly acknowledged and recognized the provisions of the 14th and 35th of the King, above recited. Not only so, but the vote of 1818, and the corresponding *act* of 1819, are to all intents and purposes a declaratory law upon this subject; for that vote and that act clearly and explicitly acknowledge a fund "already appropriated by law, and expressly renounce all right of interference with any monies in the hands of the Receiver General, except those raised, levied and collected under and by virtue of any act or acts of the Legislature of this Province." There being no change either in these laws, or in the general or constitutional circumstances of the Province, it appears, therefore, passing strange to every intelligent mind, upon what foundation in common sense, equity, or justice, the House of Assembly have ever since been endeavouring to rear such a huge and shapeless fabrick of pretensions to the disposal and control of the entire funds of the Province without distinction. Every honest man, who views the subject impartially, is amazed at such proceedings; and naturally concludes, that, as there appear no good or just grounds for such presumption, some *bad* and erring principles must inevitably be at work. "Nevertheless," from the year 1819, to the year 1829, the house of Assembly have never ceased nor slackened in their endeavours totally to throw aside the authority of the 14th Geo. III. cap. 88, and to invest themselves in the entire revenue of the Province. That they have been resisted and obstructed in their seditious and rebellious march—that they have been corresponded with, argued with, and reasoned with, by every power in the state, from the King on the throne to the humble individual who now addresses them—alas the journals of the legislature and the press of the country bear ample evidence. Nor has this resistance been confined to certain periods or individuals. The Duke of Richmond, who succeeded Sir John Coape Sherebrook, as Governor, adhered to the principles laid down in the estimates of his predecessor; but *his pretensions*, though borne out by the Legislative Council, who very properly threw out an infamously unconstitutional bill of supply sent up to them by the Assembly, failed in receiving the concurrence and approbation of the Assembly. In the last speech of that excellent and high-minded nobleman to the Legislature, he plainly and candidly stated, "It is with much concern I feel myself compelled to say, that I cannot express to you, Gentlemen of the Assembly, the same satisfaction, nor my approbation at thu general result of your labours, (at the expense of so much valuable time) and of the public principles upon which they rest, as recorded in your journals. You proceeded upon the documents which I laid before you, to vote a *part* of the sum required for the expenses of the year 1819; but the bill of appropriation which you passed was founded upon such principles, that it appears from the journals of the Upper House, to have been most constitutionally rejected." Was this, let us here again ask, "*a* pretension *put forth by the* late *Administration?*"

We now approach the "commencement *of the late* administration; those of Mr. Monk and Sir Peregrine Maitland being too short to admit of squabbles on the subject of finance, though impossible to be so much so as not to admit of any topick of Legislative difference. *Lord Dalhousie* arrived in Canada in 1820, on the anniversary of the *Battle of Waterloo!* We are not superstitious—no, not we; but this was an event which we have always considered as ominous, if, indeed, of bad, still of good. The great conqueror of *Waterloo* had arduous physical and scientifick duties to perform. But he who attempts, like *Lord Dalhousie*, to eradicate *French* ignorance, and conquer *French* prejudica, will have a still more difficult task to execute. However, now that the two heroes are once more together, let us hope, they will between them, at least put an end to the legislative differences of this Province, if not to the whole difficulties that surround us.

What the "*late* administration" itself said, or did, or *pretended*, with respect to the public revenue of this Province, we shall not refer to, but appeal direcly to those supreme and acknowledged authorities in the state which all parties affect to respect, however reluctant to obey. On the instructions and despatches furnished to *Lord Dalhousie* in 1820, and 1821, were founded ALL his measures on the financial question. Whatever may have been the individual sentiments of

His Lordship on that subject—and we have reason to know that they were as sound as they were constitutional---*they* were not obtruded on the legislature ; no communication having been made to that body, especially the House of Assembly, which was not the counterpart of instructions received from His Majesty's Imperial Government. Had the case been otherwise, and had his Lordship acted from no other construction of the constitution than his own, and obeyed no commands but the dictates of his own mind, he was exceedingly happy in the constant and unhesitating approbation of his Sovereign. As it was, his conduct could not be otherwise than approved of by the same source whence both his instructions and the whole basis of his public conduct emanated. The extent and importance of this approbation, we shall now consider.

The first intimation which reached the Assembly of the real sentiments of the Imperial Government on the subject of the financial disputes, was contained in a despatch from the Colonial Minister, Lord Bathurst, to the Lieut. Governor, Sir Francis Burton, dated the 23d November, 1824.* These despatches are accompanied by the official opinion of the law-officers of the crown, to whom were referred a report made by the Assembly upon the provincial accounts," in which a question is raised as to the right of government

* Lord Dalhousie, was in England on leave of absence at this time.

to apply the proceeds of the revenue arising from the 14th Geo. III. cap. 88, as they have invariably been since the passing of the act, towards defraying the expenses of the administration of justice, and the support of the civil government of his Majesty, without the intervention of the Colonial Administration! His Majesty's Law-Officers, who were the present Lord Chancellor and Attorney General, then go on to state:

"In compliance with your Lordship's request, we have taken the same into our consideration, and beg leave to report for the information of His Majesty, that by the 14th Geo. III. cap. 88, the duties hereby imposed are substituted for the duties which existed at the time of the surrender of the Province to His Majesty's Arms, and are *especially appropriated* by the Parliament to defray the expenses of the Administration of Justice, and of the support of the Civil Government in the Province.

"This Act is not repealed by the 18th Geo. III. cap. 12, the preamble of which declares that Parliament will not impose any duty, &c. for the purpose of raising a revenue; and the enacting part of which states, that from and after the passing of this act, the King and Parliament of Great Britain will not impose and accept only, &c. the whole of which is prospective, and does not, as we think, affect the provisions of the Act 14th Geo. III. cap. 88. It may be further observed, that if the 18th Geo. III. had repealed the 14th Geo. III. the duties imposed by the latter act must immediately have ceased; and the Act. 18th Geo. III. cannot affect the appropriation of the duties imposed by the 14th Geo. III. since the 18th Geo. III. is confined to duties *thereafter* to be imposed, and imposed also for purposes different from those which were contemplated by the Legislature in passing the 14th Geo. III. viz. the regulation of commerce alone.

"We are further of opinion, that the act 14th Geo. III. cap. 88, is not repealed or affected by the 31st Geo. III. cap. 31. It is clear that it is not repealed; in fact, as we observed, with respect to the 18th Geo. III. if the act had been repealed, the duties must immediately have ceased; and as to the appropriation of the duties, or the control over them, nothing is said upon the subject either in the 46th or 47th section, or in any other part of the Act 31st Geo. III. cap 31.

"With respect to any inference to be drawn from what may have taken place in Canada, within the last few years, as to these duties, it may be observed, that the duties having been imposed by Parliament at a time when it was competent to Parliament to impose them, they cannot be repealed, or the appropriation of them in any degree varied, except by the same authority.

We have the honour, &c.

(Signed) J. S. COPLEY,
CHAS. WETHERELL."

Earl Bathurst, &c. &c.

Colonial Department, Downing Street,
26th June, 1823.

8*

Nothing can be more distinct and explicit than this. It is the highest legal authority in the nation; and when sanctioned by a long course of practical operation of the law itself, and the general opinion of sensible men, ought to be irresistible. Nor was it hid in a corner; for upon the meeting, in 1824, of that session of the Legislature in which the Lieutenant Governor presided. *His Excellency* gave *verbal communication of it to the Speaker* and *many Members of the Assembly.* But the Assembly were not to be driven from a position so long and tenaciously maintained by a mere declaration of the opinion of the law officers of the crown. The interests of the Province, they said, were at stake; and their own ideas, they *thought*, were fully adequate to the maintenance of those interests. In proceeding, therefore, during that session, to discuss a Bill of Supply, they entirely overlooked this communication, and passed a bill, founded on their old claim of exclusive right to the disposal of the permanent revenue of the crown, and calculated to raise the greatest alarm among the friends of the constitution. How this bill passed the Legislative Council we shall leave to be explained by *those* who are better acquainted than ourselves with the *intrigue* by which the measure was effected; having no curiosity to penetrate into the sanctuary of state chicanery, especially when the results do not reflect credit on the public business of the country. In the despatch which accompanied this bill to England, the Lieut. Governor expressed his "infinite satisfaction, that the differences which had so long subsisted between the legislative bodies on financial matters, had been amicably settled," and "that the Assembly had decidedly acknowledged the right of the crown to dispose of the revenue arising out of the 14th Geo. III." It is very evident, from the whole strain of this despatch, that the Lieut. Governor thought sincerely what he wrote. But upon perusing the bill, the Colonial Minister was of a very different opinion; and in his long explanatory despatch of the 4th of June, 1825, to the Lieutenant Governor, and communicated by message to the Assembly by Lord Dalhousie, on the 14th March, 1826, the Minister says,---"*I regret that it is* not in *my power* to consider *this arrangement as* in *any degree satisfactory*. The special instructions which had been given by His Majesty's command to the Governor General, in my despatches of the 11th of September, 1820, and 13th September, 1821, had imposed upon him the necessity of refusing all arrangements that went in any degree to compromise the integrity of the revenue, known by the name of the *permanent revenue*; and it appears to me, on a careful examination of the measures which have been adopted, that they are at variance with those specific and positive instructions." The minister goes on to say, "the appropriation of the permanent revenue of the crown will always be laid by His Majesty's command before the House of Assembly, as a document for their information, and for the general regulation of their proceedings. They will therein see what services are already provided for by the crown, and what remains to be provided for by the Legislature, and they will be thus assured, that the proceeds of the revenue of the crown, (whether more or less, or from whatever sources derived) will exclusively and invariably be applied under the discretion of the King's government, for the benefit of the Province." His Lordship concludes thus---"As the bill is limited to one year, I shall not think it necessary to recommend to His Majesty to disallow it, but confine myself to instructing his Majesty's representative in the Province of Lower Canada, not to sanction any measure of a similar nature." Again, "*was this a pretenson set forth at the* commencement *of the* late administration?"

But this is not all---The Assembly and their friends out of doors, finding by the stern determination of Lord Dalhousie to abide by the instructions thus and otherwise conveyed to him, got up petitions to the imperial government and parliament in aid of their pretensions. In a country, like Canada, where the bulk of the people are ignorant, uneducated, and credulous, this is an easy business on the part of their representatives, who to secure belief, have only to state their own view of the subject, no matter however wild or improbable; their constituents being grossly ignorant of the publick affairs of the country, except as represented to them through the distorted channel of ambitious and designing demagogues, who alone, from national communion of language and manners, can secure any kind of access to the minds of the French Canadians. The petitions, which may be said to be only the petitions of a party in the House of Assembly, were entrusted to three Delegates, who proceeded to England, and laid them before the King and parliament. The English population of the province, actuated by the proverbial confidence of Britons in the integrity, wisdom and liberality of the Imperial parliament, and resting satisfied with the mere truth and justice of the cause which they espoused, being that of the King's Representative, proceeded no further than a simple expression of their sentiments in addresses to that distinguished nobleman; approving generally of his conduct, but especially applauding his unswerving perseverance in resisting the pretensions of the Assembly. Matters were now at issue before the Imperial Parliament. Mr. Huskisson, whilst there stating the views of His Majesty's Ministers on the legislative difficulties existing in this province, and soliciting a select committee to take them into consideration, with respect to the question under discussion, explicitly stated, that the duties levied by the act of 1774, in lieu of the old French duties were *bona fide, the permanent revenue of the Crown.* He then goes on to say:---"I believe there is no lawyer in this country, nor indeed any one in the least acquainted with the relative situation of the parties. who will deny, that as long as the Crown appropriates that revenue to the administration of justice in Canada, and to its civil government pursuant to the act of 1774 ---as long as it fulfils all the conditions required by good faith towards the Canadians, no one, I say will deny its *right* to prescribe the mode in which the revenue, consistently with that act, shall be expended. There *is*, I am sure, none who will not say that the pretensions of the Legislative body to take the whole management of this money into its own hands, are neither founded in law nor practice."---There was not an individual in the House of Commons who could contradict this. Nor did the *Canada Committee*, as it has been called, venture on opposite grounds, however much disposed, from party views, to side with the House of Assembly. The report of the Committee on this subject, is in these words :---" From the opinion given by the law officers of the crown, your committee must conclude, that the right of appropriating the revenues arising from the act of 1774, is vested in the crown." And, founded on all these legal and legislative opinions, the late message to the House of Assembly distinctly declares, that "*His Majesty is not authorised to place the revenue under the* control *of the Legisla*ture *of the Pro*vinct."

More we will not, and need not say upon this subject. All we ask of the candid, the generous, and the unprejudiced, is, to peruse our narrative; and brief and incomplete as it is, we have no manner of hesitation to abide by their judgment; assuring ourselves they cannot do otherwise than say with us, that the "*pretension*" said in the Resolutions of the Assembly to have been "*put forth at the* commencement *of the late Administration*," was not the pretension, if pretension it may be called, of that administration, or any particular period of that administration; but of the King, the Imperial Parliament, His Majesty's Ministers, and of every Administration of this Province since the conquest!

It has, however, been asserted by the advocates and partizans of the Assembly, that the house have never denied either the existence of the 14th Geo. III., the interpretation put upon it, or the powers with which its enactments invest the Crown; and that their claims only extend to the appropriation and control of the whole revenue of the Province when a vote of supply is solicited by the Crown; or, in other words, that when the Governor lays the accounts and estimates of the year before them for the purpose of obtaining supply, they have the undoubted right of saying, "we cannot vote a supply unless you permit us to appropriate the whole revenue; for we find, that of the duties levied under the 14th Geo. III. you have been too lavish, and might have made a far more proportionable and economical use of these funds. You have taken too much to yourself; you have given too much to the Chief Justice and the other Judges; the salary of your Secretary is, by far, too high ; and, in short, your Excellency has been much more liberal with the revenue at your disposal than the services of the public officers deserve. We can get the business done on a much lower scale ; and the less we give of the permanent funds of the Crown, the less also it will be necessary to supply from our own funds."

With respect to the first part of this position which affects not to deny the existence of the 14th Geo. III. and the consequent right of the Crown to appropriate the funds created by that act, it is so far correct, that when in 1826, Lord Dalhousie laid the despatches of the Colonial minister and the opinion of the Crown Lawyers before the Assembly, their committee reported, that they were "not *aware that the truth of these propositions had ever been contested*." But the misfortune is, that all the votes and resolutions of the Assembly upon this subject have been mere cobwebs ; manufactured to gratify the excited disappointment of the moment, and anon to be broken through for the purpose of facilitating a more ambitious and important object. We have carefully perused all the recorded resolutions of the Assembly upon this subject, and here declare that we have not seen the report of any committee which does not contain less or more resolutions asserting the non-existence of the 14th Geo. III. We could cite every one of these resolutions ; but it will be sufficient at present to state, that Mr. Cuvillier, the father of almost all of them, strongly maintained, during the late debate, that this act did not exist. His words are important: "When the 14th Geo. III. was passed, the country was too poor to supply the deficiencies in the revenue; and it is only a few years since it has risen to such a state as to be able to provide for its own wants. During that time it would have been absurd to repeal that statute; it was the only provision we had; but he would contend it was virtually repealed, not only by the act of 1774, and the constitutional act, but by others." We shall not certainly place Mr. Cuvillier's opinion in competition with that of the law-officers of the Crown, or any of the other authorities which we have already cited and detailed. As to the last postulatum with regard to the mode of voting the supplies, it will only be necessery to observe, that if, as we are certain we have made out a case with respect to the existence and force of the 14th Geo. III., nothing could possibly be more absurd than the pretension to any powers, of whatever nature, not authorised by the act itself; and nothing more at variance with the principles of our constitution, than transferring the rights and prerogatives of the Crown to a popular and clamorous Assembly. In one word, if this act be still in force, let it be obeyed, and its dictates held sacred to their purposes: if it be in force, and is nevertheless unconstitutional, let its formal repeal be prayed for at the proper bar in a legal and constitutional way; and not by inference, inuendo, misapplication, and forced construction, as has unfortunately been the practice in this province for the last ten years.

As to a vote of supply this session, we have no hopes of it. How can we? The Message declares that the permanent revenue is by "Law placed at the disposal of the Crown; but the Resolutions declare this to be a persisting in the "*pretensions*" of the "*late Administration*," and of consequence illegal; and, ergo, a supply would be a legal sanction of this illegality. "What then, is to be done?" say a thousand tongues, and not a few publick officers. Nothing, our well-beloved friends, but simply this: The Governor, by message---*The Message*---has already informed the Assembly, that he has £38,100 at his disposal. If the government stand in need of more, which it will unquestionably, His Excellency will call upon the Assembly for the balance---say, thirty or forty thousand pounds. If the Legislature vote this supply, without any questions as to the appropriation of the £38,100, good and well; and their doing so will be one good symptom of a turning back to a sense of duty and constitutional conduct. If not, the Governor must do as he best can, pay away his 38,100, as far as it will go; and then tell the poor unfortunate devils who call afterwards, that they are too late; for that the House of Assembly have locked the door of the Treasury!

We now come to the Declaration of Independence---by far the most important question that can be agitated in a British Colony.

The Resolution involving this declaration, is couched thus :

"5. *That no interference of the British Legislature with the established* Constitution *and Laws of this Province, excepting on such points as from the relation* between *the Mother* Country *and the Canadas can* only *be* disposed *of by the paramount authority of the* British *Parliament, can in any way* tend to *the final adjustment of any difficulties* or *misunderstandings which may exist in this Province, but* rather *to aggravate and perpetuate them.*"

The *only good* that can be said of this Resolution, is, that although it was intended to assert a denial of the supreme legislative authority of the Mother Country in every respect, it had neither the courage to avow such revolutionary sentiments in plain terms, nor to join the hue and cry of the demagogues out of doors, who themselves fearlessly deny, and teach—*industriously teach*—their more peaceable neighbors also to deny, the supreme legislative powers of the Imperial Parliament. It is, indeed, we are sorry to say it, only in an ignorant and illiterate colony, like Lower Canada, disturbed as it at present is, by an infamous and revolutionary faction, exposing by every step the rotten malignity of its mental barbarism, that such unworthy sentiments could for a moment be entertained. But we have ourselves alone to blame; at least the British government will alone be responsible, should the evil consequences of such sentiments ever come to maturity, which God forbid. We have no earthly desire to throw odium either on men or ministers; but this much we must say—and say it boldly—that if ever there existed publick measures calculated to instil improper notions of constitutional authority into the minds of an illiterate people---inflate them with undue notions of their own national consequence---imbue them with ideas of contempt of the authority and stability of the principles of the British government---and embolden them to deeds of irregularity and violence, they have been the callous, timid, vascillating, wavering, and unjustifiably conciliatory conduct of Great Britain towards Lower Canada! We do not mince the matter. Truth alone can elicit propriety and principle in conduct; and of the fact now stated, there is ample evidence in every page of the history of this Province. The eleventh hour, however, has not yet arrived. In the mean time let us hope, that the anarchy which at present reigns in this Province will excite the more immediate attention of the Imperial Government, and ultimately secure to us the tranquillity, peace, and prosperity which constitute the inherent rights of a British Population.

But how stands the matter with respect to the legislative authority of the Imperial Parliament over the people and Legislature of this Province, *not* a native colony, but a conquered one? For our own part, we think it most clear and certain, that this authority is omnipotent and unbounded, with the single exception of local taxation without metropolitan representation. This seems not only to be a general inherent principle of the connection which subsists between the mother country and her Colonies, implying protection and obedience, but the dictates of the declaratory act, 6th Geo. III., and the Constitutional act of this Province. The first expressly declares, "that the said colonies have been, *are*, and of right ought to be, subordinate unto, and dependent on, the Imperial Crown and Parliament of Great Britain; and that the King and Parliament of Great Britain, had, HATH, and of right ought to have, full power and authority to make Laws and Statutes of sufficient force to bind the Colonies and His Majesty's subjects in them, *in all* cases *whatsoever*. And it is further declared, that all Resolutions, votes, orders and proceedings in any of the said Colonies, whereby the *power and authority* of the King, Lords and Commons of Great Britain, in Parliament assembled, is denied or drawn into question, are, and are hereby declared to be, utterly *null and void* to all intents and purposes whatsoever." No one will assert that *this act* has been repealed. Consequently, the Resolution above rehearsed, drawing the authority of the Imperial Parliament into question, is *ispo facto*, *null* and *void*. If, therefore, the Assembly wish to enforce and follow it up, they have only to rally their partizans around them, and do so with knives and daggers at men's throats. Our own constitutional act is no less explicit; and throughout its whole enactments implies the right to amend, alter, and even take away, as well as confer rights and immunities. The second section of that act declares, that the powers thereby conferred on His Majesty and the Legislature to make Laws, shall only exist "during *the* continuance *of this act.*" Does this not imply the right to annul and terminate our Constitutional act itself, if necessary, quite contrary to the whole scope and tenor of the Resolutions of the Assembly? Learned and *honourable* gentlemen ought also to recollect that this act prescribes an *oath* which must be taken before they are permitted to sit in the Assembly; and that this oath imposes faith and allegiance upon them to their King, "as lawful sovereign of the Kingdom of Great Britain, and of these Provinces, dependent on, and belonging to, the said Kingdom." Now, this is an oath which is taken in no part of the Empire, except in the Colonies. The inhabitants of England, Scotland, Ireland and Wales, never take such an oath as this, because neither of these countries is "dependent on, *and belonging, to, the said* Kingdom, but, united one with the other, form that Kingdom upon which this Province is declared to be "*dependent.*" To deny, therefore, the dependency of this Province upon Great Britain and the supreme authority of Parliament to alter or amend our Constitution, is not only an act of the basest contempt and ingratitude, but downright perjury and treason. Nothing can possibly be more absurd than to suppose the Parliament of Great Britain possessed of powers of legislation, which, like the laws of the Medes and Persians, they could neither amend, change, nor abrogate. This would be *infallibility* with a vengeance; and which no enlightened community or body-politick will ever, we are sure, assume, without at once annihilating the best interests of society. Yet this is what the Resolutions contemplate. But happily for the country, the authors of the Constitutional act contemplated no such thing; and great and wise though they were, they never dreamed of rendering their maturest measures irrevocable. The observations of *Pitt* alone are sufficient proof of this. He said, "If the Legislature is not properly constituted *at first*, it must be recollected, that it is *subject* to *revision*, and that it might *easily afterwards be* altered." In the memorable discussion which, three years since, took place in the House of Commons on the refractory disposition manifested by the West India Colonies relative to the emancipation of their slaves, no sentiment was more unanimously acquiesced in, than the power and legislative authority of Parliament over the *internal* affairs of the Colonies. The greatest statesmen of the day—among whom was Sir James Mackintosh—joined in this opinion, the substance of which was, "Shall they the colonies—dare to resist the authority of Parliament? If they do, we shall teach them a lesson by doing for them by compulsion what they refuse to do by persuasion." We shall here ask the House of Assembly and their partizans a simple question: "Are the power and authority of the Imperial Parliament over the Colonies, less or more now than they were in 1791, when the Constitutional act was passed?" Neither the one nor the other, our good friends, but just the same supreme omnipotent authority that ever it was. If *less*, by what circumstance have they been lessened; for nothing, you will—you *must* acknowledge, could have been more fortunate to this Province than that this domination of authority did not take place *previous* to the abrogation of the 14th Geo. III. cap. 88—the *first* Constitutional Act of the Province; and an act to which the "Notion *Canadienne*," still cling with a fond grasp, similar to that of the sinking mariner, when all is nearly over, and his hopes about to perish forever. If *more*, surely the same extent of authority may *now* be granted to them which they possessed at the time of destroying an old constitution and creating a new one. By the king's proclamation of 1763, the English laws and Constitution were guaranteed to those "loving subjects" who "were or should become inhabitants" of this Province. Let us ask whether the breach of this royal promise under the great seal of Great Britain, is a greater stain in the imperial character of Great Britain, than the abrogation of the Quebec act of 1774, or any other act that has since been passed? Assuredly not! and England, whilst she has a colony to claim and own her sway, will have cause to regtet and deplore a cruel and unnatural act, by which British born subjects have been rendered *for-*

eigners—*(so they have ever been called by the French* Canadians*)* in laws, language and manners, in a colony won by British blood and British bravery. In refuting the insane doctrine laid down by the majority of the House of Assembly on the subject of the above resolution, *Mr. Ogden*, the Solicitor General, stated that "*there were duties as well as rights*" imposed upon the colonies. "I am well aware," said a great statesman, "that men love to hear of their power, but have an extreme disrelish to be told of their duty." This is, of course, because every duty is a limitation of some power. We shall, therefore, in this place, and in conclusion, lay down a few of those principles which have been pointed out for the guidance of the colonies by the greatest philosophers and statesmen that ever flourished in any country. That great authority, *Sir Wm. Blackstone*, in discussing the authority of the Mother Country over the colonies, says :---" What shall be admitted, and what rejected, at what times, and under what restrictions, must, in case of dispute, be decided in the first instance by their own provincial judicature, subject to the revision and control of the King in Council : the whole of their constitution being also liable to be new-modelled and reformed by the general superintending power of the Legislature of the Mother Country." In a note it is added, "The bare idea of a State, without a power somewhere vested to alter every part of its laws, is the height of political absurdity." There can be no gainsaying of this doctrine, especially in a conquered colony like this one; for says Lord Mansfield, in deciding, in 1774, the important case Campbell versus Hall, "A country conquered by the British arms, becomes a dominion of the King in right of the crown; and therefore *necessarily subject* to the legislature and parliament of Great Britain." "I am no courtier of America" said the great Chatham. "I am no courtier of America: I stand up for this kingdom. I maintain that the parliament has a right to bind, to restrain America. Our Legislative power over the colonies is Sovereign and Supreme. When it ceases to be Sovereign and Supreme, I would advise every gentleman to sell his lands, and embark to that country. When two countries are connected together, like England and her colonies, without being incorporated, the one must necessarily *govern*; and the greater must rule the less." In another place he adds, "At the same time, let the *sovereign* authority of this country over the colonies be asserted as strong as terms can be devised. *And be* made to extend *to every point of legislation.*"

On the same occasion, Mr. Greaville, while he reprobated the general conduct of ministry, said, "that this kingdom has the sovereign, the supreme legislative power over America, is granted; it cannot be denied." "When I proposed to tax America, I repeatedly asked the house, if any objection could be made to the right; *but no one* attempted *to deny it.* Protection and obedience are reciprocal. Great Britain protects America. America is bound to yield obedience. If not, tell me when the Americans were emancipated. When they want the protection of this kingdom, they are always ready to ask it: that protection has always been afforded them in the most full and ample manner.

Mr. Burke, in his celebrated speech, in 1774; on the motion for the repeal of the duty on tea, said, "The parliament of Great Britain sits at the head of her extensive empire in two capacities: one as the local legislature of the island, providing for all things at home, immediately, and by no other instrument than the executive power. The other, and I think her noblest capacity, is what I call her imperial character; in which, as from the throne of heaven, she superintends all the several inferior legislatures, and guides and controuls them all without annihilating any. As all these provincial legislatures are only co-ordinate to each other, they ought all to be subordinate to her. It is necessary to coerce the negligent, to *restrain* the violent, and to aid the weak and deficient, by the over-ruling plenitude of her power." "I have held, and ever shall maintain to the best of my power, unimpaired and undiminished the just, wise, and necessary Constitutional *superiority* of Great Britain. This is necessary for America as well as for us. I never mean to depart from it. Whatever may be lost by it, I avow it." "He that accepts protection" says Dr. Johnson, "stipulates obedience. We have always protected the Americans; we may therefore subject them to government." In short all great statesmen, and political writers of note, are unanimous in declaring that the mother country possesses---not a casual or eccoutriek---hot a true constitutional and incontrovertible supreme legislative authority over her colonies at all periods and in *all* points whether external or internal; and, without pursuing the subject further, we flatter ourselves we have satisfactorily proved that it is so.

If any reader have honoured us with his company this far, we have to apologize for detaining him so long upon the last subject. But, as nothing can be of greater consequence both to the mother country and the colonies, than a proper notion of their relative duties and situation; and, in particular, as nothing is so apt to promote the prosperity of a colony as a just understanding of its real rights, and a distinct knowledge of the limitations of its legislative capacity, we trust that no man will condemn our effarts to effect this desirable object on the present important occasion, however rudely the task may have been executed.

Upon the whole, like the elder Cato, who is said never to have concluded a speech but with the ominous words "*Delenda est Carthago*," we think we cannot close the present essay, as woll as those that may follow, better than with a prayer for *A legislative union of Upper and Lower Canada.*

29th December, 1828.

NO. VII.

"Watchman, what of the night?"

Perceiving that a great deal of discussion has already arisen, and is likely further to arise, on the subject of the difference between the *English* and *French* laws existing in this province; and knowing that the former ought, and should, and shall ultimately, prevail in this Province, we here think it proper to give a historical sketch of their introduction immediately after the conquest; shewing, as we go along, the right and the power of the conquering country so to introduce and maintain them. By acts of parliament, whose folly and ignorance can never be sufficiently deplored, these laws have, indeed, been since banished from the Province, and thereby stigmatized and proscribed by those who should ever be their truest and sternest supporters; but as, from a variety of concurring circumstances, it is evident that a revival of them will be necessary, in order to secure the loyalty and allegiance of the Province, we deem, that no time ought to be lost in bringing back the public to a view of their rights and privileges on so important a subject. This sketch will also serve as the basis of some constitutional topicks which it is our intention afterwards to discuss, relative to the formation of our present constitution of Government.

"The British Constitution," says an excellent writer* of the present day, "is the

---

*Lacon, vol. 2, p. 146.

proudest political monument of the combined and progressive wisdom of man: throughout the whole civilized world, its preservation ought to be prayed for, as a choice and peerless model, uniting all the beauties of preportion with all the solidity of strength." Inspired with this noble sentiment, we have taken up our humble *pen*, in the hope of being able to prove, by the mere recital of a few plain facts, that nothing can be more destructive of this beautiful fabrick, than the hateful and unnatural practice of ingrafting on its present pure and unsullied stock, the barbarous and despotick systems of foreign governments. In particular, that nothing can be less congeniel with each other than the *British Bulwark* of universal freedom, cemented and matured as it has been by the blood of the brave and the wisdom of the sage, and those gothick ruins from the midst of which, like the Phœnix, it has soared on high, the envy and admiration of the civilized world; and, consequently, that nothing could be more impolitick than conferring the privileges of our free and generous constitution on the *French* population of Canada, and permitting them at the same time the full and free exercise of those slavish and anti-commercial laws and customs which their lineal ancestors, the Salian Franks, built on the prostrated monuments of Roman grandeur; laws and customs which have happily been banished from almost every other quarter of the world, as totally unfit, in the present enlightened era, to regulate the conduct, secure the interests, or preserve the liberties of any class of people. If it be true that the French of Canada, like the ancient inhabitants of Italy, of Ireland, and of Wales, have been conquered into the enjoyment of true liberty, that conquest ought to have been completed: at least, some prospect ought long ago to have been held out to those whose fortunes are no less connected with the fate of this Province, than their affections are sincere, and their prayers ardent, for the glory and welfare of the Mother country, that some system similar to that which had been adopted so successfully in gradually admitting Ireland and Wales into a full participation of the laws, customs, language, and general polity of the conquering state, should also be followed with respect to Lower Canada. Equally unfortunate for the happiness of the province; as detrimental to the naval and commercial prosperity of the Empire at large, a line of policy, diametrically the reverse of this has ever been the guiding star of our rulers and statesmen. They found Canada, at the conquest, the subordinate and I may add, the tributary province of a despotic sovereign; and the inhabitants in a condition more resembling slavery than a free and independent people, having rights to maintain and property to defend. Beyond the food which nourished them, and the clothes which sheltered them from the inclemency of the weather, they had no desires, and with these, perhaps, that ignorance of civil and political happiness which they inherited from their ancestors, taught them to be contented. Their rules of inheritance and tenure were feudal to the core; and the gloomiest features of that barbarous code which arose in the forests of Germany, penetrated into the wilds of Canada, where they were deeply and indelibly impressed by the power of the sword. In the making of their own laws they had no voice. These were furnished ready-made from France in the same way that the manufactures of that famous country were brought to them: with this difference, that they generally came without being asked for, sometimes overstocking, but more frequently of a character quite unsuitable to the *market*. The administration of justice bore all the characteristicks of the basis on which it was founded. All that can be said in its favour, and that is no common recommendation in these days of delay and procrastination, is, that it was expeditious, which may be easily conceived when we recollect, that the sword, and putting the question by torture, were the principal instruments employed in putting the laws into execution.* It is well known, that letters *de Cachet* were in use throughout all the French dominions, without any opposition whatsoever on the part of the people, or any imag-

*It was only in 1780 that the torture, a brutal custom which had been so established by the practice of ages, that it seemed to be an inseparable part of the constitution of the

ination that any remedy could be had against them by an application to any court of justice. And it is certain, that under the French Government in Canada, the people were compelled to engage as soldiers whether they would or not, and to march to the most distant points of the country, even as far as Acadia and the Ohio, to make war upon the British or the Aborigines. The essence of the French law, as practised, and formerly enforced in this province, was well understood to be contained in these significant monosyllables, *si veut le roi, si veut la loi* ; i. e. *that which the King will, the law ordains.* If it was His Majesty's pleasure that a man obnoxious to him should be imprisoned in a particular castle, or fortress, or monastery, for any length of time, he had nothing to do but sign his letter *de* cach*et* for that purpose, and away went the unfortunate individual to the place of his confinement by a Cornet of horse, with a proper number of troopers to support him. No body ever thought of applying to the courts of justice to procure his release, nor did he himself ever venture to bring an action of false imprisonment against the persons who executed the letters *de* cach*et* against him, nor against those who detained

---

courts of France, was abolished by the humane but unfortunate Louis XVI The conquest gave Canada twenty years precadency of the Mother State, but it cannot be said which country has been most conspicuous for its gratitude.

him in confinement.† In latter times, however, (1663-4) a great sovereign council, similar in its constitution to the parliament of Paris, with subordinate tribunals and jurisdictions, was instituted. But the sovereignty of France not being yet able, if inclined, to divest itself of those despotick attributes almost indisputably enjoyed for centuries, all those courts of justice necessarily partook of the policy, which is unavoidable to all nations that have made slender advances in refinement, such as the northern conquerors, as well as the more early Greeks and Romans; and in all of them were united the civil jurisdiction with the military power. To use the expressive words of Charlevoix, (vol. i. p. 378, vide infra) they were tribunals of the sword.‡

Such is a faint and brief sketch of the civil and political condition of Canada previous to its conquest by the British arms. That despotism was the ruling power, as well in the province as in the parent country no one can possibly doubt. Both the one and the other bore the impress of that most hateful and degrading system of Government. In

---

†See Mazere's Collection.

‡"Telles ont ete les attentions du feu Roy, pour procurer a ses sujets de la Nouvelle France une justice prompte et facile, et c'est sur le modele du conseil superriour de Quebec, qu'on a depuis etabli ceux de la Martinique, de Saint Dominique, et de la Louisiane. *Tes ces conseils D'Epee.*"

both the subject was told that he had no rights ; that he could not possess any property, independent of the momentary will of his prince. These doctrines are founded on the maxims of conquest ; they must be inculcated with the whip and the sword ; and are best received under the terror of chains and imprisonment. Fear, therefore, is the principle which qualifies the subject to occupy his station ; and the sovereign, who holds out the ensigns of terror so freely to others, has abundant reason to give this passion a principal place with himself.‖ How fatally those principles in political science have been realized in France, we are sure we need not touch upon. But how, upon the conquest of Canada, it ever became a question, whether this state of things should be continued in whole or in part, or, in other words, whether the inhabitants should be restored *in integrum* to all their ancient laws and usages, or these mixed up with a reasonable proportion of English laws, in such a manner as should suit the circumstances of both the old and the new inhabitants, is a thing not so easily to be accounted for. This is a matter of which history has preserved no record, at least beyond the secret unapproachable precints of the cabinets of ministers. If the evil consequences which have ensued were only to light on the heads of those who urged such a discussion, we have no doubt the world in general would be as little inclined to pry into

‖Ferguson on civil society, p. 107.

their closets for information on this subject, as the good people of Canada would be disposed to relieve them of the burden thus brought upon themselves. True it is, however, that the latter alternative was that which, after much procrastination, more vascillation, and a great deal of unstatesmanlike conduct, was in an evil hour pitched upon; and sure we are, that since chaos resigned his sceptre, mankind have never been cursed with such a confusion of *all* those laws and customs which preserve alike the civil and political interests of society.

We shall here briefly rehearse the system which was pursued in legislating for Canada, from the conquest till the granting of the present constitution; and we are convinced, that every person who will take the trouble of perusing our provincial history during that period, will agree with us in opinion, that a more bloated, a more absurd, a more unconstitutional or impolitick system, never disgraced the annals of the British Empire.

It was on the 13th September, 1759, that "*The bloody die was* cast *on the* heights *of Abraham.*" From that period, till the peace of Versailles, which took place on the 10th of February, 1763, the Province was necessarily subjected to military law.

Upon the conquest, the commander of the forces in America established Courts in the several Districts into which the Province was then divided, for the purpose of administering justice to the inhabitants. Of these institutions His Majesty was pleased to signify his Royal approbation, and to command the same to subsist and continue until a civil government could be legally settled in the Province. These tribunals continued to exercise their functions from the 8th of September 1760, the date of the capitulation of Montreal, until the 10th of August 1764, when civil government was established throughout the Province. On the 20th September following, an ordinance was passed by the Governor and Council approving, ratifying, confirming, and giving full force and effect to all orders, judgments and decrees of these Courts denominated in the ordinance, "The Military Council of Quebec and all other Courts of Justice in said Government." There was however, an exception to such cases where the value in dispute exceeded the sum of three hundred pounds sterling: in which case either party might appeal to the Governor and Council of the Province.*

Upon this subject it seems to be agreed among writers on inter-national law, that till there be an absolute surrender, military law must prevail in every country, and supersede the common law; but the moment the new Sovereign is in peaceable possession, the *merum imperium*, or power of the sword, or the *haute justice*, as the French Civilians call it, to be exercised according to common law, takes place: and this power must extend to all crimes that concern the peace and dignity of the crown. These are *mala in se*, crimes

---

* *Vide* Ordinance dated to 20th Sept. 1764.

in themselves, and universally known in every nation. Those crimes which arise from prohibitions are not known, and therefore they are not governed by penal statutes antecedent to the conquest. The *mixtum imperium* of personal wrongs and civil property must be promulgated before the ancient laws are understood to be altered.† This is the first step or era in our legislative system.

In the condition above sketched, Canada by the definitive treaty of 1763; was ceded to the crown of Great Britain absolutely; and, to use the words of the treaty itself,‡ "that

---

†Mariott.

‡"IV. His Most Christian Majesty renounces all pretensions which he has heretofore formed, or might form to *Nova Scotia* or *Acadia*, in all its parts, and guarantees the whole of it, and all its dependencies, to the King of Great Britain.

"Moreover, his Most Christian Majesty cedes and guarantees to his said Britannic Majesty, in full right, Canada, with all its dependencies, as well as the Island of *Cape Breton*, and all other Islands and Coasts in the gulf of the River St. Lawrence, and in general every thing that depends on the said countries, lands, islands, and coasts with the sovereignty, property, possession, and all rights acquired by treaty or otherwise, which the most Christian King and the Crown of France have had till now over the said countries, islands, lands, places, coasts and their inhabitants; so that the Most Christian King

in the most ample manner and form, without any restriction, and without any liberty to depart from the said guaranty under any pretence, or to disturb Great Britain in the possession above mentioned." In consequence of the powers thus vested in His Majesty, the well-known rights of the Crown, constitutionally as well as imperially, and the reservations and conditions of the capitulation for Montreal and Canada, his Majesty, on the 7th of October, 1763, issued a proclamation,* by which those who were, or *should be*-

---

cedes and makes over the whole to the said King and to the Crown of Great Britain, and that in the most ample manner and form, without any restriction, and without any liberty to depart from the said guaranty under any pretence, or to disturb Great Britain in the possessions above mentioned.

"His Britanic Majesty, on his side, agrees to grant the liberty of the Roman Catholic religion to the inhabitants of Canada. He will consequently give the most effectual orders, that his new Roman Catholic subjects may profess the worship of their religion, according to the rights of the Romish Church, *as far as the laws of Great Britain permit.*"

*This proclimation refers indiscriminately to Canada, *East Florida, and Granada.*

"And whereas it will greatly contribute to the speedy settling our said new Governments, that our loving subjects should be informed of our paternal care for the security of the liberty and properties of those *who are*, come inhabitants of Canda, were assured, *on the* royal *word*, that for the security of their

---

and shall become inhabitants thereof; we have thought fit to publish and declare by this our proclamation, that we have in the *letters patent under our great seal of Great Britain*, by which the said governments are constituted, given express power and direction to our Governors of our said colonies respectively, that so soon as the state and circumstances of the said colonics will admit thereof, they shall, with the advice and consent of the members of our Council, summon and call *general assemblies* within the said governments respectively, in such manner and forms as is used, and directed in those colonies and provinces in America, which are under our immediate government: and we have also given power to the said Governors, with the consent of our said council, and the representatives of the people, so to be summoned as aforesaid, to make, constitute, and ordain laws, statutes, and ordinances for the public peace, welfare, and good government of the said colonies, and of the people and inhabitants thereof, as near as may be to the laws of England, and under such regulations and restrictions as are used in other colonies; and in the meantime, and until such assemblies can be called as aforesaid, all persons inhabiting in or resorting to, our said colonies, *may confide in our* royal protection *for the* enjoyment *of the* benefit *of the laws of* our realm *of England*; for which purpose we have given power un-liberty and property, express power and direction should be given to the governor of the province, as soon as circumstances would admit of it, to summon and call a general assembly, with power, in conjunction with the governor and council, to make laws, statutes and ordinances for the peace, welfare and good government of the inhabitants *as near as might be agreeable to the Laws of England*, and in the meantime, and until such Assembly could be called, all persons inhabiting or resorting to the province, *might confide in the Royal protection for the enjoyment of the benefit of the law of the Realm of England.* In consequence of this publick and, I may say, *national guarantee*, that not only the English laws and judicial proceedings, but a free representative government, modelled upon that of the conquering country, had already, or, at least, were about to be established in their full

---

der our great seal to the governors of the said colonies respectively to erect and constitute with the advice of our said councils respectively, courts of judicature and public justice within our said colonies for the hearing and determining all causes, as well criminal as civil, according to law and equity, and as near as may be, agreeable to the laws of England, with liberty to all persons who may think themselves aggrieved by the sentence of such courts in all civil cases, to appeal under the usual limitations and restrictions, to us in our privy council."

force and vigour in Canada, many hundred enterprising families of both agricultural and commercial capital resorted to the province, in the firm faith, and full belief, that the change of their native for a strange and distant clime, with a few years of industrious hardship peculiar to the settlement of a new country, would complete the catalogue of their trials; and that their birth-rights, the laws and government of England, would ever be maintained in the terms set forth in the above recited proclamation.† But, to the dishonour of England, and the confusion of the Colony, they were deceived; and therefore some very important questions soon afterwards arose with respect both to the general powers of sovereignty over a conquered people already in possession of laws and civil institutions of their own, and the efficacy of the proclamation of 1763, in introducing the laws of England into the province. We shall dwell a little on these important subjects, as we think we shall be able to prove very satisfactorily, not only the right of the King of Great Britain to take away the laws of the conquered country, and substitute such other laws in their place as, either by himself or conjointly with the legislative wisdom of the nation he may think proper, but also that the laws of England were *ipso facto* introduced into Canada and the ancient laws of

†See Letter from the British inhabitants of Canada to Lord Dartmouth, preserved by Maseres.

the province, as a matter of course, wholly and in reality superseded.

With regard, in the first place, to the right of the king, on the general principles of the laws of nations, as well as of the empire, to alter and change the laws of conquered or ceded countries already in possession of laws of their own, there seem to exist no doubts whatever: and indeed, it is impossible there could be, as in all the conquests of England this right has uniformly been exercised to the entire exclusion of every other right of interference. But with regard to Canada in particular, if any doubts could at all be entertained, they are completely obviated not only by the unconditional terms in which by the treaty of peace the country was delivered over to Great Britain, but also by the capitulation with the inhabitants themselves; both of which are sacred and inviolable according to their true intent and meaning. In the forty second article of this capitulation,* the demand was that "the French and Canadians shall continue to be governed according to the custom of Paris, and the laws and usages established for this country." The answer was "*they become subjects of the King.*" The inevitable consequence was, that their laws were liable to be changed by their own act as well as by the inherent rights and

*Art. XLI. The French Canadians, and Acadians, of what state and condition soever, who shall remain in the colony, shall not be forced to take arms against His Most

powers of the new Sovereign.† There is no gainsaying this self-evident fact. A country conquered by the British arms, becomes a dominion of the King in right of his crown; and therefore necessarily subject to the legislature and parliament of Great Britain. The conquered inhabitants once received under the King's protection become subjects, and are to be universally considered in that light, not as enemies or aliens. The law and the legislative government of every dominion, equally affects all persons and all property within the limits thereof; and is the rule of decision for all questions which arise there. It is left by the constitution to the King's authority to grant or refuse a capitu-

---

Christian Majesty or his allies, directly or indirectly, on any occasion whatsoever. The British Government shall only require of them an exact neutrality.

ANSWER. They become subjects of the King.

ART. XLII. The French and Canadians shall continue to be governed according to the custom of Paris and the laws and usages established for this country. And they shall not be subject to any other imposts than these which were estabished under the French dominion.

ANSWER. Answered by the preceding articles; and particularly by the last.

†Cowper's Reports, 1774--8. Campbell vs. Hall.

lation; if he refuse and put the inhabitants to the sword or exterminates them, all the lands belong to him. If he receive the inhabitants under his protection and grant them their property, he has a power to fix such terms and conditions as he thinks proper. He is entrusted with making the treaty of peace: he may yield up the conquest or retain it upon what terms he pleases. These powers no man ever disputed: neither has it ever been controverted that the king might change part or the whole of the law or political form of government of a conquered dominion. The history of the conquests made by the crown of England, is a practical illustration of this position. At the conquest of Ireland, the inhabitants were governed by what they called the Brehon law, so styled from the Irish judges, who were denominated Brehons. The conquest of the island and the alteration of the laws by the King of England, in the twelfth and thirteenth centuries, have been variously and learnedly discussed by lawyers and writers of great fame, at different periods of time: but no man ever said that the change in the laws of the country was made by the parliament of England; no man ever said the crown *could* not do it. The fact in truth, after all the researches which have been made, comes out clearly to be, as laid down by Lord Chief Justice Vaughan,* that Ireland received the laws of England, by the Charters and com-

*Rep. 292.

mands of Henry II. King John, Henry III. and he adds an et cetera to take in Edward I. and the subsequent kings. And he shows clearly the mistake of imagining that the Charters of the 12th of John, by which, it was ordained and established that Ireland should be governed by the laws of England, were either submitted or assented to by a parliament of Ireland, as surmised by Sir Edward Coke.* Whenever the first parliament was called in Ireland, the change was introduced without the interposition of the parliament of England, and must therefore have been derived from the crown. The statute of Wales, 12th Edward I. is no more than regulations made by the King in his Council for the government of Wales, which the preamble says was then totally subdued. Though for various political causes, he feigned Wales, to be a feoff of the crown;† yet he governed it as a conquest. The town of Berwick upon Tweed was originally a part of the kingdom of Scotland;‡ and as such, was for a time reduced by Edward I. into

---

*1 Inst. 141.

†These are the words of the statute of Rhudhlan, as quoted by Blackstone:

"Terra Walliae cum incolis suis, prius regi jure fodali subjecta, jam in proprietatis dominium totaliter et cum integritate conversa est, et coronae regni Angliae tanquam pars corporis ejusdem annexa et unita."

‡Blackstone, Vol. 1. p. 98.

the possession of the crown of England : and during its subjection, it received from that prince a Charter, which was confirmed by Edward III. with some additions. From that time till the reign of James I. it was governed by Charters from the crown without the interposition of parliament. All the alterations in the laws of Gascony, Guienne and Calais, must have been under the king's authority ; because no acts of parliament relative to them are extant. The king has always exercised legislative powers in Minorca. At the conquest of New-York, (1664) in which most of the old Dutch inhabitants remained, Charles II. changed the form of their constitution and political government ; by granting it to the Duke of York, to hold of his crown under all the regulations contained in the *letters patent.* It is remarkable that although the King never exercised any legislative authority in Canada notwithstanding the promises held out in the proclamation of 1763, and the powers conferred by the letters patent containing the commission to the Governor in the same year, yet a different system was pursued in Grenada to which the proclamation indiscriminately referred. There the Commission of General Melville, as governor, is dated in April, 1764. The Governor arrived in Grenada on the 14th of December, 1764 ; and before the end of 1765, an assembly had actually met in that island. No question, says Lord Mansfield, was ever started before but that the King has a right to legislative authority over a conquered country. It was never denied in Westminister Hall; it never was questioned in parliament. Coke's report of the arguments and resolutions of the judges in Calvin's case lays it down as clear. If a King, says the book, comes to a kingdom by conquest, he may change and alter the laws of that kingdom; but if he comes to it by title and descent, he cannot change the laws of *himself* without the consent of parliament. In the year 1722, the Assembly of Jamaica being refractory, it was referred to Sir Philip York, and Sir Clement Wearge, to know, "What could be done if the Assembly should obstinately continue to withhold the usual supplies?" They reported thus: "*If Jamaica was still to be considered as a conquered island, the king had a right to levy taxes upon the inhabitants; but if it was to be considered in the same light as the other Colonies, no tax could be imposed on the inhabitants but by an Assembly of the island, or by an act of parliament.*" I shall only add, that, with the exception of Canada alone, the legislative and judicial authority in all the colonies planted by Great Britain in America, arose from grants and commissions emanating directly from the King.

Having thus generally, and with respect to Canada in particular, clearly established the right of the king to abolish the laws of a conquered country and replace them either by those of the paramount state, or such others as may deemed most advisable, we proceed, in the next place, to inquire how far the proclamation of 1763, and the subsequent acts of the imperial and provincial governments, succeeded in accomplishing the great object in view. In doing so we may be tempted into some detail; but however feebly executed, we hope it will not prove altogether uninteresting to those who may be anywise concerned in the welfare and happiness of the British Colonies.

We have already alluded to the proclamation, and made such quotations from it as may convince the most obdurate, that, at the time of its publication, it was intended not only that it should form the basis of the British Sovereignty and supremacy in Canada, but the palladium of the rights and liberties of the old as well as the new inhabitants, "*agreeably to the laws of England*."* This however has been questioned by very high authority. In a report made on the 14th of April, 1766, by the Attorney and Solicitor General, Mr. Yorke and Mr. De Grey, it was attempted to be proved, as the basis of their statement, that this proclamation was only meant to be introductive of select parts of the law of England, and not of the whole body of laws; and that the criminal laws of England, and of personal wrongs, were almost the only laws that came under the terms made use of in the proclamation; and that the laws of England relative to the descent, alienation, settlement, and incum-

---

*Vid. Proclamation.

brances of lands, and the distribution of personal property in cases of intestacy, and all the benefical incidents of real estate, in possession or expectancy, were not comprehended under the proclamation It is very remarkable, that in pronouncing such an opinion—an opinion which involved the happiness of millions, and, perhaps, the peace of empires—the learned reporters did not cite one principle or maxim of national or municipal law in their own justification. They merely proceeded on the abstract principle, that to change at once the laws and manners of a settled country, must be attended with hardship and violence; and therefore wise conquerors, havin provided for the security of their dominiong proceed gently, and indulge their conquered subjects in all local customs, which are in their own nature *indifferent*, and which have been received as rules of property, or have obtained the force of laws. These observations might serve as a text to a very large volume upon national law and justice; but we shall rid ourselves of them by a very few remarks. The reasoning made use of by the learned gentlemen might indeed suit a purpose when the proclamation first became a topick of discussion at the council-board, or at any other time or place previous to its being issued. But this *ex post facto* reasoning came rather too late after hundreds and thousands had left their native country with all their resources and emigrated to Canada, where they purchased lands, planted, settled, and carried on trade and commerce to a very great, and, in Canada at that time, a very wonderful extent,* on the faith of the king's royal proclamation, guaranteeing to those who might resort to the new province "*The enjoyment of the benefit of the Laws of England.*" As to the honour which the learned gentlemen have done Canada by placing it in the rank of settled countries at a time when the population† scarcely exceeded that of some manufacturing villages in England, I shall only observe, that even if it had been a settled country at the time of the conquest—and, alas! the greatest part of it still remains unsettled, and so will ever remain until the present system both in laws and general polity be changed—such a circumstance could neither justify the erroneous view taken of the proclamation by the Attorney and Solicitor General, so widely different from that of every other individual in the empire; nor destroy those rights which, as we have seen, the law places so firmly within the grasp of the king. And, lastly, with respect to those wise conquerors, who we are told proceed gently in

---

*Vid. Memorial from the English inhabitants of Quebec to Lord Dartmouth.

†The following progressive view of the population of Lower Canada may not be uninteresting:—

1663— 7,000,	1775— 90,000,
1714—20,000,	1784—123,727,
1759—70,000,	1814—335,000,
	1825—420,179.

the imposition of their own laws upon their conquered subjects, and indulge them in their local customs, we shall only observe, that we should on all occasions sit down to the study of history, with increased and increasing pleasure, if we were assured that her stores contained a *single page* which exhibited the conqueror as more disposed *to* sanction the customs and prejudices of *the conquered*, than to gratify his own vanity and ambition. But, with the exception of the solitary and unfortunate instance now under consideration, the whole course of history is a standing evidence against the assertion; and it is good that it is so, for otherwise mankind would never have emerged from the rudeness and barbarity in which they had been originally sunk. The arts, the eloquence, and the poetry of Greece and Rome would never have arisen, as they have done, like the sun in his glory, on the other benighted nations of the world, and spread knowledge and elegance through the uttermost parts of the earth; seducing in their course the savage from his cannibal revelry, the barbarian from his never-ceasing wars, the robber from his plunder and his den, and the assassin from his nocturnal mareedings. The sacred names of Liberty, Justice, and Civil Order, which now resound through the universe, would have been buried amidst the ruins of Jerusalem, Athens, and of Rome; still, perhaps, leaving man the dupe of his folly and the victim of his passions. Let us, however, listen for a few moments to history on so important a subject.

The *Greeks* not only imposed their laws upon the provinces subjected by their arms, but compelled the unfortunate inhabitants to repair to the capital of the conquering state to obtain justice. In truth, there never existed in civil society such pitiless tyrants as those who composed the Democracies of Greece, in respect both to their conquests and natural colonies, terms more frequently synonymous than distinct. Any pretence served them to rob their Allies, as they sometimes affected to call those victims of their ambition, of almost every blessing that they enjoyed, whether consisting of pecuniary riches, domestick comforts, or publick splendour; and their rapacity could not be exceeded by the most avaricious Turkish Pasha that ever existed. For a number of years they continued to raise six hundred talents *annually* from the Asiatick Colonies: yet not a single talent of this enormous and unjustifiable exaction was ever expended for the benefit of those upon whom it was levied; but, on the contrary, sent to fill the coffers of the parent or conquering state in order to minister to her corruption and extravagance. Thus, Plutarch informs us, the sum levied on the colonies, all of whom came under the denomination of tributary provinces amounted to thirteen hundred talents. Yet when these states revolted, which these unfeeling and unjustifiable exactions frequently induced them to do, they were punished by the *Mother* City with the utmost severity. The authors of the insurrection were put to death:

their property was confiscated; and a heavy fine imposed upon the *whole* community. By what process of trial all this was done, we leave to the decision of those who still administer justice by hard blows rather than by the dictates of truth and reason; and thank our stars that, however much indebted to the arts and learning of Greece, we are none of her dependencies. In the fifth year of the Peloponesian war, the territory of the island of Lesbos was, on an occasion of this kind, partitioned among the Athenian citizens. On the breaking out of a similar mutinous humour, the inhabitants were condemned to pay two hundred talents. By such tyrannical exactions, Athens could at one time boast of a treasury of ten thousand talents. The high chivalrick, and in many instances, the mistaken notions which from childhood, we are accustomed to entertain of Grecian liberty and patriotism not only tend to prevent us from viewing with impartial severity the dark side of the picture which has been handed down to us of that nation's character, but go a great way in prevailing upon us to disregard even the assurance of well-accredited history as to the extent and enormity of the tyranny of Greece alike over her colonies and conquests. Yet such were the excesses committed in this way under the sanction of the boasted popular institutions of the Grecian republics, that it were well if some modern patriots and politicians would seriously reflect before holding up for our imitation governments whose theory was always at variance with their practice, and the ingenuity of whose patriots and ministers is much more to be admired, than either their morals or their manners. At any rate it is not for *us* to borrow from Grecian polity. Their colonies and conquests instead of being fostered with the care and liberality of a wise and polite nation, and their necessary wants of every description supplied when occasion required it, were harrassed with incidental levies and burdened with the most oppressive taxes. Their commerce and industry were also heavily assessed; and their local institutions, alike civil and religious, were frequently abolished, that the attention of the people might be more constantly directed to those of the mother city, and that all pecuniary emoluments, and other advantages accruing from them might go to enrich and aggrandize the avaricious parent. "The people of Athens," says Xenophon, "desire to acquire at once all the wealth of their tributary states, and can hardly be pursuaded to allow their subjects to retain what is barely sufficient for their subsistence. They permit not their allies to have *tribunals for deciding causes* between one man and another, but *oblige* them to have recourse to Athens for their determination. Hence they govern them without any trouble to themselves and ruin in the Courts of Justice every one who appears to bear ill-will to the Athenian people. Besides this advantage, the particular citizens who happen to be Judges, get a considerable increase of fees because they are in preportion to the number of causes which they decide. They profit also by letting their houses and servants to such strangers as are obliged to resort to Athens for *obtaining Justice*. The State itself is a gainer by an augmentation of tax called the hundreth, which is paid at the Piræum.* And all the citizens in general obtain much honour and respect; for if the *allies* were not obliged to plead their cause in Athens, they would pay regard to our generals, ambassadors, and sea-captains, and them only. But at present they obey honour and respect every Athenian citizen; they even kiss his hand as a mark of submission due to the man who at some future time may be their Judge." Sparta, when she became the paramount state, was no less strict and imperious in imposing her own laws and government upon those who fell in her power; but I shall not detail the desolation and horror with which she filled all Greece after the Peloponesian war, as it will answer my present purpose simply to say, that she dissolved the democratical governments in Italy and Sicily, and established tyrannies every where in their room. To conclude, Isocrates, in his panegyrick, greatly extols his countrymen for their policy with respect to their conquered allies; and adds these remarkable words: "*We established, over all*

*The Piræum being the sea-port of Athens, it is very evident, that none but the maritime and transmarine dependencies were subjected to this slavish extortion.

Greece, the same system of policy which we ourselves enjoyed." Such were the principles that actuated the Greeks in their conquests!

As to the policy of the *Romans*, in respect to *their* conquests, it is so generally known, and so completely subversive of the doctrine laid down by the Attorney and Solicitor General, that we shall merely allude to it in as general terms as possible. It has been said of the Turks, that in the propagation of their religion, the sword is the only expounder of the Koran. Well may it be said of the ancient Romans, that, in extending their empire, the same celebrated and irresistible logician was the best definer of their laws. Where the sword of Rome gained possession, there her sovereignty, language, and laws took root. "Wherever the Roman conquers he inhabits."† The security of the government, and the interests of individuals co-operated in seizing the strongest, or the most fertile, situations for the establishment of colonies, to be occupied by Romans or their conciliated subjects who, in the capacities of soldiers, farmers, and traders, reaped the greatest advantages, which could be derived from the property of the soil in the conquered territories, while the original proprietors were compelled to cultivate their own lands for the emolument of their new lords. What laws but the laws of Rome could be the rule of conduct in such settlements? All those unfortunate people who became subject to

---

†Sen. Consol. ad Helviam, c. 6.

the Romans were immediately exposed to every kind of hardship. Their lands were seized and given to the veterans, among whom the Roman laws were introduced, for they knew none other. The inhabitants, strangers to the power which the arts of civilization placed in the hands of an enemy naturally warlike, and whose most honorable profession was arms, soon experienced their own weakness and disproportion to the Roman forces, and reluctantly acquiesced in the dominion of their masters; gradually incorporating as a part of that mighty Empire, whose laws, customs and manners they were compelled to embrace in silence, tho' in pain. Liberty, says Montesquieu, speaking of the Roman government, was at the centre, and tyranny in the extreme parts, meaning the Colonies or Provinces. While Rome extended her dominions no farther than Italy, the people were governed as confederates, and the laws of each Republick were preserved. But as soon as she enlarged her *conquests*, and the Senate had no longer an immediate inspection over the Provinces, nor the Magistrates residing at Rome were any longer capable of governing the Empire, they were obliged to send prætors and proconsuls. Then it was that the harmony of the three powers was lost. Those who were sent on that errand were intrusted with power which comprehended that of *all* the Roman Magistracies, *nay* even *that of the senate and the* people. They made their edicts upon coming into the Provinces. They were *despotick Magistrates*. They exercised the three powers of the metropolitan government, and were the husbands of the Republick. While the city paid taxes without trouble, or none at all, the *Provinces* were plundered by the Knights, who were the farmers of the publick revenues. All history abounds with their oppressive extortions, "All Asia" says Miltiridates, "expects me as its deliverer; so great is the hatred which the sapaciousness of the proconsuls, the confiscations made by the officers of the revenue, the quirks and cavils of judicial proceedings, have excited against the Romans.* Nothing, however, can convey a better idea of the conquering policy of the Romans, than the account given by Tacitus of their conquests in Britain in his life of Agricola. "The Britons themselves," says he, are a people who cheerfully comply with the *levies of men*, with the *imposition of taxes*, and with all the duties enjoined by government; nor have the Romans any farther subdued them than *only to obey just laws*." But the best representation extant of the grinding and oppressive conduct of the Romans towards the Britons, is to be bound in the famous speech which the same author has recorded as having been made by Galgacus to his army previous to engaging with the Romans at the foot of the Grampian Hills. I shall make a short extract from it; and whether actually spoken by

* *Montesquieu*, L. XI. c. 8.

Galgacus, or written by Tacitus, it is in my opinion, equally a proof of the savage and merciless principles on which Rome extended her imperial yoke over the world: "Already the Romans have advanced into the heart of our Country. Against their pride and domineering, you will find it in vain to seek a remedy or refuge from any obsequiousness or humble behaviour of yours. They are plunderers of the earth, who, in their universal devastations, finding countries to fail them, investigate and rob even the sea. If the enemy be wealthy, he inflames their avarice; if poor, their ambition. They are general spoilers; such as neither the eastern world nor the western can satiate. They only of all men search after acquisitions both poor and rich with equal avidity and passion. To spoil, to butcher, and to commit every kind of violence, they style, by a lying name, Government, and, when they have spread a general desolation, call it *Peace.* Dearest to every man are his children and kindred, by the contrivance and designation of nature. These are snatched from us for recruits, and doomed to bondage in other parts of the earth. *Our* wives and sisters, however they escape pollution and violence as from open enemies, are debauched under the appearance and privilege of friendship and hospitality. *Our fortunes and possessions they exhaust for* tribute, our *grain for their provisions.*"

The conquering system pursued by the Norman *Usurper*, is familiar to every reader of English history; and what was said of Clovis, not long since, may with truth and justice be applied to William---that he had been cast in the true mould of conquerors. I may add, that the latter was in every sense as great a barbarian as the former; for he who could neither appreciate nor respect the free and glorious institutions reared and consecrated by the great Alfred, which now happily form the basis of that masterpiece of human wisdom, the British Constitution, but demolished them in order to make room for his own gothick system, was in truth more rude and ignorant than he who disputed the possession of the chalice of Soissone with a common soldier. William not only changed the laws, but the language of England; for they were equally obnoxious in his eyes; as free and popular institutions must always be to the tyrant who has no ambition to gratify but his own, and no other notion of freedom than the power of enslaving thousands that one man may shake the rod over all. He introduced into England the feudal law, which he found established in France and Normandy. He partitioned all the lands, and conferred them, with little reservation on his followers. Those who held immediately of the Crown, shared out a great part of their possessions to other foreigners, who paid their lord the same duty and submission in peace and war which he himself owed to his sovereign. Thus was the feudal system of government established in England; a system under which she groaned for centuries; but from which she at last shook herself, rising in glorious triumph, as from a new epoch, above the base thraldom and slavish subjection to arbitrary will and law, to which she had been so long exposed. Yet this is the order of things which some are still desirous of perpetuating in Canada, at a time when it has been pursued with all the contumely and revenge of civilization from every other region of the world.

We might here wind up this tedious but necessary episode with an account of all the must splendid conquests of the world; but we think we have said enough in practical confutation of the abstract proposition of the Attorney and Solicitor General. We shall only add, that it has been always laid down as a well-established principle by writers, on the laws of nations, that natural law establishes neither distinction of persons not property, nor civil government; it is the law of nations which has invented these distinctions, *and* rendered *all* those *who happen to be within the territory of* slate, subject to *the jurisdiction of that state*. When a nation takes possession of a distant country, and settles a colony there, that country, though separated from the principal establishment, or mother country, naturally becomes a part of the state, equally with its ancient possessions. Whenever, therefore, the political laws or treaties make no distinction between them, every thing said of the territory of a nation ought also to extend to its colonies. We have thus, we hope, satisfactorily proved, first, that power being the natural consequence of property, all nations have been guided in their conquests by the same maxims, and have never scrupled to expel the ancient laws of a vanquished people in order to impose their own: secondly, that it is the undoubted and constitutional inherent right of the King of Great Britain to follow a similar plan, and give such laws as he may think proper to a conquered country, having done so from the earliest periods; and, *thirdly*, that he was therefore fully justified in issuing the proclamation of 1763, being the only mode then in use for establishing the constitutions of the colonies. It now only remains to be proved, that, in consequence, the laws of England had been absolutely and with scarcely any reservation introduced into Canada.

We have already said that the proclamation was issued on the 7th of October, 1763. The commission to General Murray, as Governor, is dated the 21st day of November following, the bill not being signed by the Attorney General, for the commission of letters patent till the 22d of October; and on the 14th of November, the privy council made an order for interlineations of some necessary words. On the 10th of August, 1764, it was published at Quebec.* This commis-

* Quebec, August 16th.---Friday the 10th instant, His Majesty's letters patent, constituting and appointing the Honorable *James*

sion, as well as the instructions which accompanied it seemed every where to pre-suppose that the laws of England had already been in force in the Province since the conquest; being, as Marriot observes, full of allesions and references to those laws on a variety of different subjects; and did not contain the least intimation of a reservation of any part of the old laws and customs of the Province. At the time of passing those instruments, His Majesty's Ministers appear to have been of opinion, that by the refusal of General Amherst to grant to the Canadians the right of being governed by the custom of Paris; and by the reference made, in the fourth article of the definitive treaty of peace, to the laws of England as the measure of the indulgence intended to be shown them with respect to the exercise of their religion, sufficient notice had been given to the

---

Murray, Esq. Captain General and Governor in Chief in and over His Majesty's Province of Quebec, and vice admiral of the same, were read to a numerous concourse of people in the square fronting his Majesty's Castle of St. Louis, where the troops were drawn up under arms; after which, the cannon from the ramparts was fired, and answered by the men of war in the harbour, and by volleys of small arms from the regiments in garrison here, and the day was concluded with the usual demonstrations of joy and universal satisfaction.---*Quebec Gazette.*

conquered inhabitants, that it was His Majesty's pleasure, that they should be governed for the future according to the laws of England; and that the inhabitants, after being thus apprized of the King's intention, had consented to be so governed, and had borne testimony to this consent by continuing to reside in the country, and taking the oath of allegiance, when they might have withdrawn themselves from the Province, with all their offeote, and the produce of the sale of their estates, within the eighteen months allowed by His Majesty, in the treaty of peace, for that purpose.

Thus formally installed, the Governor, without delay, proceeded to the execution of his high and important functions. The first thing done, was the nomination of eight Councillors, whom he was authorised by his commission and instructions to make choice of.* Thus constituted, the Governor and Council in virtue of the said commission and instructions, found themselves invested with powers and prerogatives of no ordinary magnitude. The most important of these was the power "to summon and call general assemblies of the freeholders and planters" of

---

*The gentlemen nominated were the following:

William Gregory,	Walter Murray,
Paulus Emilius Irving,	Samuel Holland,
H. T. Cramahe,	Thomas Dunn,
Adam Mabane,	Francis Mounier.

the Province, to be called the Assembly of the Province of Quebec; with the advice and consent of which Council and Assembly, after being duly qualified, the governor was empowered to make laws for the publick peace, welfare, and good government of the Province, such laws "not to be repugnant, but, as near as may be, agreeably to the laws and statutes of this our Kingdom of Great Britain." But it may be asked, if the governor really possessed the power of convoking a general assembly and enacting laws in the manner here set forth, why, instead of proceeding to do so in a legal and constitutional manner, did he restrict the whole legislative power of the Province to himself and his Council; and seeing, that neither his commission nor instructions empowered him to make laws otherwise than with the advice and consent of the *Council* and *Assembly*, how could the laws actually made by the *Governor* and Council alone, being only *two* of the constituent branches of the prescribed Legislature, be binding upon the people? This is, indeed an important inquiry, and which, considered abstractedly, might involve alike the fundamental principles of good government and the dearest rights of the people. But in so far as it concerns the present disquisition, the objection can easily be obviated.

With respect to a general Assembly, the fact is, that though one had been summoned and chosen for all the parishes but Quebec, it was discovered upon reference to the commission, that it could not sit, in consequence of the restrictions therein contained, arising from the Test Act of the 25th Charles II. which prevented the measure of an Assembly being executed in a Colony where all the principal old inhabitants were of the Roman Catholic religion.* No discretionary powers were given to the Governor with respect to the administration of the oaths prescribed by this act; and as the Assembly could not proceed to transact business without being duly qualified agreeably to the commission and instructions of the Governor, it was deemed advisable to abandon the measure for the present, and await further and better defined instructions from the Imperial Government. Besides, as the governar, by his commission, was not enjoined peremptorily to summon a general assembly, such a step being merely optional, "so soon as the situation and circumstances of the Province would admit thereof," it was thought advisable not to do so, the present circumstances of the Province rendering the measure by no means necessary. It would also be premature, it was thought, and attended with many great public inconveniences; as the people of Canada were then, as they still are to a proverb, extremely illiterate, and not yet ripe for so great and sudden a share of liberty and of legislative power; it being doubted whether there were more than four or five persons in a parish in general

*Marriott.

who could read. It was, therefore, most reasonably apprehended, that the calling of an Assembly so composed, instead of remedying and regulating all the causes of complaint, would have created new ones, and become the source of distempered and ignorant factions highly injurious to the welfare and happiness of the people; a truth which was unhappily realized soon after the granting of the present Constitution; producing evils which nothing but the speedy intervention, power, and legislative wisdom of the mother Country can ever effectually cure.

As to the legality of the ordinances and laws passed by the Governor and Council, thus engrossing to themselves the whole legislative power of the Province, whatever lawyers might say of them on general principles of constitutional government, especially such of them as did not receive the express sanction of the King, no authority, except the highest in the state, could impugn the legality of the ordinances made for the establishment of the laws of England in the Province, and the necessary tribunals and officers for administering them. The Governor's commission contained the most ample powers on this head:---"And we do by these presents give and grant unto you, the said *James Murray*, full power and authority, *with the advice* and consent *of* our said *council*, to erect, constitute, and establish such and so many courts of judicature and publick justice within our said Province under your Government as you and *they* shall think fit and necessary for the hearing and determining all causes, as well criminal as civil," &c. Even if an assembly had been called, as originally intended, the powers thus conferred could not be called in question; for they are entirely and absolutely confined to the Governor and Council; and therefore, whatever laws were made for the establishment of courts of justice in the Province, must be held binding on the people, and looked upon as the foundation of their rights and the best security of their persons and property, until abrogated by the King or Parliament.

Accordingly, on the 17th of September, 1764, a law, entitled "*An ordinance for regulating and establishing the Courts of Judicature, Justices of the Peace, Quarter Sessions, Bailiffs, and other matters relative to the distribution of Justice in this Province,*" was passed, part of which I shall make no apology for transcribing *verbatim*:

"Whereas it is highly expedient and necessary for the well-governing of His Majesty's good subjects of the Province of Quebec, and for the speedy and impartial distribution of Justice among the same, that proper Courts of Judicature, with proper powers and authorities, and under proper regulations, should be established and appointed:

"His Excellency the Governor, by and with the advice, consent, and assistance of His Majesty's Council, and by virtue of the power and authority to him given by his Majesty's Letters Patent, under the Great Seal of Great Britain, has thought fit to ordain and declare; and His said Excellency, by and with the advice, consent, and assistance aforesaid, doth *hereby* ordain *and declare*,

"That a superior Court of Judicature, or Court of King's Bench, be established in this Province, to sit, hold terms in the town of Quebec, twice in every year, viz. one to begin on the 21st day of *January*, called *Hilary* term, and the other on the *21st* day of June, called *Trinity* term,

"In this Court His Majesty's Chief Justice presides, with power to determine all civil and criminal causes agreeable to the laws of England, and to the ordinances of this Province; and from this Court an appeal lies to the Governor and Council, where the matter in contest is above the value of £300 Sterling; and from the Governor and Council an appeal lies to the King and Council where the matter in contest is of the value of £500 Sterling, or upwards.

"In all trials in this Court, all His Majesty's subjects in this Colony be admitted on *juries* without any distinction.

"And His Majesty's Chief Justice, once in every year, to hold a Court of Assize and General Gaol Delivery, soon after Hilary term, at the towns of *Montreal* and *Trois Rivieries*, for the more easy and convenient distribution of justice to His Majesty's subjects in these distant parts of the Province.

"And whereas an inferior Court of Judicature, or Court of Common Pleas, is also thought necessary and convenient. *It is further ordained and declared by the authority aforesaid*, that an inferior Court of Judicature or Court of Common Pleas, is hereby established, with power and authority, to determine all property above the value of £10, with a liberty of appeal to either party to the superior Court, or Court of King's Bench, where the matter in contest is of the value of £20, and upwards.

"All trials in this court to be by jovies, if demanded by either party; and this Court to sit and hold two terms in every year at the town of Quebec, at the same time with the superior Court, or Court of King's Bench. Where the matter in contest in this Court is above the vulue of £300 Sterling, either party may (*if they shall* think proper) appeal to the Governor and Council immediately, and from the Governor and Council an appeal lies to the King and Council, where the matter in contest is of the value of £500 Sterling or upwards.

"The Judges in this Court are to determine agreeable to equity, having regard nevertheless to the *laws of England*, as far as the circumstances and the present situation of things will admit, until such time as proper ordinances for the information of the people can be established by the Governor and Council, *agreeable to the laws of England*.

"The French laws and customs to be allowed and admitted in all causes in this Court, between the *natives* of this Province, where the cause of action arose before the first day of October 1764.

"The first process of this Court to be an attachment against the body.

"An Execution to go against the body, lands, or goods, of the defendant.

"Canadian Advocates, Proctors, &c. may practise in this Court."

The rest of the ordinance is taken up with the appointment of Justices of the peace, and the inferior officers of the Courts of law throughout the Province.

It soon, however, appeared evident, that notwithstanding the full and ample, as well as explicit, manner in which this ordinance established in the Province the *English* Courts of Law and forms of procedure, the intended enactment would have been incomplete without some legislative measure relating to the tenure and conveyance of *lands*. Accordingly, on the 6th of November following, an ordinance was passed declaring *That until the 10th day of August* then *next, the* tenures *of lands, in* respect *to* such grants *as were* prior *to the* cession *by the definitive treaty of peace, and the* rights *of* inheritance *as practised before that period*, should remain *to all intents and purposes the* same. "The consequence," to use the words of Sir James Marriott, "after the expiration of this date is obvious, *that the rights of inheritance and* tenures *would be* changed *to the laws of England, so far as this* ordinance *and declaration* could *legally change them*." On the same day—6th November, 1764—another ordinance was passed "For registering *grants*, conveyances, *and* other *instruments in writing*, *of or concerning any lands*, tenements *or hereditaments within this Province*." This ordinance, termed the *Registry Office* law, and which, had it remained in force till this day, might well deserve the proud appellation of the *Magna Charta* of Lower Canada, contained the following clause;—"And every deed or conveyance of or concerning any lands, tenements, or hereditaments in this Province, shall within the space of forty days next after the respective dates thereof, be registered in the said Office in words at length; And for want of such registry, every such deed or conveyance shall be judged fraudulent against any subsequent purchaser for a valuable consideration." The Quebec Gazette of the 25th February 1765, contains a public notification of this ordinance, dated "*Register's Office*," the same day.

Thus it is evident, that the *English laws* were legally introduced into this Province both in form and in practice; and so continued during the space of ten years without any material objections, except those arising from national prejudice and pre-conceived aversion to a system of laws but little understood amongst a more enlightened people than the French Canadians. This foundation of just laws and a liberal government, so wisely and judiciously laid by the Governor and Council of the Province, and *sanctioned by the approbation of His Majesty, ought never to have been disturbed*. Yet the contrary was done by the impolitick and tyrannical *Quebec Act of 1774*; an act that will ever reflect disgrace on its authors and the Empire at large; and an act that must at no distant period give place to more patriotick and enlightened counsels. We conclude in the memorable words of Sir James Marriott;—"After certain new regulations have been submitted to with patience by His Majesty's new Canadian subjects for a space of thirteen years, though with some such complaining as is natural upon a change of masters, the foundation which has been laid for an approximation to the *manners* and *government* of the new sovereign country, must either er continue to be built upon, or otherwise the whole that has been done must be thrown down, and the Canadians must be restored *in integrum* to all their ancient laws and usage; a manner of proceeding as inconsistent with the progressive state of human affairs, *as with the* policy *of any* possible *civil government, which* cannot *revert*, but must necessarily take up things and go on the state of existing circumstances at the time it intervenes; for it can as little stand still at any given point, as it can decide that the flood of times shall go no further. *As men move forward, the laws must move with them*, and every constitution of government upon earth, like the shores of the sea from the agitation of the element, is daily losing or gaining something on one side or the other."

29th January, 1829.

NO. VIII.

" *To depart in the minutest article, from the nicety and strictness of punctilio, is as dangerous to* NATIONAL HONOUR, *as to female* virtue." —JUNIUS.

To Louis *Joseph Papineau, Esq.*

SIR:—When I last addressed myself personally to you on the subject of your conduct at opening the present session of the Provincial Parliament, I did not expect I should thus early be under the unpleasant necessity of paying you a similar visit. I then convicted you, in the face of your country, of having gone officially into the presence of the Representative of our most gracious Sovereign with a base and designing falsehood on your lips. But though, amidst my hopes of wiser measures and happier times, I did not anticipate any very particularly glaring act on your part deserving a direct and immediate visitation on mine; yet, had I called to mind the philosophical maxim of the poet, that one false step forever demos the rest, I ought to have been assured, that a career like yours, commenced in malice and iniquity, must inevitably terminate in crime and confusion. You are, indeed, Sir, a public criminal of no ordinary character. Intoxicated with impudence, there is no end of your rudeness: frantick with rage, there are no bounds to your malevolence. The high and the low, among such as do not coincide with you in opinion, are equally objects of your hatred and resentment. No character, however pure, is safe from your envy and falsehoods: no virtue however exalted, is secure from the base instruments of your jealousy and revenge. The very air is tainted with the poison of your malignant disposition; and the country resounds with your abuse of characters not only your superiors in manners, but in rank and dignity, virtue and patriotism. Sir, you seem to traffick in defamation. You move in an orbit of publick slander; and have rallied round you as satellites all the baser feelings of a rancorous and diabolical heart. Stand up thou malicious demagague---thou insolent defamer of Governors, Executive Councillors, and all men in this Province having authority in the administration of justice and government! Come forth, I say: and if we cannot penetrate into the rancour and rottenness that perpetuallly agitate thy turbulent bosom, let us, at least, behold that brazen countenance capable only of reflecting the basest and most distorted images. Yes, there thou art! We view thee, but despise thee: we behold thee, but spurn thee: we contemplate thee, but loathe thee, as a reptile to be shunned if possible; but, if met to be trampled upon.

In the debate which took place on the resolutions for expelling Mr. Christie, your are reported, in the third person, to have made use of the following language:

" Mr. Speaker trusted few persons could entertain such servile sentiments, or lend themselves to be the instruments of such a man as Lord Dalhousie, a man who was deaf to every sentiment, but those of pride, prejudice, and despotism, sentiments that were fostered by those who surrounded him, and which deservedly stigmatised him as the author of all the evils which had been inflicted upon this country. A man who had been deservedly recalled with disgrace---a man disgraced in the eyes of his Sovereign, of his country, and of the Province he had so deeply injured."

Sir, that you uttered this language in your place on the occasion alluded to, I have no doubts whatever. Of this I am well advised, as well through other channels of information, as by the printed report of the debate. But were the case otherwise, I could easily have recognized it at the offspring of your heated imagination and insolent temper. It bears the very impress of your soul. It is the foul abortion of your malignant heart, and carries along with it every characteristick of that spirit of enmity which it has long been your study how to wreak on a great patriot, a great hero, and a great man: a man, to use your own mode of expression, whose life and character are as far beyond the reach of *your* petty malevolence, as his rank and dignity are superior to plebeian vulgarity and rudeness. Nor is it my purpose at present to defend him from the attacks of so despicable an assassin as you are. Lord *Dalhousie* neither needs, nor will he thank me for so unnecessary a piece of service. My present object has a different tendency. It is not to defend, but to punish; not to save, but condomu. It is, first to exhibit you to your country and to the world as a designing and systematick calumniator and defamer of public worth and integrity; and, in the second place, to transmit your name to posterity, as one every way deserving infamy and disgrace, scorn and derision.

With the conduct of the House of Assembly in the expulsion of one of its own members for delinquencies, over which, if even proven, I maintain they possess no jurisdiction, I shall not at present interfere, though, perhaps, I may take another opportunity to express my sentiments on a measure fraught with danger to the Constitution and alarm to the Country. I shall only, in the language of Lord Chatham, say, that it was the eet of a mob and not of a senate. It resembles in a remarkable degree, the p [illegible] of the judge of hell, as described [illegible] :---

'Gnossius hæc Rhadamanthus habet durissima regna
Castigatque, auditque dolos, *subigitque fateri*.'

Sir, my charge against you is three-fold—*falsehood, defamation,* and scurrility. You say, that Lord Dalhousie was deservedly recalled with disgrace, and that he is a man disgraced in the eyes of his Sovereign and country. Sir, were you a man whose veracity was undoubted until now, I should be apt so far to give belief to your assertion, as to call upon you to produce proof of year averments. But when honest men meet with such a follow as you are, branded as you have for years been as the personal enemy of Lord Dalhousie—his defamer in publick, and traducer in private life, they very naturally put their own construction upon your statement, without troubling you for proof; being satisfied that he who will malign without cause, will stab without justice—that he who scruples not to asperse in gratification of personal resentment, will have no hesitation to arraign without evidence. But, how stands the fact? Do you really dare to affirm in your place in the Assembly, that Lord Dalhousie was recalled with disgrace? If you do, I thank God that your notions of *disgrace* are different from mine. I shall here say nothing of my right to maintain, from aught that we have seen or heard to the contrary, that Lord Dalhousie has not been recalled at all, and that his Lordship is to this hour Governor and Chief of these Provinces. But granting that he has been actually recalled, I will thank you to show me the marks, the emblems, or the tokens, of his disgrace. I presume you conceive it to be an extraordinary mark of disgrace to be called from the pitiful government of a pitiful people like the *Nation Canadienne*, having neither knowledge of their rights, nor gratitude for their privileges as a British people, to the military command of a quarter of the Globe—a command which the proudest era of Rome could not confer. Is it upon men in disgrace, that such honors and benefits are bestowed in this generous and just nation? But which of the scullions in the King's kitchen told you, or some of your friends lately in England, that Lord Dalhousie was disgraced in the eyes of his Sovereign? When and where was this disgrace earned and consummated? Was it when his Lordship was nobly fighting the battles of his Country in Egypt, in the West Indies, in Spain, and in France? Was it when he was shedding his blood in the cause of Europe and of Freedom? Or was it when, like a man and a patriot, and in the exercise of the delegated functions of that Sovereign in whose eyes you say he is disgraced, he withstood you and your desperate despairing crew, when you so clamorously and insanely assailed the constitution and the dearest rights of every true Briton in the province? Was it when the minister, in his place in parliament, before the country and the world, and in the sight and hearing of your co-adjutors, Messieurs Nelson, Viger, and Cuvillier, declared "that the still higher situation the noble lord would soon be called on to fill, would be the best *proof*, that he had not incurred the disapprobotico of government?" Was it when Mr. Stanley, whom I dare say you will not accuse of flattory to Lord Dalhousie or deceit to yourself, said, in his place in the House of Commons, that "he could not refrain from doing the Noble Earl who was at the head of the government in Canada the justice of observing, that he (Mr. Stanley,) *felt* convinced that the Noble Earl, if he had not the good fortune to give satisfaction to the *petitioners*, had acted in conformity with the instructions he had received from government?"* Was it when his lordship last embarked with such distinguished honours for his native country; carrying in his hand the recorded approbation, as Governor in Chief of every loyal and enlightened man in the province, and in his heart a deep sense of the good wishes of every individual of humanity and respectability? Or was it when his lordship was so graciously received by the King and his ministers with the report of his administration? Truly, Sir, if this be disgrace, it is a disgrace rarely to be experienced even in this age and country. But you have said that Lord Dalhousie is disgraced in the eyes of his country. What country? If you mean Great Britain, you state what is not only false, but malicious. There is not within the whole compass of that great nation, distinguished as it is above all others for worth, virtue and talent, a nobleman who is more highly respeeled, or more extensively beloved than Lord Dalhousie. But if you confine his disgrace to what you call your country only, the *Nation Canadienne*, I understand you, and find myself at no loss to comprehend the extent, magnitude, and consequence of such disgrace, when promulgated to the world by you, the hired, the well-paid calumniator of the publick as well as private character of Lord Dalhousie.

---

*See Debate in the House of Commons on the Civil government of Canada, 2d. May, 1828.

So much for the *falsehood* of your statement, I come next to its *defamation*. You assert, with an audacity very suitable to the whole tenor of your character and conduct, that Lord Dalhousie is a man deaf to every sentiment, but those of pride, prejudice and despotism. Most excellent judge of sentiment and character, tell us we pray thee, where you have culled the information upon which you found your statement? I fear this is a thing which you will take credit to your prudence for withholding. It is most true that a thievishly-inclined menial discharged by his Lordship, was once of a time much and fondly caressed for authentick information with respect to his master's private character and bearing. Was it from this despicable scoundrel—this suitable pander to your vulgar curiosity—that you collected your information? I will not say absolutely that it was; but from whatever source you got the tale, it is most certain, if one might judge from its nature and extent, that it could not have come through a much purer channel. Your own personal observation, with whatever intelligence and scrutiny it might have been exercised, I beg leave totally to exclude and deny. What your notions of society really are, I have no means of being acquainted with; though from a variety of circumstances, and the company whom you court and keep, I fear, as a gentleman, that I must estimate them at a very low rate. Your natural sphere, therefore, is as far beneath that of Lord Dalhousie, as you conceive your own cur to be beneath yourself. Such men as you herd not with the noble and the great. It is true that the same planet gave you birth. But there are orders and distinctions of men as well as of beasts; and in the same degree that the croaking, crawling toad is inferior to the majestick lion, so are you different from Lord Dalhousie. You early felt your own insignificance and this inferiority. I know not whether it proceeded from the envy of your nature, or the clownishness of your birth; but his Lordship was but a little time in this province when you shrunk into your own native atmosphere; and the only remedy left to a person in your condition was the pitiful and unmanly undertaking of pulling after you those who stood above you, but especially his Lordship, because he stood above all at the top of the gradation. Now that his lordship is gone, and you conceive yourself exalted a little beyond your natural sphere, you have the cowardice and baseness to reduce his character and publick reputation to a level with your own. But, Sir, you have undertaken a difficult task: a task which neither yourself nor the whole myrmidons of your faction congregated around you will ever be able to execute. Lord Dalhousie sits secure in the midst of an impregnable fortress of private worth and public esteem—reared by his deeds, fortified by his integrity, and embellished by the approbation of his Sovereign and country, against which neither the clamour of party nor the poisoned shafts of malevolence can ever prevail. Yet tell us, whether it was you or your friend Mr. Cuvillier, in a late private discussion of the merits of the present administration, who observed, that after all, the only difference between it and that of Lord Dalhousie, was, that the Canadians had now a man who would shake hands with them! My information does not authorize me to state positively that you are the author of this most ungenerous sneer and uncomplimentary remark towards *Sir James Kempt*; and, indeed, you are, upon the whole, an animal whose ears are too long to be saddled with any observation of point. But Mr. Cuvillier, is an auctioneer, and, of consequence, a *licensed* wit by profession. At all events, this shaking-hands business shews in a most extraordinary light your *very weighty* reasons for accusing Lord Dalhousie of pride and prejudice. Let me ask you whether it is pride and prejudice in any honest man to decline shaking hands with a personal enemy and a common calumniator of his fame? Are you not a personal enemy of Lord Dalhousie and have you not publickly avowed yourself to be so? The little honour that may be left to you after such an avowal, will not allow you to do otherwise than to answer in the affirmative. Have you ever meddled with Lord Dalhousie's character in private, or calumniated his reputation as a governor in public? Dare you hesitate for an answer?

If you do I will send for proof of the first to your friends, and of the other to your own manifesto, and speeches in and out of parliament, as well as those midnight rhapsodies which you are said to have uttered preparatory to the complaints sent home against his lordship. Did you ever pollute the walls of Downing Street with your scandal? And do you now suppose that you, or any of your gang, are fit to be taken by the hand by such a man as Lord Dalhousie? His Lordship is too much of a man of honour, too much of a gentleman, and too little of a politician to grasp by the hands those whom he cannot trust with his fame. I once had the mortification to see a drunken scavenger, with his dirty broom on his shoulder, come up to a peer of the realm, and for no other cause or provocation than his being a lord, abuse him in the most opprobious epithets. To myself and others who stood by, this was a scene of disgust and abhorrence; but to the nobleman himself it was only one of merriment. He gave the scavenger a crown, and his abuse was immediately changed into expressions of praise and gratitude. Sir, if you will have the goodness to transfer that mace from the table before you to your shoulder we shall behold an exact representation of the scavenger, and his broom, with this exception, that you have not yet been paid the crown, otherwise your clamour against Lord Dalhousie would long ere now have ceased, and be probably turned into abject adulation. But I have been told that you are a man of extensive reading. If so, you can be at no loss in what part of *Paradise* Lost to find a more apt parallel. You will there find your own counterpart as faithfully depicted, as *Eve* found herself reflected when she first beheld her shadow in the pool.

As to your *Scurrility*, Sir, it is worthy both of yourself and the cause which you advocate. In the vocation of scurrility, you appear to be exceedingly well versed. It seems to be your native element, as filth is that of vermin. You have been thought eloquent. I think so too. But it is only in scurrility. Did I not know, by your principles, that you were brought forth and educated in this Province, I should have no hesitation, from the style and character of your language, to apply at Billingsgate for a certificate of your nativity. But scurrility is a trade so low, so gross, and so loathsome that no man, however equivocal his reputation, can be injured by it; and it is only the grubs of the earth that traffick in it. At the end of the session I presume you will be able to tell us the amount of *your* gains. If your profits be equal to your industry, you will be able to lay up a capital that will enrich your posterity, without rendering them either the envy of others or respectable in their own eyes. As to the principal object of your inveterate malice, his escutcheon is too pure, and his coronet too exalted to be any ways stained or disturbed by such ribaldry as you are master of. If you intend that it should have any effect, I would, therefore, advise you to vend your poison among your own circle. There it may do good to all parties. Whilst its use will serve to convict the utterer of baseness, the circulators will be punished as accessaries. Their punishment will indeed, be dissimilar, but equally effectual. The latter will die an ignominious death and be forgotten. The former will undergo an ignominious death too ; but his memory will live to be deplored by his posterity, and execrated by his countrymen.

But who are you, Sir, who thus stand forth as the head and champion of all the disaffected and dissensions---of all the evil and ignoble spirits in the Country ? By what right of inheritance have *you* thus become at once the advocate of sedition and the calumniator of all men in legitimate authority ? If you have any other titles but those of a cowardly heart and a manevolent disposition, produce them, I entreat of you. But conscience whispers to you, that you cannot. She also tells you, that, with the exception of a few acres of ground, and a disrelish of British government and superiority, you have no other inheritance. *You* will not, of course, and the publick is not bound, to take my word for this. I shall therefore prove it. In doing so, I shall adduce as my first witness a gentleman whom I dare say you venerate very much, and whose veracity I presume you will [illegible] disposed to call in question. All I know of [illegible] gentleman myself, is, that he is reported to be a rank democrat, and to have taught you the elements of your politicks. He was himself, too, in his time a noted politician, and for some time held a seat in that branch of the legislature of which you say *yourself*---for I deny the fact---you are *Speaker*. In that capacity the venerable gentleman in question said something rude and insulting to a brother representative. This representative was not to be overdone in acts of benevolence of this kind, and accordingly sent a civil *message* to the venerable and honourable member begging his company at a certain place next morning to meet one or two friends. It is a very extraordinary circumstance, and has never yet been accounted for, though this affair took place many years since, that the venerable member, though imbued with the characteristick politeness of his countrymen, neither availed himself of the invitation of his friend nor sent any apology for his absence. It is sagely presumed that some family concerns called him away rather hurriedly. Be that as it may, he was never again seen in his place in the Assembly ; and his seat is now occupied by a descendant every way worthy of the sire.

What relation you, Sir, bear to this venerable man of the people, I will leave yourself and others to determine. Let me only add, that if you do not inherit his flying propensities, you are fully his equal as well in giving as in receiving invitations of honour. The whole province laughed at you when Mr. M. pulled you by the nose in the lobby of the House of Assembly, and you had the courage to tell him that you would prosecute him? You may think me personal.* But do you really think that any thing can be more personal, than telling a man that he is deaf to every sentiment but pride, prejudice and despotism. Do you not in effect and in fact call such a man a coward? Do you not denounce him as a man destitute of every sentiment of honour and principle of justice? And what man of honour or courage would take taunt or insult from you, who inherit neither by birth, and upon whose heart no good example or custom can make any impression through life.

Without doors, to use a parliamentary phrase, the province has yet to learn the grounds of your pretensions to the invidious office of public censor, and still more infamous profession of general calumniator. Whence, tell us, this singular assumption of precedency. Whence this robe---these emblems of authority with which you have invested yourself; for that authority must, indeed, be great which gives you a censuring and condemning power over the highest and gravest offices of government. What new dignity is

---

*In a letter from Pope to Arbuthnot, dated 26th July, 1734, he says :---"To reform, and not to chastise, I am afraid, is impossible; and that the best precepts, as well as the best laws, would prove of small use, if there were no examples to enforce them. To attack vices in the abstract, without touching persons may be safe fighting, in-

this which you have exclusively appropriated to yourself. Produce your patent, I beg of you; for it has hitherto eluded all our senses of touch and vision. From which of the great and virtuous actions of your life has it emanated? I have known you for many years, and to none of those can I trace it. I know not what *you* esteem as acts of virtue and humanity, but I will tell you one or two that I do not consider in that light. I do not esteem it either virtuous, generous, or humane in you to have shut your heart and your purse against the claims of the sufferers from the New-Brunswick conflagration at a time when every other heart and purse in the province and in the empire were thrown open to their necessities, and when, as Speaker, you had pocketed many thousand pounds of the publick money. Their solicitations, though made by gentlemen every way your superiors, were received with the cold inhuman remark that the sufferers were but *des Anglois*, undergoing the pains of a terrestrial ordeal preparatory to an infernal one! Deeds of charity ought to be done in private; nor will I insult the leading object of your malice by contrasting his conduct on this occasion with yours. It will be sufficient to say, that were I to do so, the pub-

---

deed, but it is fighting with shadows. My greatest comfort and encouragement to proceed has been to see, that those who have no shame, and no fear of any thing else, have appeared touched by my satires."

lick would be at no loss upon whom to fix the stigma of pride, prejudice, and despotism. Lord Dalhousie's charity has ever been munificent. Yours has always been confined to a *vote* in the House of Assembly. He always gave away his own in elemosynary gifts. You were contented and gratified by disposing of the property of others. Do you remember——But why should I insult the publick with a catalogue of your crimes? Are they not already well-known? Do we not find ample proofs of them in every countenance at the bare mention of your name? Is not the name of *Papineau* a by-word and a proverb? Is it not held in derision by all who wish well to the country? Is it not synonymous, not only with *pride*, *prejudice*. *and despotism*, but with every thing that is ridiculous, bigotted and obstinate? Are not the very *cahots* now called *Papineaus?* But let us behold you in another character; let us behold you *within doors*, as the phrase has it.

You were brought up to the law; a most noble and respectable profession in which, dull as your forensick talents are, you might have succeeded and dragged out a life, if not of splendour or affluence, at least of comparative innocence and retirement. But the courts of law, were too contracted a field for a man of your ambition: you found their dignity, order, and subordination incompatible with your views, and destructive of your aspirations. In an evil hour you deserted the bar, and betook yourself to the more precarious trade of politicks. How you have hitherto succeeded in your new employment, an ignorant and discontented people—an idle and famished peasantry—a disgraced and ruined country, bear ample testimony. Sir, the restlessness of temper which made you a legislator has proved injurious to yourself; but the ambition which placed you in the Speaker's chair, has, I fear, destroyed your country. We shall be overwhelmed if you do not desert the senate as you did the bar, and immediately retire to your original obscurity.

Your career in the Assembly, but especially as Speaker has been remarkable for a variety of strange circumstances. In what publick capacity does the province ever hear of you as a politician? Your publick identity is confined to the Hastings and the Assembly; and the chart of your travels scarcely extends farther. We never behold you as a member of any literary or scientific society. We never see you mix with the gentlemen of the country in giving aid, countenance and encouragement to the youth of the times in their endeavours to store their minds with useful and ornamental knowledge. Neither our museums nor our Libraries owe yoh any donation: not even one of those speeches and pamphlets in whose praise yourself and your friends are so clamorously eloquent. No; we never behold you, but in a dull round of plodding intriguing politicks. No scene has any charms in your eyes but the gloomy walls of the house of Assembly; no station but the chair, the table and the floor of that venerable fabrick. Your oratory, too, like your person, has its *locale*; and we scarcely ever hear of you as a speaker, but when the mace and a thousand pounds are glittering in magnified rays before your eyes. Who ever thought before that *avarice* had been a constituent part of eloquence! Sir, I know not whether you keep a mistress; but if you do, you are much beholden to her for initiating you so perfectly in the abandoned trade of prostitution. Have you not prostituted all the little talents that you possess to the gratification of a party? Have you not made it the object and study of your life to please that party in their endeavours to obtain the mastery over the government of the province? Have you not sacrificed with them at the shrines of Bacchus, of Pluto, and of Mercury? Have you not, in fact, become the High-Priest of their political revelries? Have you and they not turned the House of Assembly into a house of bad fame; in which the character, reputation, and circumstances of every honest man in the country are nightly investigated and discussed? But you have done worse than opening a banqueting house for scandal. Have you not established an inquisitorial tribunal over the lives, liberties and privileges of every British subject in the province? What man is safe from your illegal and unconstitutional scrunity? What private family is secure from your jesuitical mode of procedure? Is there a father in the province who does not tremble for his offspring if they are anywise connected with the publick business of the country? Is there a son who does not do the same thing for his father? Who, that differs in opinion from the House of Assembly, is not made an object of insult and persecution? Who, in the honest discharge of his duty happens to give offence to the Assembly, that is not dragged before them with every indignity, and compelled to undergo, not a fair and legal trial, but contumely, scorn, and disgrace? In the name of British Liberty, what age and country is this that we live in? Britons! can you longer endure this! Do you live in a British colony, and submit to have your rights thus wrested from you! Can you live, and forfeit the liberties for which your fathers bled? Is the cause of Sidney and of Hampden no longer yours? You are loyal and brave. Be resolute and courageous; and rest assured, that the evils you now complain of will soon have an end. I declare, in the face of my country, that the House of Assembly, as at present constituted, is corrupt and an intolerable nuisance. The people have a right—a well defined constitutional right—to recall such representatives. Let that be done. Let us peaceably and respectfully petition the Governor to dissolve the present parliament. *There can be no right without remedy.* There are limits to the privileges of the House of Assembly; and when these limits are over-stepped, I maintain that even the Legislative Council—that traduced and much abused body—have a constitutional right to join the people in preserving the constitution. They are as much the guardians of the public welfare as the House of Assembly; and they are therefore bound to assist us when our rights and liberties are at stake. It has been said that dissolutions do no good in this country. I care not. Let the forms and powers of the constitution be maintained when the rights of the people are in danger. Who is the physicina that would not administer medicine when the body is diseased and in danger, though he were assured that no benefit should result from it?

But, Sir, I have lost sight of you for a little. Yet, were you a thousand times of more importance than you really are, who could preserve any remembrance of you when his country was in jeopardy? No wonder, then, if I have forgotten you for a moment. But though I forgot you personally, the miseries which you have entailed on the province were fresh in my memory, and its real interests deeply engraven on my heart. I had a right, therefore, to rally around me all the loyalty and sterling principles which I know the country to be yet possessed of. I did so; and I have not so mean an opinion of myself as to think that my efforts will have been altogether in vain. But I know not that I should, at present, add any thing more to the truths which I have told you. I have convicted you of *Falsehood, Defamation and Scurrility*; and I think that the transmission of this record to posterity, will be ample punishment. I should be sorry, however, to send you down to futurity wholly unaccompanied; and therefore beg leave to introduce to you the very acceptable names of Viger and Vallieres---names connected by alliteration as well as by a community of feeling, principle, and profession :---

"Two bookful blockheads ignorantly read
With loads of learned lumber in their head."

They both participated with you in your assault upon the character of Lord Dalhousie; and it is but right and just that they should share in your punishment. Mr. Viger is also reported to have said, in the debate on Mr. Christie's illegal and unwarrantable expulsion, that "for his part he felt it painful even to name such a man as Lord Dalhousie." No wonder! He knew that Lord Dalhousie was a gentleman; which he is not himself. He knew Lord Dalhousie to be a soldier; which he also is not himself. The skulking exploits of a Niger behind a tree in the battle of Chateauguay, have not yet been forgotten. They yet serve as an amusing tale to beguile the long winter nights in the neighbourhood of that famous field. As to *Mr. Vallieres*, the "damnable *system*," which he spoke of on the same occasion, has served to give to the country a better opinion of his religious principles than have been hitherto entertained. This is the first intimation the publick have had of his belief either in heaven or hell. The province rejoices at the conversion of so great a man; and the church, that reared him from a destitute orphan to his present exaltation and popularity, cannot do otherwise than perform high mass and *Te Deum* for the return of so undutiful and long-lost a prodigal. However, were he now wearing, as he expected, Judge Tachereau's three-cornered hat, the publick will do him the justice to believe, that, "be the administration of Lord Dalhousie" what it would, we should hear him extolling it to heaven instead of sinking it to hell.

Adieu, for the present, false and defamaeory *Triumvirate!* Adieu, wretched calumniators of a man of acknowledged honour, virtue, and integrity! Adieu base slanderers! If you ever renew your work of malice and vindictiveness, depend upon it, that you shall hear again from

THE WATCHMAN.

28th February, 1829.

NO. IX.

"The well-being of a State is wholly dependent on the character of a people."

To John Galt, Esquire.

In fulfilment, my dear Sir, of my promise to communicate to you whatever information I might deem of importance respecting this distant, but interesting portion of His Majesty's dominions, I have often revolved in vain on a subject befitting both your own superior talents for inquiry, and those means of improving them which you could not fail to have enjoyed during your residence in the country. This residence, however, though of the utmost consequence to the future glory and prosperity of the Empire, must necessarily be too short to enable you to investigate with that truth and accuracy, for which your researches have ever been remarkable, every subject claiming the attention of the philosophick traveller; and there being few topicks which require a more penetrating eye, a keener spirit of investigation, or a more intimate acquaintance, in order to be able to draw a true representation of their various degrees and shades, than the character and manners of a strange people. I have, therefore, as an eye and an ear witness of several years, had the boldness to attempt giving you a *Sketch of the Manners and Customs of the French Canadians*. But I beg of you always to remember, that it is only a *Sketch*, and the very feeblest of Sketches; for, although few, indeed, I may say no one, has treated the subject as I, with due humility, propose to do, yet I shall only look upon my reminiscences as a sort of Dædalean clue for extricating a greater stranger than myself out of that most intricate of all labyrinths, the erring and winding ways of man. It becomes me at the same time, to assure you, that nothing shall be stated but with the utmost possible deference to truth; than no trait shall either be heightened or shaded in its colouring beyond the bounds of its legitimate and peculiar characteristicks; that no sentiment shall willingly or maliciously be distorted or exaggerated; that foibles and blemishes, if they do exist, being inherent to every class and denomination of mankind, shall not be brought forth in order to be treated with contemptuous severity, but merely to elucidate more forcibly the sources whence they spring, and the evils to which they lead; that folly and presumption will be pitied rather than blamed; that if crime or immorality should unfortunately meet us on our way, they shall not indeed be either shunned or palliated; but neither will they be treated in any other way than as the fatal engine of the ruin and destruction of society; and, in a word, that however much the pencil may be wanting in art and dexterity, it will be my endeavour to make it up in an undeviating love of truth and persevering effort at accuracy, so far as the means of my information extend.

And here I cannot help expressing my surprise at the extreme paucity of our information regarding the customs and manners of the French Canadians, who, with respect at least to the British publick, are, at this moment, a people almost as much detached as they were when Wolfe planted the British ensign on the Heights of Abraham, or even as much so, in several instances, as it is possible for the savages of the woods to be, whose estrangement is not so very unconquerable as it is generally imagined, and whose aversion to Englishmen, in particular, is not loaded with half the prejudices that are to be found among the Canadians. This want of information, insignificant as it may at first appear, has been the source of many national and local evils, as well as political blunders. For had the love of freedom, susceptibility of improvement, respect to British institutions, and, in numerous instances, docility of temper so natural to the Canadians, been better understood and brought into operation during that eventful period, from the conquest till the passing of the Canadian *Magna Charta* in 1791, our legislators and law-givers should not, at this late season, have to encounter so many stumbling-blocks as, you must be well aware, daily spring up in their way to reformation and improvement. The enlargement of the book of knowledge, would not only extend their views, but give an impetus and a proper direction to all their plans. But, without this, those who have the superintendence of national affairs, especially those of colonies situated at a distance from the mother country, must always be groping in the dark, and blind leaders of the blind, till some fearful catastrophe meet them in their way and plunge them into irretrievable ruin. It will then be too late to look for the proper path, or for careful guides to lead them through it, for the quagmires and vortices of the slough of political despond may have already swallowed them, with all their ambitious, but ill-directed, hopes and projects.

I do not assert, that any thing of this has, as yet, taken place in Canada, and I sincerely hope it never may; because I perceive many things going on around me which betoken the most auspicious improvements, nay, which, I trust, will ultimately avert the fears of the most solicitous regarding this part of the British empire. Yet who can look upon the beggarly fund of information which a Briton can boast of with respect to this country, and the difficulty which he always experience in drawing upon it for however small an amount, without absolutely hesitating as to the actual dependency of such a vast territory upon the British crown, and loudly exclaiming against that false and short-sighted policy which should thus, by a piece of the most cruel and culpable negligence, sacrifice the best interests of a large body of the finest people in the empire, and perhaps, the ultimate welfare of the empire itself! I am no stickler about voyages and expeditions to Tombuctoo, the sources of the Niger, the north pole, or even to the moon, if such a trip could be accomplished, of which, by the way, we need not despair, considering the many wonderful things that are done in this our day and generation, provided such expeditions and voyages would either add to our knowledge of science, or serve to maintain unsullied and undiminished British valour and intrepidity. But when I behold tome upon tome, and quarto upon quarto full of thrice-told savage wonders and Indian legends, and descriptive of rocks and stones —of rare birds and wild animals with which the learned world has been familiar for ages, while scarcely an authentic page can be produced on the subject of the moral and physical character of nearly half a million of British subjects—a subject of all others the most important to an enlightened nation—I positively marvel at the great want of judgment which it discovers in a quarter from whence better things might be expected, and become really amazed, that the consequent myopy has not been productive of far greater evils than those which we so justly complain of. Let me ask you, if such a state of things be not for once, at least, an ample and decisive proof of the justice of a maxim in the last book of Aristotle's physicks, which says, that whatever was below the moon was abandoned by the gods, to the direction of nature, and chance and necessity?

You are of opinion, that whatever prejudices exist among the Canadians to the general character, opinions, manners, and public institutions of their neighbours of the United States, ought to be fostered as the surest pledge in the time of need. that they will not fail in the most faithful discharge of their duty to themselves and their country. I believe I had the pleasure verbally of convincing you how cordially I agreed with you upon this point to a certain extent, and it will be my duty, in the sequel, to show you how far these prejudices at present obtain. But if you will maturely consider this important subject in all its bearings, I think you will, in your turn, agree with me in the conclusion, that the more you promote and foster these prejudices, without at the same time inspiring those who entertain them with sentiments of national pride and patriotism of wider bounds than those of Canada, and almost extending to the utmost verge of the British dominions, the higher and the thicker you will build that fatal wall of partition which has so long divided the interests of the English and French inhabitants of Canada, and entail upon the country those very evils which, by a more extended field of information, we assure ourselves would inevitably and irremediably be destroyed. The prejudices of an enlightened people against foreigners, such, for instance, as those entertained by the British against all foreigners, but particularly against the French, do not appear to me to arise so much from hatred and contempt as from that conscious superiority, that unalterable love of country, and that flattering self confidence which, as being the most acceptable unction to the vanity of human nature, it would be as easy as it would be prudent to instil into the minds of every independent nation. These prejudices, if they may be called such, seem to be the true foundation of genuine patriotism. But how is this generous and chivalric passion to be cultivated in the bosoms of a conquered or collateral people, occupied with peculiar notions of their own at perfect antipedes, perhaps, with those of the mother country, and confined to what I may term the exclusive system of a corporation that has no interest, and desires to enjoy neither interest, nor influence beyond the bounds of its own contracted sphere? Simply, in my humble opinion, by a strict and impartial inquiry into the general character, springs of action, susceptibility of change, bias to any particular order or system of society, capability of instruction, natural love of country, fondness of general knowledge and, in a word, into any prominent feature characteristick of a free and industrious people. Such an inquiry conducted, under the auspices of such a government as ours, by such men as yourself—no flattery, believe me—would afford to the philosopher and the politician a sort of moral chart which would enable them to carry with safety and success into the bosom of the Canadians any measure calculated to promote the general welfare of society, or the political prosperity of the empire; and enable them to lay the foundation of almost every public and private virtue.

By this means, without entering into many particulars, the somewhat useful, but I fear rather dangerous prejudices to which I have been alluding, would certainly be eradicated; but I hope you perceive, that they would gradually be replaced by prejudices far more important and enlightened, if I may say so. We should exchange the prejudices of gross and barbarous ignorance for the more manly and useful ones of education and real love of country. The one species of prejudices—that of rudeness and barbarism—though deeply rooted can only be nourished by sloth and brought into useful operation by flattery; while the other, because it contains the principle of action within itself, is always ready to be brought into operation whenever circumstances may render it necessary. The one, in short, degrades, while the other exalts human nature. The one debases the soul of man to a level with the brutes that perish, while the other cherishes every noble sentiment, and serves to raise the mind to the highest and the proudest pinnacle of the temple of fame. I have said that the prejudices of ignorance must always be flattered before they can be made to produce any useful results. Let me be more plain, and say, that the prejudices of my fellow subjects, the Canadians, as they are of the worst possible kind, must always undergo this degrading operation in order to render them productive of any good effects, even such effects as are only calculated to administer to their own personal interests and feelings. But is not this a most melancholy feature in the character of any people? Is it not a most deplorable circumstance—nay, disgraceful to human nature itself---to think, that, in order to render any particular vice serviceable, and what is the prejudice of ignorance, but a vice, it is necessary to call it into active existence by the application of another vice equally, if not more debasing? Yet who will deny the fact? In all the eventful emergencies of war and invasion to which we have been almost unremittingly exposed on this continent, either by our own folly, or the avidity and ambition of others, by what means did we prevail upon the Indians to take an interest and a part in our affairs? Why, by imposing, in the first place, on their credulity, and in the next, flattering their vanity and and corrupting their native love of country. Their prejudices were strong, but not so strong as to enable them to resist the more powerful grasp of bribery. For our own sakes, and not on account of any love we bore to them, we approached them as we would a man out of his reason or half distracted with rage, easily seducing them from their own more natural and legitimate allegiance by those means which gave to knowledge in all circumstances the superiority of ignorance. Thus the poor unfortunate creatures become a sort of Cis-Atlantic Swiss, ready to barter to the highest bidder those services which their rudeness, ignorance and prejudices prevented them from applying to the salvation of their country. It is just so with the Canadians, whose prejudices, as I said before, are, in a many respects, as narrow and deeply rooted as those of the Indians; and whose notions of patriotism if they have any notions at all upon the subject, are solely confined to their own narrow circle and circumstances. The ridiculous jealousies of the Canadians prevent them from extending their views. This prevents them from associating with their more enlightened fellow subjects, by whom alone they can be taught those genoroes sentiments by which all great nations are almost spontaneously actuated. They are thus strangers to their most important duties, as members of this great empire. In time of danger, therefore, a sense of this duty must of necessity be forced upon them. But how is it possible to do this, except by that identical process which was used with respect to the poor savage? It is therefore but reasonable to suppose, that a people of such confined views and such unseemly sentiments should become, at times, the prey of those most dexterous in plying them with those hopes and fears most congenial to their prejudices. Indeed the strongest, whether friend or foe, will become their master; and they will cry out like the Italians, God save *the conqueror*; passing, in all probability from one allegiance to another in the course of a Campaign.

Thus our duty at once to ourselves and this

sprightly but rude people, becomes plain and evident. They must be inspired with *British* sentiments and *British* feelings. Though permitted to retain the free exercise of their manners, language and religion they must be taught to look upon themselves, not as a distinct people having no community of interests or feelings with the rest of the country, but as an integral, important and substantial part and portion of the nation. They must not be taught, as they have hitherto unfortunately been, by those claiming influence over them, to look upon Englishmen as foreigners and invaders of their country, but as brethren whose rights are neither superior nor inferior to their own, and whose prosperity is not a whit dearer to government than theirs. They must not be allowed to imagine that the sole business of Englishmen in coming to this country, is to crush and extinguish them, but, on the contrary, to improve their own condition in life, and in doing which, they are always willing that the Canadians should go along with them side by side. They must be taught, that our laws are equitable, humane and salutary; that government, especially such a government as ours, and which we have most liberally imparted to them in its fullest vigour, is not the engine of tyranny or despotism, like that from which we have emancipated them, but of freedom the most perfect, and of power the most extensive; that our protection is, in every respect, unquestionable; and that, instead of loading them with public burdens for that purpose, we do it gratuitously, and relieve them from every imposition, except those calculated to promote their own immediate improvement and prosperity. But, above all, they must be mentally instructed. The iron barriers of ignorance and superstition must be broken down, so as to admit the genial rays of education and learning. The mind must be illuminated.

If all this be done, we shall soon discover the Canadians to possess all the virtues that we can reasonably desire, and a strong disposition to amalgamate with every thing laudable in British sentiments and feelings. When we have occasion for their services, instead of finding it necessary to address ourselves to the prejudices of a poor and selfish people in a state of semi-barbarism, we shall find them meeting us half way, mutually fraught with indignation at the country's wrongs, and inspired by every sentiment becoming a great and free people. We shall no longer be obliged to *treat* with them for their assistance as with foreigners whom we wish to become our allies, in order to avert the approaching danger; and it is not by trucking, higgling and bartering for the services of her own sons, that England has attained her present elevated station, and, in a great degree, become the protectress of the civilization of the world. Let the Canadians persevere in calling themselves a *Nation*. If there is any charm in the title, let them enjoy it in its fullest extent. But let it be enjoyed as an integral part of that of *Britain*, in the same way that the inhabitants of the Roman provinces, while they preserved their own national appellations, claimed, and were proud to obtain, the more important and dignified title of *Roman* Citizen. This, I dare say, you will say, is still ministering to those local prejudice which I am so anxious to see destroyed. It is so. But if we permit any kind of prejudices to exist—and there is no nation, and God forbid there should be any nation without certain prejudices—this harmless one ought to be the first to be tolerated and fostared. There is, as you well know, a peculiar charm in the nicknames which different countries sometimes give themselves. With what electrifying emotions do the various appelletions of *John Bull*, *Sawney* and *Paddy*, strike the ears of the different inhabitants of England, Scotland and Ireland! No one will deny that this is a prejudice; but who would be so cruel as to seek its destruction? If, therefore, the Canadians can be made happier by an indulgence so common among their fellow-subjects, let them enjoy it in the same manner that *they* do—the mere emblem of good humoured distinction, but at the same time, of true hearts, united courage, and undeviating loyalty.

But it has been objected to the mother country, that it is neither her *right* nor her *policy*, in any manner to interfere with the Canadians so as to force upon them any change of manners, customs, or laws, however conducive to their moral and political improvement. Nor is this the vague and idle surmises of a day. It has, as you partly know, become of late the business of a very influential party—and a *party* it is in every sense of the word—to instil such dangerous doctrines into the minds of a people, whose proverbial ignorance and credulity render them above all others the easy dupes of political intrigue and factious principles. It is daily uttered in pamphlets, newspapers, and all those other popular means of corruption by which wicked and dissolute men have in all ages been able to poison a certain portion of the public mind. As to this country, such indescribable enormities have been committed on the glorious liberty of the press, that great palladium of British freedom, that it is now scarcely possible for it to disgorge any thing that can disgust, however much it may contaminate; for every liberal and generous act of government, every act calculated to raise this colony in dignity and importance, has the misfortune to encounter in almost every direction a mountain of resentment and abuse sufficient to astonish if not horrify any reasonable being. But that the pure press of England should be sullied as it has of late occasionally been, by the slime, and filth and putrid saliva, and leprous bile of Canadian factions, is rather too much for our patience and fortitude to bear; and is a convincing proof, that neither place nor time is two sacred or unsuitable for the purposes of those who have no business but error, and no ambition but to be distinguished as the misleaders and corrupters of mankind. It was in this manner that what is *fashionably* termed the American *revolution*, commenced. It was by the preaching of this *identical* doctrine, that the Apostles of confusion and rebellion prepared the minds of weak and uninformed men for despising the parental authority of the mother country, and of driving Britons to the madness of imbruing their hands in each other's blood. It is evident to every impartial observer, that Canada is fast approaching towards some important crisis, and that, too, a crisis not the most satisfactory to the lovers of order and good government. A political storm has for years been gathering in this country, which, if longer submitted to, must inevitably carry us down the tide of inextricable ruin; but which, if resisted in time, and manfully stemmed, must yield to our perseverance, and burst harmless long before it approaches to that destructive maturity which it at present portends. It is, therefore, of the highest consequence both to England and Canada, that their true relative situations should be distinctly traced out; that the authority of the one and the duty of the other should be impressed on every mind and made legible to every capacity; and that, in short, the rights of Sovereign and vassal should be so ascertained as to render the least deviation from them as dangerous to the one party as to the other. In the event of revising our present constitution for the purpose either of remodelling it, or devising better means for promoting the peace and improvement of this part of the British dominions, this—I mean a clear and distinct understanding of the *relation* subsisting betwixt us and the parent state—is the first thing that ought to be done; for whether we know our own interests or not, and whether knowing them, we pursue them in the right or the wrong way, nature herself will teach us to resent, and that in no very mild or delicate terms, every reprimanding voice and every blow of correction, except those alone which proceed from recognized and well-defined authority. If this first principle in the government of Colonial possessions be not attended to, we may well despair of every step that may be taken in their amelioration, where prejudice and interestad views—a thing unheard of—do not go hand in hand with philosophy. If, therefore, in humbly submitting to your consideration a slight view of the deplorable state of matters in this province, and the mode in which, in my opinion, they can only be extricated from their present jeopardy, I shall be tempted to go somewhat into detail, I trust you will forgive me, and credit me when I say, that nothing but an ardent desire to see Britain flourish in all her departments and dependencies could have induced me to lead you into discussions which I fear will, to you at least, be far more tedious than profitable.

Trusting to future opportunities and more ample leisure than I at present enjoy for the fulfilment of my promises on the subject

here touched upon, I must
present, and only add that I al

Yours, truly,

THE WA

7th March, 1829.

NO. X.

" *When the blessings of the* British *Constitutian were* granted to *this Province, you received them with the* recorded *experience of centuries of practice: there is* no *question of doubt or of difficulty that may* not *find its* precedent *in the* records *of the Imperial Parliament, and I* cannot *think that any wiser* guide need *be* desired."

Lord *Dalhousie's prorogwing Speech.* 17*th March*, 1821.

The late Session of the Provincial Parliament.

Although we have already expressed our opinions on some of the leading questions which have occupied the attention of the Legislature, still the session offers us abundance of materials for further observation. It the most important session that has been held under the present Constitution. On its decisions hung not only the peace, welfare, and prosperity, of the Province, but the very existence of this Constitution itself; which, from the atrocious nature of the proceedings that distinguished and characterized the session, and the monstrous issue of its termination, has, in a manner, been destroyed and annihilated. What is the Constitution but a rule of conduct? If that rule be once broken or encroached upon, by what other means shall society be held together, and our rights and liberties preserved from destruction? In undertaking to review a session pregnant with such momentous consequences, we are not ignorant either of the ardour of the task which we have imposed upon ourselves, or the fate which awaits us---the fate of all those who distinguish themselves by opposing number, power, and prejudice. We know right well to what animadversions and imputations we expose ourselves. We know what a speaker or writer has to expect in these days who advocates the cause of the constitution and the rights and sentiments of those true Britons who have the misfortune to live under it in this Province. We know we live in a country where, though subject to British rule and British dominion, the very countenance of an Englishman is beheld with aversion, and where he is esteemed a greater enemy than even an alien from any other quarter of the world. We know we live in a British Province which affects to raise itself to the character and standing of a Nation, and that he who resists the impotent and ridiculous claim, runs the hazard of being branded as an incendiary and outlaw. We know we live in a country upon which the blessings and privileges of the British Constitution have been conferred, but where the authority derived from those blessings and privileges has been made subservient to the most infamous and iniquitous purposes. We know, as we have said on a former occasion, that there may be a Political as well as a Religious Inquisition, and that there is at this moment a *Political Inquisition* in this Province! We know all this, and a great deal more which we will not now recapitulate; but still we flinch not from our duty; and never shall, even if the whole power and menace of this Inquisition were arrayed against us, until we behold a purer and a brighter sun arise on our political horizon. Thank God! we are strangers to that grovelling cowardly spirit which has of late characterized the *Press* of this Province. That Press has abandoned a good cause and betrayed a great man and munificent patron. We proclaim this to the world in the sight and hearing of that Press. We thus give it an opportunity of vindicating its conduct if we have arraigned it unjustly; but we fear that its condemnation has already been pronounced by the publick. It is true that *we* have come later into the field than any Press now in Canada; but it is also true that our inducement to remain so long in it, is the desertion and flight of those who ought to have died on the spot rather than forsake the cause which they adopted with so much seeming zeal and loyalty. We are aware that we are fighting almost alone: but has the justice of a cause ever been estimated by the force arrayed on either side? But what is our cause? The principles of the *British Constitution!* This is a cause in which the civilized world is interested. Yet, how sad a thing it is, that in Lower Canada, whatever may be thought or uttered by individuals in private, scarcely a voice is publickly raised in its favour. Heaven forbid that such a state of things---that such degrading and despicable apathy---should continue to disgrace a British Province any longer, and that only *one* solitary "*Watchman*" should be found at his post in a time so perilous and desperate. What has become of "Setter," of "*Delta*," and "*A British Settler?*" Are those voices *now* mute which were wont to sound the alarum when the Constitution was in danger? In the name of *British Liberty* we call upon them once more to stand forth, and rally around them the friends of the Constitution. Our rights never stood in greater jeopardy than they do at this moment; and unless we array every *British* heart in their defence, we are undone forever.

"Thy spirit, *Independence*, let me share,
Lord of the lion-heart and eagle-eye,
Thy steps I follow with my bosom bare,
Nor heed the storm that howls along
the sky."

In the meantime let us do our duty. We have undertaken a task and must perform it. Bold in the integrity of our intentions, and stern in the consciousness of our honesty and independence, it is not the unpopularity of an individual, or the unfashionableness of a doctrine, that shall deter us from defending the one or maintaining the other. We say this because we detest all kinds of innovation, tyranny and malicious abuse. A Legislature can be tyrannical as well as a King:

and we detest one tyranny as much as the other. We also detest inconsistency, avarice, and intrigue ; and if we can shew, in the course of these strictures, that it is to those detestable propensities and passions, we principally owe our present state of political degradation, who will blame us for making use of that just but severe language which renders the moralist the best guardian of virtue, and the patriot the best safeguard of his Country. Our sentiments as well as our language may be thought irksome and disagreeable to some men, and even to men of standing and authority. Yet we shall make no apology. We are too well acquainted with our Constitution and with British liberty not to know, that we cannot be better employed than in defending our rights and privileges as freemen, and in resisting all invasions of those rights and privileges, whether they emanate from government or the legislature. Unconstitutional measures must be withstood as well as those of tyranny and despotism, because the first are always the precursor of the second. But to animadvert on measures in the abstract, without tracing them up to their authors, would be at once useless and endless. *We* shall not therefore attempt it. It is, indeed, impossible to do otherwise than deplore the general features of the measures of the late Session ; but, in pronouncing an opinion upon them, we must have recourse to their authors, as alone responsible to us and to the country at large.

Before proceeding farther, it will be necessary, for the full understanding of the subject, to draw a sketch of the state of parties in this province.

When the Sovereignty of *Canada* was transferred from his Most Sacred to his Britannick Majesty, nothing could be more vociferous than the joy of the Canadians. It was like the emancipation of a Colony of slaves. The chains of French despotism once struck off, it was thought that no submision could be greater, and no gratitude more deep and lasting than those of this people towards their new Sovereign and Country. Every voice was raised in lamenting the injuries which they had so long endured under a military system of government, and in praise of the freedom which they breathed, and the protection which they felt from the influence of the British Constitution and laws. Such sentiments, worthy of a wise and prudent people, they were not only content to utter among themselves, but frequently to convey to the foot of the throne, as well as to every intervening power and authority.* This excess of kindness," say they in a petition to the king from which an extract is given in the note below---" This excess of kindness towards us we shall *never* forget. These

*" Sire, vos tres-soumis et tres-fideles nouvaux sujets de la province de Canada prennent la liberte de se *prostener* au pied du throne, pour y porter les sentiments de respect, d'amour, et de soumission dont leurs

generous proofs of the clemency of our benign conqueror will be carefully preserved

---

cœurs sont remplis envers votre auguste personne, et pour lui rendre de treshumbles actions de grace de ses soins paternels.

Notre reconnoissance nous force d'avouer que le spectacle affrayant d'avoir etc conquis par les armes victorieuses de votre Majeste n'a pas longtems excite nos regrets et nos larmes. Ils se sont dissipes a mesure que nous avons appris combien il est doux de vivre sous les constitutions sages de l'empire Britannique. En effet, loin de resentir au moment de la conquete les tristes effets de la gene et de la capture, le sage et vertueux General qui nous a conquis, digne image du Sauverain glorieux qui lui confia le commandement de ses armees, nous laissa en possession de nos loix et de nos coutumes. Le libre exercise de notre religion nous fut conserve, et confirme par le traite de paix; et nos anciens citoyens furent etablis les juges de nos causes civiles. *Nous n' oublirons jamais cet exces de bonte ces traits genereux d'un si doux vainqueur* seront conserves *precieusement* dans nos *fastes: et nous les* transmettrons *d'*age *en age a nos derniers neveux.* Tels sont, Sire, les doux liens qui dans le principe nous ont si fortement attaches a votre majeste: liens indissolubles, et qui se reserreront de plus en plus.

Petition of the Catholick Inhabitants of Canada to the King, December, 1773.

in the annals of our history; *and we shall transmit them from generation to generation to our remotest posterity.* These Sire, are the pleasing ties by which, *in the beginning of our subjection* to *your Majesty's government,* our hearts were so strongly bound to your Majesty; ties which can never be dissolved, but which time will only strengthen and draw closer." Similar to these were the sentiments uttered by the same people in August, 1764, to General Murray, the Governor in Chief:—" At last," say they, "our *most* sanguine *wishes* are gratified; we have been the faithful witnesses of the prerogatives granted to your Excellency by the greatest of Kings, in the commission of Governor in Chief of the vast Province of *Quebec.* Permit us to vent our joy, which is too great and too perfect to be contained. We are already certain, that we shall see peace, justice, and equity reign in our province: every circumstance assures us of the freedom and security of trade. He is no more one of those conquerors of the province of Quebec, who formerly managed the thunder-bolt of war with so much skill in the conquest thereof: as mild in peace as dangerous in battle, his only occupation is to dispense happiness. Such is the pleasing idea we entertain of the happy government we are to enjoy under your Excellency: an idea founded on the unanimous testimony of *all* the inhabitants of the ancient government of Quebec."*

*Vide Quebec Gazette, 23d August, 1764.

Such were the praiseworthy sentiments expressed by the French population of this province for some time after the conquest. That they felt at that time what they uttered, we will do them the justice neither to doubt or deny. If ever a people experienced the advantages of conquest, it was the Canadians. If ever the people felt the benefits of the transition arising from a state of penury, thraldom and misgovernment to a state of freedom, industry, and wealth, it was the people of this Province. Nothing, therefore, could be more natural than their readiness to give utterance, on all occasions, to the sentiments which were uppermost in their hearts; and nothing more honourable and becoming than the assiduity with which they cultivated the esteem and protection both of the new paternal state and the British population who came to reside amongst them. That they looked upon these as superior beings, carrying along with them the blessings and privileges of a free and generous mode of government, unparalleled in the history of the world, cannot for a moment be doubted. As we look forth at the termination of winter for the harbingers of spring and renovated nature, they beheld *them* as the real messengers of national peace and prosperiity. They esteemed them as the patrons of every thing great and happy; at once the active promoters of enterprise, and the fearless defenders of public right and justice. They esteemed it a boon of no little importance to be ranked as equal in privileges with such a people : to be counted bone of their bone and flesh of their flesh; to be joint-heirs of the inheritance secured to them by the British Constitution. Nor did they waive their rights nor shun their station. They embraced their new fellow-subjects as brothers, and lived with them as such on the most cordial terms of ease, peace, and good will.* But favours may be too munificent and protection misapplied. The seeming docility of the Canadians; the sentiments of joy which they universally exhibited at passing from a despotick and tyrannical government to a free and constitutional one; the gratitude expressed on all occasions at this event;

---

*In a petition proposed to be sent to the King in 1773, by both his old and new subjects in Canada, we find this passage:— "Your petitioners, though they entertain different opinions upon matters of religion, have nevertheless lived in a friendly intercourse with each other ever since the conquest of the Country. They are all of them unminted with Jacobite principles: they are and ever will remain, good and faithful subjects to your Majesty: they acknowledge no title to the Crown, but that of the illustrious house of Hanover: they desire to be united and connected by the same ties, which will preserve both them and their posterity to the latest generations, in a state of perfect obedience to your most Excellent Majesty, and your heirs and successors to the British Government."

their apparent simplicity of manners; and their willing submission to the new laws imposed upou them, induced the supreme govcrament to believe that no indulgence shewn to their new subjects, however incompatible with the just rights and interests of the British population settling in the province, and destructive of the ultimate benefits arising from Colonial possessions, could be attended by any of those evil consequences which have often disturbed the peace, and not seldom proved destructive of the integrity of extensive empires. The result was, that, though the laws of England, both civil and criminal, had been introduced into the province; though the rule of government and mode of exercising it, had been proclaimed by documents emanating immediately from the Crown, still the ancient laws, language, and prejudices of the Canadians were fostered in a manner which shewed clearly, that if Britain really understood the true interests of her colonies, she for once either lacked the wisdom of carrying her views into effect, or the courage of enforcing them. However, it must be stated in her justification---if indeed, any thing can justify such conduct ---that, being then in free and full possession of the whole continent of North America from the Mississippi to the St. Lawrence, throughout which immense region her own language was spoken and her laws executed, she probably imagined, that but little injury could result from permitting the Canadians, a small people of no ambition, commerce or enterprise, to enjoy undisturbed their own institutions and usages. This notion, if really entertained, might have been supported by the fact, that, having the whole *English* colonies before them, few emigrants from the mother country would think of settling in a newly-acquired province, possessing but little sympathy of manners or habits with them, and enjoying but few resources for a stirring and commercial people. What Briton would think of settling in Canada, whose government and laws were not yet established, whilst such a tract of country as the New-England and other British Colonies, in the full enjoyment of almost every moral and political advantage, lay open to his ambition? In fact, before the American rebellion, few Englishmen settled in Canada. Few men thought of expending capital in a country whose laws were not only foreign but fluctuating; and fewer still deemed it prudent to cultivate a soil shackled and burdened by feudal tenures and taxes. The consequence was, that the Canadians began to look upon themselves as *individualized*, if we may be permitted to coin a word. They never entertained much mutual sensibility with the English Colonists, and the long wars in which the two nations were perpetually engaged, served not only to separate them as aliens to each others' sentiments and feelings, but to render them natural and irreconcilable enemies. Thus left to themselves, the Canadians also began to feel their own importance. They studied and became acquainted with the rights of British freemen. Had they done so, unbiased by native prejudice, this province would long before now have been the happiest spot on the face of the globe. But, unfortunately, the insignificant notions attached to the Canadians themselves as a people, and the little value attached at the time to that part of the country which they occupied, in consequence both of being but little known, and considered of small commercial or political importance in comparison of the extensive sea coast already in our possession, his Majesty's new subjects were left almost entirely to the freedom of their own will: and permitted to speculate on the future in any way most agreeable to their interest or ambition. Though they were well aware that the British government wore not only desirous of establishing on a permanent basis the lowa and government of Canada, but had adopted active preliminary measures for that purpose, yet they readily perceived symptoms of delay and hesitation on the part of the mother country, which led them to believe that both in a moral and political point of view, they were considered of much more importance than they were in reality. They watched the signs of the times; and it must be confessed that these proved as favourable to the *exclusive system* to which they already began to aspire as their utmost ambition could possibly wish. In consequence of the attempts made by the Imperial Parliament to raise a revenue in the *Old Colonies*, the publick mind there became disturbed. Men began to talk high of their natural and political rights: and to refuse obedience to laws in which they had no voice in framing. The result is well known: it is one of the most momentous eras in the history of mankind. Neither the interests nor the passions of the Canadians being immediately concerned in the awful struggle which ensued, it was deemed far from being impracticable to render them willing and powerful instruments in the coorceive measures that had been finally adopted by the Mother Country against her native but rebellious colonies. The ancient feuds subsisting between the Canadians and those colonies, and their mutual jealousy and animosity of one another, were thought grand and infallible excitements in the Canadians towards the due execution of the intended blow. As a collateral incitement, it is a well known fact—and a fact which very much disgraces the history of the time---that the old subjects of his majesty who had resorted to the province with capital, and who had by that means already given it a commercial aspect, which it never enjoyed before, were considered as disaffected to the Mother Country, and dangerously tainted with the spirit of riot and sedition which raged with such fury in the neighbouring Colonies. In truth they were not only suspected, but watched; and the ordinary language of a British freeman, if coming from them, was construed into the jargon of disaffection and rebellion. Such sentiments, proceeding frequently from the highest authority in the province, gave an air of truth and reality to the suspicions entertained which they could otherwise never obtain; and the Canadians, already on the alert for an opportunity to justify the confidence which began to be placed in them, most readily chimed in with these unworthy surmises.* There certainly were not at this time many men among the Canadians who entertained such rooted prejudices to the laws and government of England as to trouble themselves much as to their introduction

*We have heard an anecdote of General Murray, which if true, confirms all that we have said in relation to the reflections cast on the English settlers in the province. The General, with the view, no doubt, of putting a timely stop to the disaffection which he supposed to exist at this period, sent an *Orderly* to desire the immediate attendance at the Castle of all the British merchants in Quebec. Upon coming up and waiting some time in the ante-room, the General entered in great wrath and told them, that he sent for them merely to tell them from his own mouth, that they were all a set of d——d villians; and that, if they did not behave themselves better, he would ship them off from the Colony by the first King's vessel that should be ready to sail for England. The only way in which such proceedings can be justified, is to recollect, that General Murray had just succeeded to the authority anciently possessed by the *French Governor*.

finally in whole or in part; and the great majority, understanding little and caring still less about abstract rights, were willing to obey any law or government that might be conferred upon them. But there was at that time, as there is now, a *party* among the Canadiens of almost unlimited influence---of an influence which had only to command in order to be obeyed, and to lead in order to be followed. This party, with the acuteness peculiar to faction, clearly and distinctly perceived their vantage ground; and left no effort untried in order to possess themselves of it. They assailed both Governors *Murray* and Carleton with assurances, that if the Canadians were reinstated in their ancient laws and customs, every exertion should be made, if necessary, in coercing the old Colonies and in putting down their new pretensions. These were favourable omens to the military ambition of a General Commanding in Chief in Canada; and we may be assured, from the result, that he did not fail to turn them to account in his correspondence with the Imperial Government. We accordingly find that the measures which had been adopted in England for the establishment of a permanent government, *on the basis of the English laws*, civil, *mercantile*, *and criminal*, were from time to time suspended, according to the extent and increase of the refractoriness of the Colonies, until at last they were abandoned and wholly superseded by one of the most unjust and tyranical acts that ever emanated from the British Parliament. This was the impolitick "*Quebec Act*," 14th Geo. III., Cap. 83 which, at one "fell swoop," annihilated the Laws of England, though in full force and operation in the province during the preceding ten years; and restored the Canadians, *in integrum*, to their ancient laws, customs and prejudices: a state of things as destructive of Colonial prosperity, as injurious to the interests of the Mother Country itself. This was all that the Canadians wanted or wished for. They now beheld themselves a distinct people, having no community of interests or feelings with any other part af the continent. Whilst the old Colonies were in a state of insurrection against the authority of the Mother Country, and in arms in defence of their supposed rights, *they*, however averse to British rule and dominion, found themselves encouraged and protected in every thing that could render them a people alien to true British principles and sentiment. A passion for exclusive domination took possession of their souls, and every nerve was strained to perpetuate a system, which, in their opinion, surpassed all others in wisdom, energy and stability. They now congratulated themselves upon being a French Nation on British soil; and eagerly looked forward to the period when no bounds should exist to their independence as a distinct and separate people. But the views of those who were instrumental in securing these supposed advantages to the Canadians, were grievously disappointed, and their hopes most unmercifully overcast. The British Government, found that they had been the dupes of deceit, as well as the silly panders of overweening ambition. *The Canadians would not fight!* They said they had no objections to defend their own fire-sides; but no inducement could prevail upon them to join the country that had just exhibited such marks of indulgence to them, in quelling the unnatural rebellion raging in the other provinces of the continent, and Britain was obliged to fight her battles the best way she could, without any aid front the Canadians *even when Canada itself was invaded!* It was now that the genuine principles and loyalty of the despised English Merchants were properly understood. *They* forsook not their country in the day of peril: but manfully and successfully resisted the tide of rebellion when the Canadians cowered at its approach, and seemed not unwilling to submit to its laws, notwithstanding the indulgence manifested to them. Nothing could be more suitable to the boon than such craven and ungrateful conduct; and though Britain bled at every pore, she saw with shame and confusion, that she had been the dupe of an adopted child of foreign birth and extraction, upon whom she had lavished every favour, while her own legitimate offspring were stripped of their natural rights and cruelly abandoned to their fate. This was a lesson in experimental *government* which ought never to have been overlooked or forgotten by the parent state. However, a period of intestine commotion and the hurry and tumult of war, is not the time for revising the errors of government or of establishing laws on a solid and lasting basis. It was not till after the peace of 1783, therefore, that any attention had been paid to the state of Canada; and it is more than probable that a longer period would have elapsed before the exercise of this necessary act of government, had not the old Colonists, who preserved their allegiance and crowded into Canada for protection, become clamorous for the re-establishment of those laws and government of which they found Canada had been bereaved by the act of 1775. In the petitions addressed to the King and Parliament in 1784 for the repeal of the obnoxious *Quebec Act* and the establishment of a free representative government, many of the Canadians joined; but with what views we know not, considering the satisfaction which they had always expressed at the privileges conferred upon them by that unfortunate law. If they foresaw that their distinction as a people would be still more confined, and the powers of their concentrated force better maintained by a free government, we will do them the justice to say, that they exhibited political talents to which their English fellow-subjects were totally strangers. Be this as it may, it is a well known fact, that the great majority of the Canadians never anticipated any very extensive influence, even in the contemplation of a popular Assembly. They felt, perhaps, their gross ignorance of free legislative discussion; and were ready to resign any talents that they might have for business to those who, by their knowledge of the British Constitution, knew best how to direct and apply it to the best interests of the colony.*

The British population of Canada, well aware of their natural rights, and the extent and importance of the security afforded to these rights by the King's Proclamation of 1763, never ceased to urge their claim to a free representative government, notwithstanding the cruel disappointment they experienced in the "Quebec Act." Ever since that act passed, a committee existed in the province, whose business it was to solicit

---

*" You will perceive, Sir, upon the perusal of this petition that in it the Canadians make you join with them in requesting his Majesty, that they, as being the greater number of his Majesty's subjects in this province, and possessed of the greatest share of property in it, may be represented in the Assembly by a greater number of members than his Majesty's British subjects in the province. But this request ought not to alarm the British subjects. For, if you will consider the matter with temper, you will soon agree with me, that this privilege of the Canadians, of having the greater number of members in the assembly, will, in its consequences, prove to be a thing of form only, that cannot be attended with any substantial effects. For I will suppose by way of exam-

by every legal means its repeal; and it is to the industry and perseverance of this committee that the Province owes its present mode of government. But neither did this committee nor the petitioners of 1784, ever contemplate such a Constitution as that of 1791, which, while extending to Canada a free representative system of government, divided the country into two distinct Prov-

---

ple, that two-third parts of the members that compose the assembly were to be Canadians, and the other third part Englishmen, it is next to certain that the English third of such an assembly, being so greatly superior as they are to the Canadians in abilities and knowledge, and capacity for public business, would in such case easily obtain the suffrages of the other two third parts of it to whatever measures they should propose. You will say, perhaps, that this is paying no great compliment to my countrymen, the Canadians. I confess it. But unfortunately I am but too well acquainted with their great want of knowledge and capacity to presume to speak of them in any other manner. This request of theirs, therefore, in the petition I have now sent you, ought not to deter the English inhabitants of the province from signing it. These are the sentiments of my Canadian friends concerning an assembly."

Letter of F. J. Cugnet, Esq. to Malcom Fraser, Esq. 1st September, 1773.

laces ; leaving the French population in full possession of their ancient laws, language, habits, and manners, to the entire exclusion not only of *British* rights, principles and feelings, but of all those other means calculated to premote a great and flourishing Colony : a thing now rendered doubly desirable on the part of the Mother Country in consequence of the great national and political loss which she sustained in the independence of her native Colonies. The real causes of these violent and unnatural measures have never been discovered ; but their evil effects, *as had been foreseen,** have been deeply felt and frequently deplored. For ourselves nothing has ever

*"The bill now under the deliberations of this honourable House proposes, in the second and subsequent enacted clauses, to separate or divide the Province into two governments, or otherwise to erect two distinct Provinces in that country, independent of each other. I cannot conceive what reasons have induced the proposition of this violent measure. I have not heard that it has been the object of general wish of the loyalists who are settled in the upper parts of this Province ; and I can assure this honourable House, that it has not been desired by the inhabitants of the lower parts of the country. I am confident this honourable House will perceive the danger of adopting a plan which may have the most fatal consequences, while the apparent advantages which it offers to view are few, and of no great moment.

puzzled us more than this solecism in legislation and government. *Pitt*, the minister of

---

"Sir, the loyalists who have settled in the upper parts of the Province have had reason to complain of the present system of civil government as well as the subscribers to the petitions now on the table of this honourable House. They have been fellow sufferers with us, and have felt all that anxiety for the preservation of their property, which the operation of unknown laws must ever occasion; a situation of all others the most disgreeable and distressing, and which may have engaged some of these people, who could not perceive any other way to get out of such misery, to countenance the plans of a fowt individuals, who were more intent to support their own scheme than to promote the true interest of government, in the general tranquillity and prosperity of that extensive country.

* * * * * *

"Sir, in the positions now on the table from my constituents, inhabitants of the Province of Quebec, this honourable House will observe they have complained that the Province has been already greatly mutilated; and that its resources would be greatly reduced by the operation of the treaty of peace of 1783. But, Sir, they could not have the most distant idea of this new division. They could not conceive that while they complained of the extent of their country being already so

the time, was a great man ; but this is one of the prices which nations frequently pay

---

much reduced, as materially to prejudice their interests and concerns, it would be still farther reduced and abridged. If at the time they penned their petitions they could have supposed or foreseen this proposed division, it would have furnished them with much stronger reasons of complaint, that their interests would thereby be injured. Sir, I am sure this honourable House will agree, that a Province ought not to be divided into separate and independent governments, but on the most urgent occasions, and after having seriously and carefully weighed all the consequences which such a separation is likely to produce: For if from experience the division shall be found dangerous to the security of government, or to the general interests of the people, it cannot again be re-united. The strong principle of nationality or national prejudice, which at present connects the people of that province to one another, as being members of one state, who though scattered over an immense country, yet all look up to one centre of government for protection and relief, is of the utmost consequence to the security of government, in a country where the inhabitants are so much dispersed. It is that political connection which forms such a prominent feature in the character of all nations: by which we feel at first sight a degree of friendship and attachment which inclines us to associate with, and

for a long servitude of unparalleled genius and talent. Lord Grenville, who framed

---

to serve a subject of the same kingdom, which makes us look on a person from the same country or province as an acquaintance, and one from the same town as a relation; and it is a fact which the history of all countries has established beyond the possibility of a doubt, that people are now united in the habits of friendship and social intercourse, and are more ready to afford mutual assistance and support, from being connected by a common centre of government, than by any other tie. In small states this principle is very strong: but even in extensive empires it retains a great deal of its force; for, besides the natural prejudice which inclines us to favour the people from our own country, those who live at the extremities of an extensive kingdom, or province, are compelled to keep up a connection or correspondence with those who live near the centre or seat of government, as they will necessarily at times have occasion to apply for favours, justice, or right; and they will find it convenient to request the assistance and support of those whose situation enables them to afford it.

"I might here compare the different situation of Scotland, now united to England, and governed by the same legislature, with some other of the dependencies of the British empire; but I consider it to be unnecessary,

our present constitution, is a living witness both of its glaring errors and dismal consequences. The only atonement which his Lordship can now make to the country, is, to declare the reasons and motives which existed at the time for concentrating and perpetuating *French prejudices and exclusive domination*; AND WE CALL UPON HIS LORDSHIP TO DO SO. He owes it to his publick character, and to the reputation which he is desirous of leaving behind him.

The Constitutional Act had scarcely gone into operation, when the evils which it has entailed on the country, became manifest. Even the first act of the popular branch of the legislature, that of choice of Speaker, was made subservient to the all-engrossing spirit of that body. A Frenchman, who scarcely understood a word of the language of his sovereign, was called to the chair; and who, on his first official appearance in the presence of the representative of that sovereign declared, "*that he* could only *express himself in the primitive* language *of his native country*."* The House of Assembly

---

as the object must be present to the recollection of every member of this honourable House."

Mr. Lymburner's Speech *at the Bar of the House of* Commons, 23*d* March, 1791.

**Vide* that most valuable and learned work, "*Political Annals of Lower Canada*,

consisted of thirty-five French Canadians, and fifteen Englishmen. The former, indeed, composed the *majority*, but the latter were the *men of business*; and, during the first and second sessions, the prognostications of Mr. Cugnet in his letter to Mr. Fraser, with respect to the inferior capacity of his countrymen, may be said to have been realized. But where ignorance and prejudice reign not only uncontrolled, but are fostered by the supreme authority of a state, and when the physical power is altogether on the side of such degrading characteristicks, what authority can check---what force resist their evil effects and consequences? It is not surprising therefore to find, that, in the course of a few sessions, the aptness for business, and superior constitutional knowledge of the English members of the Assembly, gradually gave way before an overwhelming majority of voices, backed and led by the worst principles that can possibly actuate the human heart---self-sufficiency, ambition, and national prejudice. These passions, springing up, living, and flourishing among the constituents of this majority, nothing could now eradicate or control; and every succeeding event ministered to their increase and aggrandizement. Nothing contributed

---

by a British Settler:" a work that ought to be in the hands of every man who has any regard for the prosperity of this part of his Majesty's dominions.

more to this state of things than the exercise of his Majesty's prerogative, however necessary and constitutional, in calling up from time to time the English members of the Assembly to seats in the Legislative Council. Of the twenty five members *at present* composing this second and important branch of the legislature, at least *twelve* have been withdrawn from the Assembly in this way. Their superior information, experience, and capacity for business, have indeed, rendered their presence in the Council absolutely necessary, because, without prejudice to the claims of the native Canadian gentry, there was no other source in the province from which stations so high and important could be supplied. But the injury sustained by the real interests and happiness of the province, has, beyond all comparison, been great and serious. The Assembly, thus left to themselves, and to the dictates of an *exclusive system* of ascendency over British laws and constitutional principles, set no bounds to their errors, ignorance, wickedness, ambition and presumption. What power and authority have they not from to time arrogated to themselves? Not content with a voice in the general legislature of the province, they claim the right of ruling and directing every other branch, to neither of whom will they allow the common dictates of honour and humanity; and endeavour by every possible means, to infuse their own popular and republican notions into every department of government. They have declared acts of the imperial parliament, under which they themselves "live, and move, and have their being," as annulled and of non-effect. They have denied the prerogative of the Crown in almost every instance recognized by the constitution; and have assumed to themselves the right of appointing and paying, according to caprice and pleasure, every officer under the Crown. They have in effect declared war against the sister province; and not only denied her rights, but deprived her of them, until checked by the intervention of the mother country. They have declared native born subjects of Great Britain "*Strangers* and Foreigners!"*

Need we say more to characterize in their true light the spirit and principles of this abominable party---of this accursed and monstrous faction, whose deeds have ever been the disgrace of this otherwise happy province, and whose late attempts to rule and ruin the country make them absolutely to stink in our nostrils! May heaven, in its mercy, preserve this province from the tyranny of this lawless faction! They have of late, too, experienced more support and countenance from the other branches of the legislature than *we* ever expected to have witnessed, notwithstanding the dismal view in which we have been accustomed to be-

**Vide* Debates of last Session generally; but especially the malicious and mouthing declamations of Messieurs Papineau, Vallieres and Viger.

hold the affairs of the country; and unless the king's government *now* enforce the existing constitutional laws, with the full intent and purpose not only of stopping the career of this atrocious faction, and of rescuing his Majesty's British-born subjects from their despotick sway, but of establishing a more direct and pressing *British influence* over the hearts and actions of the majority of the people of this province, we shall be *utterly undone*. It were far better, in obedience to the advice of Admiral Coffin, to tie a millstone round our necks and throw us into the bottom of the Ocean! It were far better to sell us to the Yankees, who would treat us more like men and Englishmen, than those wretched and degenerate sons of France to whom we are now enslaved. At all events, it were far better in the imperial government and parliament at once plainly and candidly to inform us what are their real intentions with respect to this province, if they *have* any intentions, than leager to permit us to worry and cut each others' throats, with as little hopes of a permanent settlement of our disputes as the Guelphs and Gibbilines had at the commencement of *their* wars. This is a piece of information with which, we humbly maintain, the mother country is bound to furnish us, and that without delay. Allegiance and protection are the bond which connect us together; but the national obligation which does not specify *internal* as well as external protection, may not indeed be void and null, but it is surely deficient and nugatory. We therefore claim the information as a matter of right due to us by a kind, indulgent, and munificent parent: a parent of whom we are justly proud, and a parent whom we know will not abandon us in the day of trial. Let her conduct be parental, and she may rest assured, that ours will be filial. When the people of England are advised to come to Canada, they are not told that on their arrival, they are to be subjected to French laws, and enslaved by a French faction who loathe the very sight of a Briton." It is therefore but common justice to the sons of England on both sides of the Atlantick, to tell them, what is to become of Canada?---Whether this system of tyranny is to be continued, and engrafted on the rights of British freemen, or whether it is to be checked and abolished in such a manner as to secure the liberty and independence, as well as the spirit and enterprize, of *those alone* who are capable of rendering it a colony of worth and consequence---of value and importance to the mother country?

That there is any power, party, or influence in this province possessing sufficient strength to resist and finally annihilate the torrent of popular and republican usurpation which threatens to overwhelm us, is a notion fraught with absurdity and madness. In a House of Assembly consisting of fifty members, there are only *three* who may be depended upon as the stern, undeviating supporters of British principles and constitutional legislation; and these three are Englishmen in birth or origin! To such a pass have the imperial statutes of 1775, and 1791 driven this province! Had a more wise and enlightened line of conduct been persued, we should long ere now have been a British Colony in reality as well as in name. No British emigrant of capital, prudence, or industry will ever settle in Lower Canada, while the laws continue to be French, and the popular branch of the legislature *republican*, in spite of the drivelling nonsense of the emigration committee of the Assembly "to the contrary notwithstanding." With the exception therefore of the *fifty thousand* inhabitants of British origin in the Townships, *who are not* represented *at all*, and the British population settled in the towns and cities of the province, amounting to about *eighty thousand* souls, the French population are in entire and uncontrolled possession of *universal suffrage*. They send whom not *they*, but their leaders, please to the Assembly; and it is no wonder if those who elect themselves in defiance of their constituents, who have no other choice except among the despised and heretical English, should also endeavour to usurp, as they have frequently done, the whole functions of government. Nothing therefore, as we have said, can be more absurd and insane than to suppose, with those vulgar and partly-politicians, the *Humes* and *Labouchères*, that Canada can set itself to rights, and work out its own salvation. The contest going on here is not a contest of *men* but of *principles*, otherwise we could soon and easily settle the matter. This being the case, we have drawn upon the Mother Country for an acknowledgment and declaration of our rights, and patiently await her award. We have done all that we could constitution*ally*. We trust we shall never be driven to the necessity of doing more, in justification of our rights and privileges as Britons.

We will now leave these matters, and, without paying much attention to order or method, glance at a few of the most important questions which came before the Provincial Parliament during the late momentous session.

The first question we shall allude to, is that which was raised in the Assembly with respect to the conduct of *Mr. Griffiu*, as Returning Officer of the West Ward of *Montreal* at the last general election. It is not, however, the *intrinsick* importance of this question itself, nor its constitutional bearings that induce us to notice it, but the glaring light in which it exhibits the inconsistency, the party-spirit, the fury, and partiality of the "*leaders*" of the House of Assembly,---for to deny that the house is *Led*, and that in away the most disgraceful and degrading to human beings having the smallest particle of brains in their sculls, would be as absurd as to deny the light of heaven at noon-day. Here is a petition from certain individuals residing in Montreal---whether respectable or not, is nothing either to us or to the subject---complaining of illegal and unwarrantable conduct on the part of the Returning

Officer of the West Ward of Montreal, whereof the unparalleled *Mr. Papineau* is one of the representatives, whilst the *Election* itself is held forth as pure, immaculate and incontrovertible! This was a question which corresponded exactly in character with the general tenor of the proceedings of the Assembly, and they accordingly embraced it as such. The petition was referred to a Committee; the Committee reported by Resolutions to the House; and the House concurred in the Resolutions.* These Resolutions, which ought to be held in everlasting remembrance, not only accuse Mr. Griffin of Not having taken the oath *Required* by law, but declare him *Unqualified* as Returning officer of the west ward of Montreal. Yet "the *Return* made by him of the two mem-

*Resolved—That Henry Griffin, Esq. Returning Officer for the West Ward of the Town and City of Montreal, has not taken the oath required by the *formula* of the Law of the 5th year of His Majesty's Reign, Chapter thirty-three.

"Resolved—That, notwithstanding the oath taken at the late Election by Henry Griffin, Esq. the Returning Officer for the West Ward of the Town and city of Montreal, was not in the form prescribed by Law, the return made by him of the twe Members elected to represent the said West Ward is nevertheless good and valid, the Electors having enjoyed full and entire libertyof suffrage."

bers elected to represent the said west ward is Nevertheless declared "good and valid!" This will not be believed in England nor in any other Country of the least pretensions to national honour, justice, or equity. But still it is a fact, and a fact which makes us absolutely to shudder at the prospect which it opens to our eyes of the deplorable condition of this province. Had Messieurs McGill and Delisle been returned instead of Messrs. Papineau and Nelson, we ask if such would be the result of the deliberations of the Assembly on this petition against the Returning Officer? No, no. The House could not stand without Mr. Papineau, and every principle of law and justice must consequently be sacrificed in order to secure a seat for him. Under similar circumstances the election of *any other* individual uninitiated in the plans and views of the *Faction*, would have been declared null and void, his seat vacated, and the unfortunate Returning Officer voted incapable of serving in the like capacity for ever. But in the present case, as stated by *Mr. Solicitor General*, the object was to condemn the Returning Officer and to approve of the representative. Surely no principle of right and justice can be more plain and clear, than that he who invests himself with any official character without due authority and legal qualification, renders every act performed by virtue of such false authority, *ab initio*, null and void. Nothing therefore seems to us more strange and unseemly, than to say, as was said and done in this case, that the conduct of the man was *wrong* and its consequences *right!* We have no notion, thank God, of such decisions. They are not sufficiently even-handed for us. They carry neither decency nor decorum in their aspect; neither justice nor stability in their effects. They are vicious in practice and monstrous in precedent. But as in every other case where plausibility rather than strength of argument is necessary to ensure success, a reason was assigned for these anomalous proceedings, and it was this:---that "*any Governor wishing to eject a* particular member *had only* to appoint *an unqualified Returning Officer, and his purpose was effected.*"* We shall say nothing of the indecent insolence of this reasoning, which supposes the Governor of this province to be at all times inimical to the views of the Assembly, and opposed to their rights. It shews the real sentiments of the "*Leaders,*" and is a convincing proof, that they are altogether strangers to that principle of the constitution which has only the *public* good for its object; mistaking, in their gross ignorance, individual interests and party prejudices for the first and noblest of virtues. As to the reasoning itself, it is beneath contempt. Is it not the object of the law to secure the rights and privileges of all parties, when it says, that no man can legally act as Returning Officer but on the conditions and under the qualifications therein specifi-

*Vide Debate on this question, 10th December, 1828.

ed! Are these conditions the mere *dicta* of the Governor, and can the *governor* appoint "an un*qualified* Returning Officer!" This doctrine supposes the mere act of appointment a sufficient qualification. But it is not so. After the appointment, the law steps in, and says, "Sir, you cannot proceed to the execution of your office unless you perform such and such conditions: you must qualify yourself, for unless you do so, all the acts performed under your commission become null and void." No man can accept or perform the duties of an office which he is naturally and legally incapable of performing. Has an alien any suffrage under our constitution? Can an elector vote without the necessary qualification? Can a judge ascend the bench without the usual oaths of office? Nay, can Mr. Papineau become speaker without the appropriation of his Majesty's representative? If then, as stated in the Resolutions, Mr. Griffin was not duly qualified for acting as Returning Officer of the west ward of Montreal, by what authority have his deeds been rendered good and legal? Not, surely, by a vote of the House of Assembly. It is the Assembly, therefore, and not the governor, that act an illegal part in the present instance; for how, or by what right, a member can lawfully sit amongst them who had been sent there illegally and without due authority, is to us incomprehensible. But the truth is, that both the election and the Returning Officer were perfectly legal and constitutional; and nothing degrades the Assembly more in the eyes of the country, than the false and insidious distinction which they have drawn in this case, and the unmanly and malignant attack which had thus been made on the character of a highly honourable and respectable individual, who, it is well known, discharged his duty as Returning Officer in the most fair, candid, liberal, and impartial manner. It is to his political sentiments, and not to his misconduct as Returning Officer, that *Mr. Griffin* owes the cowardly treatment which his character and feelings experienced in the House of Assembly. Had he been a partizan of the "*Leaders*" he would have been treated very differently; and his conduct, instead of being condemned and separated from its effects, would have been lauded to the skies. But the mind of *Mr. Griffin* is too honourable, and his principles too truly loyal and British to render him the tool of any *party*; far less of an atrocious and loathsome *faction* that pollutes as well as destroys the best interests of the country. He is too much of a man to be led, and too much of a gentleman to be corrupted. We cannot drop this subject without noticing the indecent manner in which *Mr. Papineau* obtruded his sentiments on the House during the discussion of this question. One would think that a sense of delicacy would alone have prevented him from speaking when his own name and condition were the subject. But this man has long been lost to all sense of shame in his publick conduct. Having fortified his mind in insolence, he thinks that all things become him. His overweening opinion of his oratorical powers, induces him to take the lead in every question, and the gaping admiration of his satellites, swells him beyond endurance with pride and arrogance. As speaker it is highly unbecoming in him to be a party-man; far less the leader of a faction in the legislature. Who can expect dignity in the *proceedings*, or impartiality in the decisions of the House whilst such a man sits in the chair! What man, opposed to him either in sentiments or politicks, would trust his life or reputation to his casting vote. For our own part, we should sooner submit to a tribunal of the most barbarous race of Esquimaux, with the most savage Cannibal at their head, than to *Mr. Papineau* surrounded by his blind and subservient gang. We would, once for all, strongly urge upon him the propriety of squaring his conduct and opinions as Speaker with those of his prototype in the House of Commons. He will there find dignity of *Manners*,* propriety of conduct, impartiality of decision, and avoidance of party-spirit so combined as to produce the happiest effects on the proceedings of the House, and benefits the most lasting on the higher interests of the empire.†

Of the same stamp and character with the

---

*This is a pun which we hope its truth alone will warrant on such an occasion as this.

†We will here read a lesson to *Mr. Pepineau*, from that learned man and consistent

foregoing decision of the Assembly, was the vote for printing *four hundred* copies of "*The Imperishable Monument*." Some of our readers will, no doubt, be curious to learn, what this "*Imperishable Monument*" means?

Speaker, SIR FLETCHER NORTON, who so long and so ably filled the chair of the House of Commons. On the 13th of March 1780, the whole House being in a Committee on MR. BURKE's famous *Economical* bill, and a great difference of opinion having arisen with respect to the right of the Commons to resume or control any part of the civil list, MR. FOX called so loudly and repeatedly for the opinion of the Speaker, that his secretary rushed through the side gallery, and called him from his Chamber to the Committee. It is not our intention in this place to give any account of the sentiments expressed by the Speaker, on the *merits* of the question before the house. We shall confine this note to what he conceived to be his duty in regard to *speaking* to questions in general; and we hope *Mr. Papineau*, and all other Speakers will confine themselves to the judicious and excellent axioms there laid down. *Sir Fletcher Norton*, said, "since he had the honour of presiding in that chair, (pointing to it) he had on every occasion avoided as much as possible, giving any opinion respecting matters which came before the house. His duty and inclination led him to adopt that mode of conduct. His duty, lest from the respectable and honourable station he filled, his

Dear friends? the "*Imperishable Monyment*" means the *Report of* a Select *Committee of the House of Commons appointed to inquire into the state of the civil government of Cana-*

---

mixing in debate, without arrogating any thing to himself, might be supposed to create an IMPROPER INFLUENCE, in some of his hearers; and his inclination forbad him, because he knew from experience that whatever he might support as an individual member, *might be apt to bias his judgment in his other character, that of* Speaker, *when he came to preside in the House.* It was true that the mode and order of proceeding, did not preclude him from Speaking in a *Committee.* The House was now in one, consequently within the most rigid rules of order, he was as much at liberty to deliver his sentiments as any other member, and he was ready to acknowledge that he had more than once, soon after he was called to his present honourable station, exercised that right. But he could not say for what reason, but so it happened, that he found whenever he *had* exercised it, that his conduct was liable to misinterpretation, and that whatever he offered as arising from his own faclings and judgment, was deemed rather as taking a step OUT OF THE PROPER DUTIES OF HIS OFFICE, *which were said to be a strict observance, of whatever might tend to impress on the House the most strict impartiality and indifference.* He was not prepared to say, but this he was ready to acknowledge, that he had experi-

da; and has been thus denominated by a member of the House of Assembly, the fumes of whose enthusiasm got the mastery over his judgment on the occasion. It was well observed during the conversation which took place on this subject, that nothing could be more ridiculous than printing *four hundred* copies of this Report, even if at all necessary, whilst *fifty* were quite sufficient to enlighten all the members of the House; thereby subjecting the country to an expense of *a thousand* pounds, which would have been much better employed in relieving the poor during a season of unusual hardship and severity. But no mendicity is so clamorous and unsatiable as ungratified party-zeal. It was in vain, therefore, that the *individual* who opposed the manufacture of the four hundred copies of the "*Monument*" resisted the preposterous claim. The members themselves must be edified; the Demagogues without

---

enced in himself a propensity to wish success to that side of the question which he had supported in the Committee, as soon as the House was resumed. He felt his mind warped, and a certain bias hanging on it and bearing it down, consequently, though he might not be converted to the opinions of those who wished him to be silent upon every occasion, *he was satisfied* that *the seldomer he mixed in debate, the* more *likely he would be to avoid* giving *offence to* either side *of the house.*" *Parliamentary Register, Vol.* 17. *pp.* 319, 320 *and* 321.

must be instructed and gratified with the perusal of a document which reflected so much bonour of the Triamvirate Delegates, and confusion on the late administration. As to the *people*, God help them, there were not *four* hundred of them, as stated by Mr. OGDEN, who could read! This was a terrible cut; it was absolutely a gash; and joined to that of Mr. Huskisson, who discovered that out of 87,000 there were only 9,000 individuals who could write their own names, was a tickler which could only be overcome by shame, confusion and blushing. Alas! the *Schoolmaster* and *Primer*, of *Mr. Brougham* have not travelled thus far. The people are now as ignorant and unlettered as they were in the reign of Louis the XIV., who had always a greater regard for soldiers than scholars; and a higher respect for steel and gun powder than for the "*Schoolmaster* and *Primer*." This, to be sure, was not denied in the Assembly: ignorance—gross and total ignorance was admitted to reign triumphantly over the minds of the people. Even *Mr. Neilson*, the great apostle of education, reform, radicalism and republicanism, admits this fact; and he had good right to do so, knowing what it has cost him to educate his sons in Scotland, the land of their fathers. Yet the Assembly—magnanimous, generous souls, are not to blame—not they, heaven-born patriots! With the dignity which becomes their rank and station, they throw the blame from themselves, and fix it on the shoulders of the *King*—God bless him—because he will not surrender at discretion the estates of the Jesuits, which he inherits by right of *Conquest*; and of the English clergy, because they patronize the *Bible* and the *English language*! But all this is desperate drivelling. We shall not in this place speak of the measures adopted during the session for the purpose of establishing a better system of education in the country. But what can possibly be more absurd and ignorant, than to suppose that the Legislature must do *every thing* with respect to education—and that no people can be educated without the intervention of the Legislature? Monstrous! The best educated people in the world—that is, the brave and honest people of Scotland—never trouble their heads about the Legislature. They are determined that their sons and daughters shall be educated, and they *are* educated accordingly. To be sure they have the parish schools; but what are these in the wilds of the Highlands and in populous towns and cities? Absolutely nothing. Yet the people are educated. "*The Schoolmaster and his Primer*" are to be seen in every family, glen, and hamlet. There, every child sucks in education like his mother's milk; and no man bothers his head about what the Legislature can do for him. If Scotland were to remain stock-still until it had pleased the Legislature to adopt a system of education which would yield universal satisfaction throughout the country, she would at this day be as ignorant as Canada, and her fame for morality and virtue---the real fruits of education---would have been unknown and unsung. Let her example be followed in Canada, and we shall soon find, that the share which the legislature will have in arranging or promoting our education must be truly insignificant. No man can make the unthirsty ox drink: no legislature can drag to school urchins whose parents are unacquainted with the value of the institution. But the time will soon come when the people of this province will be governed by another and a better spirit. The time is at hand when the people will take the matter into their own hands; and in spite, of the drivelling of the Assembly, on this and other topicks, secure such an education to their children as will render them virtuous men, and good citizens. This, and not the Report of the Canada Committee, will then be the "*Imperishable Monument*;" and it is such a monument as this that ought to excite the solicitude and urge the zeal of the Assembly, and not the trash in the report, which ministers so largely to their prejudices and party spirit. But let us say a few words of the "*Monument*."

No doubt but the architects of this wonderful edifice entertain very sublime notions of their own skill and dexterity, and imagine that they have reared a superstructure as durable as the *British Constitution*. They think, that, like the artificers of the plain of Shinar, they have built a tower whose top will reach unto heaven, and have made a name to them selves, lest they be scattered abroad upon the face of the whole earth. But we venture to tell them that their object not being the public weal nor national honour, but party spirit and faction, their work will not stand; and that, like their patriarchial prototypes, they will ultimately be scattered abroad on the face of all the earth. Besides, they were divided among themselves; and a house divided against itself *cannot* stand. Let us speak more plainly. The views of *Mr. Huskisson*, in soliciting a Committee to inquire into the present state of Canada, whatever may be said of the general political principles by which he has been actuated, were truly patriotick, and in accordance with his duty and responsibility as Colonial Minister. The speech in which he introduced his motion is a master-piece of talent, knowledge and discernment. In it he displays more real and intimate acquaintance with the condition of this province in particular, and true Colonial policy in general, than many who have studied the subject for years. It does his head and his heart infinite honour; and is a convincing proof to us, that he is a man of grasp and power, whatever the Duke *of Wellington* may think of him. That we ourselves have *always* thought well of him, we cannot—we dare not say. But, so far as respects his conduct towards this country, we not only respect and admire him, but will stand by him and defend him to the last. He sees as well as we do, that the present system of civil government in this country is vicious and unsuitable. He perceives with the eye of a statesman that it was so from the beginning.

He perceives that *French* law, French usages, and the French language are not the things that will promote the prosperity, peace or welfare of a *British* Colony, having the British *Constitution* for their rule of government. He knows that nothing can be more incongruous as well as dangerous, than to entail on this province a mixture of French feudal, and English jury, laws. He knows such a system to be fraught with the germs of future dissension and national disaster; and has therefore wisely solicited its destruction. He knows the rights of the English population of Canada: he knows that they have been unjustly deprived of these rights, and he wished to restore them. He knows that no British Colony can flourish where British language, laws, and enterprize are not fostered; and that no people can be contented, loyal, happy or industrious, who have no uniformity of laws, language and manners. He knows that though a people may have one Sovereign, they cannot be true or loyal but with *one* interest—domestick peace and external protection. He knows, that "there is no possibility of suing or being sued, except in the French Courts, and according to the *French Form* and *Practice*—no mode of transacting *Commercial* business except under *French customs*, now *obsolete in* France:" that "in Lower Canada they go upon the law and system of *Feudal* tenure; and the law is more incapable of ever being improved or modified by the progress of information and knowledge, than if it still remained the system of France and the model of her dependencies. Here, in the midst of a wilderness, flourishes the French feudal system, and the custom of Paris of centuries ago. The result is, that *Englishmen* in Canada are much like *Aliens* and *Settlers* in a Foreign land as an equal number of British subjects who should have sat down in the centre of France in the thirteenth century. It is not therefore to be wondered at that our Countrymen have had to encounter considerable difficulty in Lower Canada, and that but a slow progress has been made towards the settlement of that province."* Mr. *Huskisson* knows all this, for these are his own words, and he justly and prudently sought to annihilate a system so injurious and disreputable to the empire at large. He also knows, " that the system wished to be established by the *Canadian Legislature* is not compatible with the independence and dignity either of the king's representative or the criminal judges." He knows " it is still the duty and interest of this Country to imbue Canada with English Feelings, *and* Benefit *it with English* Laws *and Institutions.*---- (Cheers.") On these grounds he sought and obtained a Committee, which was instructed " to reconcile the conflicting pretensions of the different parties, and thus *remove the great obstacles* to the improvement of this important Colony."

There was not an individual in the House

*Vide Mr. Huskisson's speech on the civil government of Canada, 2d May, 1828.

of Commons who could either contradict a word of what *Mr. Huskisson* stated to be the simation and necessities of Canada, or throw a spark of additional light on the subject in hand. To be sure the hackneyed mouthers on the opposite side of the House *attempted* something of the kind; but their "long yarns," agitated the whole senate, must of whom were soon out of sight and hearing of the orators, leaving them to "discourse most eloquently" to empty benches. As to the ridiculous rent of Sir *James Macintosh*, nothing can be thore preposterous. What can possibly be more absurd, than to maintain, as he did, "*that nothing else can save a country from ruin than allowing the majority to make laws!*" *Sir James* once lectured in a very learned and eloquent style on the law of nations: but we do not remember that he ever advanced such a doctrine as this before. Perhaps the *extensive, enlightened* and *independent* County of *Nairn*, which he now or lately represented, may have thrown some light on this subject. *Sir James* may not, indeed, be a "*Sportsman*,"* and his sporting days may be over; but if such be his notions of Government, it is high time to tell him, that the day of his political penetration and wisdom are also over; and it would be well for his reputation if he were endowed with sufficient judgment to perceive the departure of the one as soon as the other. Who ever heard of "*The Majority*" of a people making laws but

*Vide his Speech.

in the most rank and simple *Democracies?* Such a doctrine as this might sound very fine in a dissertation on the governments of ancient Greece and Rome; and may not have been inaptly applied to the *Black Mail* laws of the *Clan-Chattan*, the Celtick ancestors of *Sir James!* but when spoken of in England, it only calls to mind the club-laws of stews and gambling-houses. We are amazed that Sir *James* was not ashamed to speak of such a thing in the British House of Commons. We are absolutely astonished that he was permitted with impunity to pollute a spot so sacred to real liberty with his monstrous abominations. If such be really his principles and his notiana of free independent government, how can he with honour to himself or benefit to his consutituents, longer sit there as a mere *Delegate?* Is he not aware that, by doing so, he is standing between those constituents and their just rights? If he think as he speaks he ought immediately to accept the Chaltern-Hundreds. If he does not, it is very easy to form a true estimate of the character of the man, who, to gratify some vain and foolish ambition would advance a doctrine in Parliament which he neither believes in his heart nor intends to practise in his life. Nothing, therefore, can lower Sir James in the eyes of the word more, than this attempt to institute *democracies* in these colonies, while the mother country continues to be governed by a limited monarchy; and nothing would sooner alienate and destroy the colonies than such a constitution as this. The great fear is---and it is a fear not ill-founded---that the political institutions in our dependencies, as they stand, are of too popular and democratical a cast, consistently with their own happiness and the legitimate supremacy of the parent state. As to Lower Canada, late events demonstrate clearly, that we are governed by a kind of Democratical Oligarchy--that the people enjoy universal suffrage—and that our government unlike both its model and what it ought to be, is not one of checks and balances. This being the case, it betrays great and gross ignorance in Sir James thus to rave like a maniack about the majority of the *people* making their own laws. This would be leasant news to the Manchester, Glasgaw, and Paisley radicals. It would be glorious intelligence to the Catholic Association. O'Connell and Sir James for ever! The Demagogues of all countries have an extraordinary sympathy for one another. How beautiful and consolatory the uniformity of their creeds and doctrines! But will Sir James be so good as tell us, in which of the *Democracies* of Hindoostan he learned this new-light? Perhaps we are indebted to his *embryo* history for it. If so, should this *great* work ever come out, which seems rather doubtful, the *Utopia* of Sir Thomas More will sink into insignificance compared with that of Sir James Macintosh. We are told in this province by that great man Mr. Papineau, that we have been better governed by Knights than by Earls. Should the doctrine of Sir James prevail that happy country, *Utopia*, will be equally well-governed. We trust the emigration Committee will not lose sight of a prospect so singularly advantageous to the surplus population of the empire. Sir James would willingly draw out a coda of laws and plan a system of government for the new colony, on which he will not fail to engraft the *French Feudal* and *Seignieural Tenure*, and the right of the "*majority*" to make the laws. We happen to *know* somewhat of Sir James. We have often admired him as a statesman, a politician, a judge and a man of learning and literary acquirements. Never therefore were we more disappointed than to behold his conduct with respect to Canada. We always looked upon him as a man of liberal sentiments and enlarged views. Never therefore have we been more surprised than in discovering in *him* the advocate of feudal barbarism and narrow prejudices. Is it possible that a sympathy for the septish domination of his native mountains still lingers around him? We have no objections to the fire and martial spirit of that renowned country; but, in heaven's name, let us never again hear of its prejudices and *feudal* barbarities. Lower Canada is the only spot in the British dominions whose sun of prosperity is still darkened by the clouds of the feudal ages. It was therefore truly unworthy of a man of the political rank and legislative acquirements of Sir James to become the blind advocate of perpetuating a system of things so little congenial with the spirit of the times, and the destinies of the British Empire. Sir James is a friend to Catholick Emancipation. So are we. But we would ask him, whether it is more honourable to unclasp the chains of political than moral darkness and depravity? We fear, nay, we are sure, that Sir James has taken the right side of Ireland and the wrong side of Canada. His conduct in opposing the union displayed great ignorance of our real wants and necessities. This ignorance is excusable, even in such a man as Sir James. But his advocacy of French laws, manners and habits in a *British* Colony, and his desire to entail upon this province all the miseries which it inherits as an offspring of Feudal and Despotick France, neither does honour to the man nor reflects credit on the politician. His speech was a compound of abstract and theoretical reasoning which was as applicable to Botany-Bay as to Lower Canada. There was not a sentiment nor an opinion in it which he who wishes to legislate for the prosperity of this province would adopt. He praises the people because they are ignorant, and abuses the Governor because he obeys his instructions. Let him reflect on such rhapsody, and say whether it would reflect honour on any statesman. It has, however, been his fate to place this province in a light in which no other man—even the insane demagogues of the province—has dared do. He has called this province the "*Foe*" of England!* It is

*Vide his speech when alluding to his opposition to the union in 1822.

very certain that in so far as regards our religion, laws and language, we are *opposed* to England, and our natural and national antipathy becomes stronger in proportion to the attempts of the mother Country to Anglicise us. But as to being the "*Foe*" of England, it will be time enough to speak of that when we become independent of her, and are able to compete with her in the field or on the ocean—a period which need never be expected until Great Britain becomes as indolent and stupid as we now are. This shews clearly that Sir James took no real interest in the affairs of *Canada*, and that he spoke at random merely to please a pack of ignorant and prejudiced blockheads, who had themselves not only been the tools of a faction, but had the art to impose upon him in accordance with the narrow views and dangerous plans of that unprincipled faction. Had the case been otherwise he would from day to day have attended to his duties as a member of the *Committee*, and not remain at home reckless at once of the fate and condition of this vast Colony. But Sir James thought that a *speech* was all that was asked from him. So it was; and we can tell him, that the oftener he utters *such* speeches, the more he will compromise his own character and risk the safety of this province.

As to the *Report* of the Committee, the best way to characterize it, is to state the circumstances which have come to our knowledge with respect to the mode in which it was got up. As soon as the evidence had been gone through, a very intelligent member of the committee was appointed to draw up the Report. He did so, and that in a manner that reflects much honour upon his information and talents. But *this* Report is not the "*Monument*." It now became evident that there was *a party* in the Committee. This party, after several numbers of the committee had left town for their country seats, under the impression that there could be no doubt as to the adoption of the draught submitted to them, drew up a *new* Report, adopting and concealing as much of the first as corresponded with their own views, and adding the famous supplement which at once closes and disgraces this extraordinary document. Yet *this* Report, to the eternal disgrace of the *party*, was only carried by a majority of *one* vote! Posterity will scarcely believe it; but it is a fact, that this majority, instead of being guided by a sense of national honour, and the principles of sacred universal justice, were solely influenced by motives of personal dislike and private resentment. Is not the character of the nation gone when we find the very Legislature---the very parliament actuated in their publick conduct by such base and disgraceful passions! We have only to look into the report itself to be convinced of the corroption that existed in the Committee. Who but a faction could interlard a state document like this with personal vituperation against charactors hitherto held sacred until fairly charged and formally convicted. It was not paying a great compliment to the King to tell him, that his Majesty's representative in Canada was a delinquent when no charge had been *regularly* brought against him; far less submitted to his Majesty. Was not this trying and criminating individuals instead of inquiring into errors and grievances? Who made the Committee a Criminal tribunal when the House of Commons itself cannot —dare not put one of his Majesty's subjects on trial before it? Thus far, at least, the Committee over-stepped their legitimate authority; and on these grounds alone, we are clearly of opinion, that the Report will never be concurred in. A decision to the contrary would eternally disgrace the *British House of Commons*. Even as respects its main points, though they contain many things that we ourselves approve of, we do not think that it will ever be received or concurred in by the House. Notwithstanding the large volume of evidence subjoined, it does not communicate a particle of information on the fundamental evils of this province; nor suggest, of course, any reformation with respect to them. It foolishly supposes the Canadians to be as susceptible of knowledge and improvement as Englishmen; and takes it for granted, that the removal of some Financial difficulties and giving way to all the wishes and prejudices of a rude and simple people, would send us down to future ages the envy and admiration of the world! Provided the

Committee could drive all the Englishmen already in the province out of it, and prevent others from coming into it, it is very probable that Lower Canada would seldom be heard of as a part and parcel of the *British* dominions. But while matters remain as they are, it is the bounden duty of the parent state not only to protect us, but to render us as happy as she herself is. But it is not at the hands of the Canada Committee that we are to expect suc happiness. If *their* Report be sanctioned and fallowed up, without amendment or modification, we shall of all people be the most miserable. In truth, we have reason to know that it never will be sanctioned in its present form. In all probability the committee, instead of being thanked for their industry and assiduity, will either be dissolved or sent back to reconsider the evidence, in order to draw a closer parallel between it and the Report; a glaring deficiency which detracts very much from the good sense and impartiality of the committee.* Yet, this is the "*Imperishable Monument*" which the House of Assembly have undertaken to print, publish, and circulate throughout the country? We shall only add,

*We decline alluding to the extraordinary character of some of the evidence given before the committee. The manner in which that part of it which has reference to the Lachine Canal, has been refuted in this country, is as honourable to one party as disgraceful to the other.

that before the printer has got the job out of his hands, it is more than probable that the "*Imperishable Monument*" shall have been dashed to pieces, and a structure more useful and durable erected in its place.

Mr. *Viger's Judicature Bill* was again lost. We heartily rejoice at this, not only because its whole machinery was cumbrous, unsuitable to the present condition of the country, and impossible to be put in motion, but because the infanticide was committed on the floor of the House of Assembly in full and deliberate conclave! This wonderful and ill-fated Bill was declared by its parent to have been the labour of *twenty-five years*; and, indeed, if we may judge from its dimensions and the number of its proposed enactments, the production is not unworthy of the time and labour bestowed upon it. It contains *seventy-three* clauses, and occupies *forty-nine* folio pages in print! The exploits of the son of Jupiter and Alcmena were nothing to this. The squeezing to death of the serpents; the destruction of the lion of Cithaeron; the destruction of the Lernaean hydra: the killing of the monster Geryon, the carrying of Cerberus from hell; killing the Centaur; the cleaning of the stables of Augeas;—in short, the twelve labours of Hercules sink into insignificance compared with this gigantic undertaking of *Twenty-five years*! No wonder, then, though he has ever since played the dotard, and wandered through the country, like a drivelling maniac, bewailing the untimely loss of the hopeful heir of his name and family. How the good, worthy people of Quebec, pitied the hoary-headed sire as he walked along their streets, in rueful and downcast aspect; bedewing the pavement with his tears, and rousing the very children from their slumbers by his sobbing and convulsive respirations! But where was *Sir James McIntosh* at this critical moment? Have the melancholy news yet reached him? Where were the petitions of grievances, with their long list of accusations against the Legislative Council for not baptizing and consecreting this loyal scion. Where were *Nelson* and *Cuvillier?* Where were the Canada Committee with their Report and its hundred lies? Alas! all—all gone. All had forsaken the unhappy and bereaved father—the father of this only child—to his fate. Why did he not, in this the hour of his calamity, do "*what* Cato *did and A*ddison *approved*," and so put an end at once to the Bill and his own miseries. But hypocrisy and cowardice are too near akin to separate on such bad terms.

Every wise man is ready to acknowledge the calamities under which this Province labours, from the want of an uniform, stable, and effective system of judicature. Justice, if pure and impartial so far as it goes, which we are ready to admit, is too distinct and purchased at too high a price, both as regards real compensation and moral consequences. The evil has been long felt, and many efforts have been made, as well without as in the Legislature, to discover a proper and effectual remedy; but hitherto in vain. It appears passing strange, that, in an assembly, composed nearly one half of *Lawyers*, no measure can be divised of sufficient force and wisdom to establish the administration of justice on that simple and secure basis which is necessary to maintain the peace and happiness, as well as the rights and liberties of every civilized people. We fear it is as bad to be governed by lawyers as by judges; and that the former are as *useless* in the Assembly as the latter are reported by the Canada Committee to be in the Council. But more of this in the sequel. In the meantime, it may be proper to state the proceedings which have taken place in the Legislature, during the last twelve years, on this important subject.

The first bill, having a better system of judicature for its object, originated in the Legislative Council: and, in 1819, was sent down to the Assembly, where it met with little or no attention, and was laid on the shelf. Mr. *Viger's time* was not yet come. *His* bill, though conceived and in embryo, had not yet been fully formed. In 1821 another bill was sent down; but after a deliberation of *five weeks*, it was drapped. The *pregnancy* of *Mr. Viger* had but little advanced. In 1823 a third bill was sent down; but though a special committee had reported upon it with amendments, the House never entered into the consideration of it. But Mr. Viger had now come to the birth: every preparation was made for the in-lying, and the case was submitted to the midwives of the Assembly. In 1825, the Assembly sent *up* to the Council a Judicature Bill, which the Council immediately proceeded to consider and amend; but before their measures, in regard to it, were completed, the Lieutenant Governor prorogued the session. In 1826, another bill containing the same provisions, was sent *up* to the Legislative Council, where it was discussed for three weeks, and so largely amended, that, on the day previous to the prorogation, it became necessary to print it for the use of the members. In 1827, the *same* Bill was again sent *up* by the Assembly; but only a few days before the prorogation, which, though read a second time in the Council, was necessarily interrupted by the adjournment of the session.* *Mr. Viger*'s *labour* now became no less tedious than painful, and his friends began to entertain great fears for his safety. There was but one alternative, and that was to consult that great Colonial *Accoucheur*, the Imperial Parliament. It was stated at the consultation,† that the Legislative Council—a term asserted by the Assembly to be synonymous with "*Executive*" —had repeatedly refused to proceed on the Judicature Bills sent *up* by that body, and that the province had suffered great and various hardships from a want of sympathy on the part of the Legislative Council towards

*Vide "*Observations on Petition of Grievance*," p. 20.

†Vide the Quebec Petition of Grievance.

the precarious situation of *Mr. Viger*, and the anxiety of his friends. The great *Accoucheur*, without pronouncing any definite opinion himself, referred the matter to a Committee of young Æsculapians, who declared that the Legislative Council were much to blame for their cruel and inhuman treatment of Mr. *Viger*, and recommended a different constitution of that respectable body. But the council have refused to acquiesce in this opinion, and declare themselves perfectly innocent of the crimes laid to their charge.* In truth, we are ourselves of the same opinion —and the little sketch which we have given of the history of this famous Judicature Bill may convince any impartial person, that the statements in the petitions of grievance respecting this matter, were as false as they were groundless. Is not the failure of the Bill in the *Assembly* itself a convincing proof of this? Who would trust in future to similar representations from the same source? Yes! The House *of Assembly* strangled the Bill in its birth and saved the Legislative Council the trouble of again legislating on a measure so incongruous, and so full at once of blunders and danger to the due administration of justice. This event however, has been the means of dividing the Assembly into two parties, now commonly known as the Quebec and Montreal parties.

The Montrealers have always supposed

---

*Vide Appendix A, of their journals for 1829.

themselves far superior to the Quebecers both in number and legal lore; but this is a proposition which the Quebec folk deny; and it must be confessed, that they have proved their superiority so far as to be able to throw out *Mr. Viger's Bill* without being capable to maintain the *Resolutions* of Mr. *Vallieres* on the same subject. Whilst this state of things continues, we despair of ever seeing a sensible judicature law pass either branch of the Legislature. We are not prepared at present to enter into the merits of the measures of either party; but we cannot refrain from saying, that, *of the two*, those of *Mr. Vallieres* are by far and decidedly superior, though still at an immense distance from the true line of judicial legislation. The observations of Mr. Solicitor General on this question will reward any one who peruses them.* They do as much honour to his candour, as to his information, talents, and research.

We are ourselves no lawyer; but with a little study and labour, we think we could be able to devise a system of judicial administration for this province which would at least be equal to that of either *Mr. Viger* or *Mr. Vallieres*. The policy of our ancient constitution, says Blackstone, as regulated and established by the great *Alfred*, was to bring justice home to every man's door, by constituting as many courts of judicature as there were manors and townships in the king-

*Vide debate, 3d February, 1829.

dom ; wherein injuries were redressed in an easy an expeditious manner, by the suffrage of neighbours and friends. These little courts, however, communicated with others of a larger jurisdiction, and those with others of still greater power ; ascending gradually from the lowest to the supreme courts, which were respectively constituted to correct the errors of the inferior ones, and to determine such causes as by reason of their weight and difficulty demanded a more solemn discussion. The course of justice flowing in large streams from the king, as the fountain, to his superior courts of record ; and being then subdivided into smaller channels, till the whole and every part of the kingdom were plentifully watered and refreshed. This seems to us to be the true basis of Courts of judicature, and is such as ought, in our humble opinion, to be adopted not only in this province, but in every other country of the least pretensions to civilization. The system was evidently borrowed from Moses, who, finding the sole administration of justice too heavy for him, "chose able men out of all Israel, such as feared God, men of truth, hating covetousness ; and made them heads over the people, rulers of thousands, rulers of hundreds, rulers of fifties, and rulers of tens: and they judged the people at all seasons ; the *hard* causes they brought unto *Moses ;* but every *small* matter they judged themselves."* It is on such a plan as this that we wish to see the judicature of this

*Exod, Chap. XVIII. v. 21.

province firmly and permanently settled. This is the true division of judicial labour. Let the province, therefore, be divided luto counties and townships. Let there be a *sedentary* judge in each of those counties and townships, having jurisdiction in real and personal cases to the amount of £30 sterling. Let these counties and townships be split into *three* divisions, and attached, according to their locality, to each of the general districts of *Quebec*, *Montreal*, and *Three-Rivers*. Let each of these general Districts have a court of Kings Bench, consisting of a Chief Justice and three puisne Judges; having a concurred original, as well as an appellate, jurisdiction over all the counties and townships attached to the District. So far as regards the appeal from counties and townships, let the decisions of these *District* courts be final. Let there be a supreme court of Appeals, consisting of the Governor and Council; that council, for *judicial purposes*, to consist of His Majesty's Representative, the speaker of the Legislative council, if he be not one of the Chief Justices, but if so, the senior member of the same council; the said three Chief Justices, the Judge of the Vice Court of Admiralty, and His Majesty's Advocate General. As to criminal matters, let all trials be had in the court of Kings Beach within whose General District the offence may have been committed. Let *all* these Judges be rendered independent; and not only permanent salaries granted to them during good behaviour, but *pensions* also, in the event of their retiring in consequence of bad health, old age, or a judicial servitude of ten years. Let the *Record* language at least of *all* these courts be *English*.* As to the laws that ought to govern the decision of cases, of course, *we* are not prepared to speak.

---

*"Identity of language is a fundamental relation, on whose influence we cannot too deeply meditate. This identity places between the men of these two countries (the United States and England,) a common character, which will always make them attach themselves (se pendre) to, and recognize each other. They will mutually think themselves at home when they travel into each other's country. They will have a reciprocal pleasure in the interchange of their thoughts, and in every discussion of their interests. *But an insurmountable barrier is raised up between a people of a different language, who cannot utter a word without recollecting that they do not belong to the same Country—between whom every transmission of thought is irksome labour, not an enjoyment, who never succeed perfectly to understand each other—and with whom the result of conversation, after the fatigue of unavailing efforts, is to find themselves mutually ridiculous.* The very part of America through which I have travoiled, I have not found a single Englishman who did not feel himself to be an American; not a single Frenchman who did not find himself to be a STRANGER." *Talleyrand's Memoir of America.*

But we venture to think, that the sooner the French feudal laws and tenures are abolished, and the English laws and forms of procedure established in their place, the sooner the province will become happy, prosperous and wealthy. With regard to the foolish dread that has been entertained in the Assembly respecting *local* judges, and their partialities to those next them in society and kindred, it is quite absurd. Has not a *local* judge the same honour and character to maintain that a District judge has? To suppose the contrary, would be to suppose him *a priori*, destitute of every principle of justice and integrity. Has not every individual a certain rank and character to uphold? In the name of heaven, why should *local* Judges be exempted from so general and favourable an idea of mankind? Are local and parish *persons* less virtuous and moral in their lives than metropolitans? It is positively a libel upon human nature to say, that an individual can be more upright and virtuous in one place than another; and that judges in the country are less impartial and honest than city judges. For our own part, we honestly declare, that, had we a case pending, we would much sooner submit our fate to a country, than to a town judge. It is very true we might be favoured with finer speeches, closer logick, and more eloquent language from the city judge; but we very much question whether we should not receive stricter and more sterling justice from the country justice. Nothing can be more childish than the reasoning of the Assembly on this subject. They have mistaken their own suspicions and prejudices for realities; and have put down, as an offence to be guarded and watched, the more surmises of their own imaginations. We trust we have assisted in exploding such futile doctrines, and that, when the Assembly meet again, their minds will be better prepared for the discussion and final adjustment of a subject which, above all others, claims their serious and undivided attention. *This*, ought not to be made a *party* question, because it is of paramount and perpetual importance. Neither Quebec nor Montreal ought to claim any honour or favour from its settlement. The whole country ought to unite in its accomplishment; and he who divides either the country or the Assembly in an endeavour to establish a wise and permanent system of judicature, ought to be execrated and banished for ever from decent society. Without a proper system of judicature, no country can be free or happy: without meekness and magnanimity, no legislature can be useful.

The Bill introduced by *Mr. Lee* for disqualifying the judges from having seats and votes in the Legislative Council, was a very silly and foolish measure; and we are happy that it miscarried. It displayed neither generosity of sentiment nor knowledge of the constitution. This is an old and favourite object in the Assembly; and of course, was thought to be irresistible on the present occasion in consequence of the complaints of the petitioners of the *Cross* on the one hand, and the remembrance of that foul monster, the Canada Committee, on the other. But, thank God, desperate as our condition is, we have not yet fallen quite so low, as to be driven from our post by every wind of doctrine that rises from the Assembly and their minions throughout the country. When the *assembly* prevail so far as to be able to say with impunity, either who *shall*, or who *shall not*, sit in the legislative council; or, in other words, dictate the spirit and the principles which ought to regulate that essential balance which the constitution has opposed to their popular passions and designs, there will be an end of the matter. Nothing, indeed, is more natural to licentiousness, faction and envy in all countries, than to unite in an endeavour to possess themselves of the whole power of the state, and we have seen that, in obedience to this general law, nothing has ever occupied the attention of the Assembly more than the means of acquiring the whole power and authority of the province. The attempt, therefore, of driving the Judges from the Legislative Council, if successful, is considered as one great step towards an end so desirable. We call upon the government and the country at large to be unanimous in their resistance to these unwarrantable and outrageous proceedings! One concession leads to another; and we may be assured, that if the Assembly succeed in their present attempts to destroy the constitutional organization of the Legislative Council, their next endeavour will be either to declare that body altogether useless, or fill it with their own creatures. Such a conjecture is not so distant or remote as some persons would induce us to believe. They who have narrawly watched the operations of our Constitution, and the process of *encroachments* and *violations* on its principles which have been going on for years, clearly perceive, that if such a system be longer persevered in, it must be yielded up, like a battered and ruined citadel, into the hands of its worst and basest enemies. In the Colonies, in particular, it behooves his Majesty's government to guard against innovation from the side of the popular branches of the legislatures. While the Assemblies possess much of the power and constitution of the House of Commons, the provinces are destitute of that rank and fortune which are necessary to secure that stable, uniform counterpoise in the Legislative Councils, which characterizes the House of Lords. The model is a good one; but it can never have fair-play in a country where the materials for forming a counterpart, do not, and cannot exist. Besides, neither the king nor government holds any patronage in the provinces, which can create attachment and influence sufficient to counteract that restless arrogating spirit, which in popular assemblies, when left to itself, will never brook an authority that checks and interferes with its own. We do not here advocate any undue influence or clandestine rewards. These are equally disgraceful at all times.

and in all places. We only refer to that weight and influence on the poblio mind which always characterize, and ought ever to follow the acceptance of posts of honour, and merited preferment. It is on these grounds alone that we warn this province of the danger that awaits it, if the House of Assembly be permitted to pull down and level every barrier which the constitution has established not only in its own defence, but for the safety and security of the rights and liberties of the people at large.

But with respect particularly to the attempts made by the House of Assembly of this province to exclude the judges from the Legislative Council, nothing can present their true character in a better light. They do not complain of the judges because they have polluted the seat of justice, but, on the contrary, because they possess, *in the opinion of the Assembly, the natural enemies of the other branches of the Legislature*, an undue influence in the Legislative Council! We do admit, that, if a case were made out shewing *one solitary* instance wherein the political character of the judges interfered with the legitimate discharge of their judicial functions, we should be among the first to second the measures of the Assembly. But when we find that the Assembly, even presumptuous and insolent as they are in all their measures, have not dared to bring a charge of this description against any of the judges, but, on the contrary, only hunt them as mere organs of imaginary political grievances, we stand on their side; and have no hesitation to say, that the minister or the Governor who consents to stigmatize a learned and honourable body of men, in subserviency to the views of the Assembly, is an enemy of the constitution and a base traitor to his country. Yet, even if there had been good and formidable grounds for excluding the judges from the Legislative Council, the *mode* in which the Assembly attempt to effect their purpose, is alike at variance with the principles of the constitution, and destructive of the just prerogatives of the crown. By the constitutional act his Majesty is authorized to call whom he pleases to the Legislative Council, except aliens and persons under twenty one years of age; and those called, hold their seats during LIFE, unless vacated and forfeited by absence from the province, treason, or allegiance to any foreign prince or power. Now, as it is not pretended that the judges have forfoited their seats, by the commission of those crimes, or by absence from the province, by what power on earth can they be disqualified, except by an act of the Imperial Parliament? It is in virtue of an act of the supreme Legislature of the empire that they hold their seats, and we know of no other authority by which they can be deprived of them. Nay, even had his Majesty *recommended* the measure in question, which we are certain his Majesty will never do, we maintain that the *Provincial* Legislature could not constitutionally proceed to enact a law upon the subject. Their doing so would be legislating in the face and in defiance of the Constitutional Act; and neither the judges themselves nor the country would be bound by their decision. If the judges in the council have committed any crime, let them be tried and convicted, and then their seats will fall as a thing of course, agreeable to the dictates of the constitution. If it *is* necessary to remove them, which we flatly deny, let the king and the imperial Parliament, the only competent authority, be solicited to perform the ungrateful task. But never let it be said in a British province, that an outrage so glaring has been committed on the principles of the constitution; and that incompetency and injustice walk hand in hand. At the risk of incurring the displeasure of the Assembly and their friends—which, by the way, we should be sorry ever to do otherwise than *deserve*—we have no hesitation in saying, that *some* of the judges are the most useful and efficient members in the Legislative Council, and that nothing could be more injurious to the real interests of the province than *their* removal, at a time when the constitution lies prostrate at our feet, and every avenue opened to the insolent and destructive pretensions of the House of Assembly. His Majesty's government will therefore do well not to part with them especially at the present juncture. They get nothing for their labour; and whilst they work the good work of the constitution faithfully and honestly without injury to their judicial character, we think that the debt is on the side of the king and country, and not on theirs. Some of the most eminent and experienced judges of England have always been found to have seats in the House of Lords, and those who have not are daily liable to be called upon for advice and instruction. Why should not the analogy be maintained in Canada as nearly as circumstances can admit? Moreover, when we consider that the Legislative Council of this province consists of *twenty six* members, and that of this number only *three* are judges, exclusive of the Chief Justice, who, it seems, *may now* retain his place,—what evil consequences could result to the country, even if these *three* formed a faction as stupid, as vile, and as democratical as the *Triumvirate* who complained of them? The fact is, that the good sense of the country has been very much insulted and outraged on this as well as on other subjects: and we are surprised that we have hitherto submitted so quietly to be told that all our judges are pure and immaculate, except those *alone* who hold seats in the Legislative Council. We think we have shewn the cause of this in its true colours; and we venture to presume that the government will fail in their duty, if they do not immediately put a stop to this base outcry against respectable individuals, who are an honour to the country and the rank which they hold in its civil and political institutions.

But who are they who raise this outcry? Why, a pack of upstart, ignorant lawyers and notaries, who compose nearly one half of the representatives of the people. While traducing the judges for meddling in politicks, they altogether overlook the fact that they are themselves committing the very same fault. Is it not as dangerous to a lawyer, who anticipates promotion to the bench to be a politician, as a judge? We at least, think so; especially when we consider the *politicks* of the lawyers in the House of Assembly, and their misapplication of that time and industry which would be much better employed in studying their cases in order to do justice to their clients. It is very clear to us, that practicing lawyers cannot dabble in politicks without injuring the political interests of the country, and disqualifying themselves for being judges; and therefore we hope the government will ever do its utmost to keep *such* lawyers in their proper sphere. We hope that political lawyers will be studiously kept from the Bench: we hope this, because we wish to see the laws purely, unerringly and impartially administered.*

We regret that the Bill, of which we present a copy below, was not introduced into the Legislative Council and passed, as it forms one of the best commentaries on the spirit and character of the lawyers in the Assembly we have ever seen. We hope the gentleman who got it printed will not fail to

*" The government of the *United* States, since its institution, has scarcely evinced any thing else but proofs of weakness; and, in future, greater vigour cannot be expected from it, as long as it is conducted by LAWYERS."

take it up next session.* We are serious in this expectation. We do not wish the constitution to be buffeted, like a rock in the middle of the ocean by every surge of democracy that these infatuated lawyers can raise against it. We wish to see honour, justice and liberality of sentiment pervade the province; but whilst *lawyers* continue to legislate for us, we despair of ever seeing the country prosperous or happy.

---

species of men the least proper to govern others, because they have nearly all a false judgement and dull character; and because with their confined ideas and mean passions they think they can govern empires, in the same manner as they would govern a club." *Beanjour's* Sketch *of the United* States, *pp.* 64 *and* 65.

**Bill for placing the* Legislative *Council and House of Assembly of* this *Province upon an equal footing.*

WHEREAS a bill having passed the Assembly for disqualifying the judges from sitting in the Legislative Council and thereby establishing the principle, that professional knowledge of Law ought to work Legislative incompetency, it is fit and proper for the preservation of the due balance of the Constitution, and of equal rights, that the two Houses of the Legislature should be placed upon the like footing: Be it therefore enacted, &c. and it is hereby enacted by the authority of the same, that from and after the passing of this act, no person being an Advo-

Upon the whole, we are firmly of opinion, that the Assembly would much better discharge their duty to their constituents and themselves in an endeavour to secure the real independence of the Judges, than thus to hunt them, *nolens*, *volens*, out of the leg-

---

cate, Solicitor, Notary Public or other practiser of Law in any shape shall be elected or sit in the House of Assembly of this Province as a Member thereof, any Law, Statute, Ordinance or Usage to the contrary thereof in any ways notwithstanding.

And whereas Physicians and Surgeons would be more usefully employed in attending to their Patients, than in composing Legislative nostrums, Be it therefore further enacted by the authority aforesaid, that no person being a Physician or Surgeon, shall after the passing of this Act be elected a Member of the House of Assembly or sit therein.

And whereas great public injury has arisen from the number of Members of Assembly resident in Quebec and Montreal, and the Counties thereof, representing other Counties, whereby their local interests and feelings are attended to instead of the public good, Be it further enacted by the authority aforesaid that from and after the passing of this Act, no person resident in Quebec or in Montreal or in either of the Counties thereof, shall be elected or shall sit as a Member of the Assembly, for any County, Town, or Borough, other than the Cities or Towns of Quebec

islative council; for even were the Judges excluded from this Council, who can say that their dignity and independence would be greater, while their commissions are held *durante bene placito*, or during pleasure, instead of *quamdiu bene se gesserint*, or during good behaviour. The first maxim of a free state, is the impartial administration of justice. But, constituted as human nature is, how can justice be impartially administered, unless the minister of justice be placed in such a situation and circumstances as will render him as indifferent to one party as the other; as indifferent at once to the king as to his subject, however mean or destitute?* In such a government as ours, the great and leading object of the laws, is the security and

---

and Montreal or the Counties thereof, any Law, Statute, Ordinance or usage to the contrary thereof in any ways nothwithstanding.

And any person being an Advocate, Solicitor, Attorney, Notary Public, or other Practiser of Law in any shape or any person resident in Quebec or Montreal or either of the Counties thereof who shall be elected a Member of the Assembly and sit therein as such, contrary to the provisions of this Act, every such person for every such offence, shall forfeit and pay Five hundred pounds sterling.

*Even in the United States, "The judges both of the supreme and inferior courts, shall hold their situations during good behaviour, and shall, at stated times, receive for their

protection of the rights of individuals, and in their impartial execution when these rights are invaded. Suppose the Crown or its officers to be the invaders: suppose a subject ---suppose *ourselves* dragged from our home, our femily, and our business, and consigned to a dungeon by a tyrant of the law in some high authority, for no other cause than a free and candid expression of our sentiments on some point of government, what justice are we to expect---in what light are we to look upon our rights, while our Judges, those men who are to sit as arbiters between us and those who may have robbed us of our liberty or property, hold their situations *at the pleasure* of these robbers and invaders? Suppose our Judges to be men well known to the community for integrity and impartiality—men fearing God and hating a bribe—may not the Crown dismiss them and appoint others in their place of less scruples, honour and integrity? Aye, and such dismissals and appointments have taken place, even in that country which boasts of the best laws and freest constitution in the world. But, thank God, the times of such evil deeds and evil men have long since gone by. The patriarchs of the Revolution of 1688, clearly saw the defect, and destroyed it for ever. By the 13th WILLIAM III. cap. 2. the Commissions of the Judges were made during good

---

services, a compensation, *which shall not be diminished during their continuance in office.*" *Vide* constitution of the U. S. ART. 3. Sec. 1.

behaviour; thus depriving the Crown of the power of appointing subservient and time-serving judges. This was one of the noblest achievements of the Revolution. By the I. Geo. cap. 23, the judges are not only continued in their effices during good behaviour, but notwithstanding any demise of the Crown; and their salaries absolutely secured to them during the continuance of their Commissions. The sentiments of the monarch on this occasion, were worthy of the sovereign of a free nation; and ought to be repeated as often as the conduct and independence of the judges become subjects of discussion:--"He looked upon the independence and uprightness of the judges, as essential to the impartial administration of justice; and as one of the *best* securities of the *rights* and *liberties* of his subjects, and as most conducive to the honour of the Crown."

It is much to the honour of the judges of this province, that they have long felt the evils and dangers of the tenure upon which they hold their Commissions. Previous to Lord Dalhousie's departure for England in 1824, a memorial was presented to him from the Chief Justice and Judges of the province, praying that their Commissions might be granted them during good behaviour, and a provision made for their retirement after a service of a certain number of years. His Lordship, while at home submitted and strongly recommended this memorial to his Majesty's government; and, upon his return to the province the ensuing year, he received a despatch from the Colonial minister, stating, "that he would recommend to his Majesty that the appointment of the Judges in this province should be placed on the footing on which corresponding appointments are placed in England, provided that the Legislature of this province should make a provision for their retirement according to the scale which is adopted in England." On the 1st of February, 1826, a Message to this effect was sent by his Lordship to both houses of the Legislature. It would appear, however, that in the Session of 1825, when the Governor in Chief was in England, the Assembly had passed a series of Resolutions on this subject, on the *basis* of which, and not on that of the Message, they now, for the first time, introduced a bill. The clauses of this bill were as novel and unconstitutional in themselves as they were at variance with the whole tenour and spirit of the Message. The very first of these declares "that from and after the passing of this act, it shall no longer be lawful for any of the Judges of the several Courts of King's Bench in this province, nor for any of the Judges of the Provincial Courts therein, to have or to occupy a seat in the Executive Council, nor in the Legislative Council of this Province." Now, is there any rational being in existence who can discover any consanguinity between this clause and any part of the Message? What had the seats of the Judges in the Legislative and Executive Council to do with their judicial independence? We have already spoken at large on this head, and shall only add in this place, that an attempt to deprive his Majesty of the right of calling to his councils, whom he will, is a direct encroachment upon the prerogatives of the Crown, and an assumption of an executive power which cannot for a moment be tolerated under such a Constitution as ours. It would at once overwhelm the just balance of a free representative government, checked and controlled by a limited monarchy. The second clause of this famous bill declares, that the Judges shall hold their office "during *their* good *behaviour*." But what have the Assembly or the Legislature at large to do with the mode in which the judges are to hold their offices? This is entirely a gift of the Crown that cannot be interfered with by the Assembly without assuming to themselves the rights of the Crown. It was not for them to say whether the Judges should or should not hold their situations during good behaviour. The Message calls for no such legislation. It only enjoins the propriety of "*a provision for the retirement of the judges;*" in which case only the minister engaged to recommend to his Majesty the appointment of the judges of this province on the same footing with corresponding appointments in England; and in which case only can the judges be furnished with Commissions during good behaviour. The next three clauses indeed, affect to establish a permanent allowance for salaries and pensions to the Judges. But whence were these to come? Why, say the

Assembly, from "the funds already by law appropriated generally for the administration of justice and support of the civil government." Surely our readers need not be told, that these are the very identical funds whose existence the Assembly at once deny and assume to themselves the right to dispose of! What infamous tergiversation is this! Were such a measure as this sanctioned, the judges would be less independent than ever. Should these "*appropriated*" funds be given up to the Assembly, as has been done towards the conclusion of the late Session, would not the judges be obliged *annually* to beg at the door of the House of Assembly for their salaries and pensions? Besides, even allowing that no such pretensions had ever been set up by the Assembly to the permanent appropriated revenues of the Crown, these revenues are far from being adequate to the payment of the judges; and the object of both the despatch and the message was, not a disposition on the part of the Assembly of these permanent funds, but a new and different "provision for the Retirement of the judges according to the scale which is adopted in England." But this was a distinction which the Assembly could not, or would not understand. They had long contemplated the hope of being one day enabled to render the judges subservient to their own popular tribunal, and this, they thought, was one step towards a consummation so devoutly to be wished. Accordingly, the sixth clause of the bill in question.

constitutes the Legislative Council as a tribunal competent to try not only the judges but every other officer guilty of high crimes and misdemeanours. Yet, they forget, that whatever instructions may have once reached this province on this subject, these were afterwards modified to such a degree as to deny to the Council any judicial jurisdiction without the express sanction of his Majesty. But we should be glad to stand face to face with the man who dared to say, that even the King himself had the right to confer a judicial character upon the Legislative Council without an act of the Imperial Parliament. To talk then of a provincial subordinate *legislature* assuming to itself powers which can only emanate from the supreme authority of the empire, is sheer downright stupidity and nonsense; and such opinions can only be entertained by a legislative body pretending to an equality of power and authority with the Imperial Parliament. Need we be surprised, then, if the Legislative Council have rejected a bill so fraught with innovation and real danger? They therefore did right in damning it; and we think that those who have found fault with them for doing so—such as the Canada Committee, their minions and witnesses—ought to be impeached as traitors to their country; at least, as base malignant traducers, unworthy of being associated with by any wise or high-minded people. Such is the state of affairs with respect to the independence of the judges; and such is the fate of the recommendations of his Majesty on a subject, which above all others, demands the serious attention of a free and enlightened country!

The *qualification* of Justices of the Peace has been an old and favourite measure in the House of Assembly; but the real object in view, is, perhaps, not so generally known as it ought to be. We shall state it in a few words. Though more than *three-fourths* of the whole magistracy of the province* is actually composed of native *French* Canadians, yet the Assembly have ever deemed it an intolerable grievance that the *whole* body of Justices of the peace does not consist of what they term their "*Countrymen*," to the entire exclusion of "*English foreigners and strangers*." They are not content with an exclusive legislative power. They must also be possessed of the civil and criminal judicial authority of the province. The only means which they have hitherto devised for effecting this object is the *qualification* of Justices of the peace; imagining, that, as the French population are the holders and occupiers of the greater part of the landed property of the country, they are alone entitled to be called upon to perform the important duties of magistrates. They cannot endure that an *Englishman* who is not possessed of real property, can possibly discharge the duties

*In the District of Quebec there are 131 Justices of the Peace; but of this number, only 56 have English names. The number of English in the other Districts is much less.

of a magistrate, however well qualified as to rank, fortune, education, talents and intelligence. All---all must yield to the *physical* strength and qualities of the Country. It cannot be endured that a man with an English face, an English name, or an English tongue in his head should sit in judgment on a Canadian, or sign a *mittimus* for committing to "durance vile" a son of the immaculate and renowned "*Nation Canadienne.*" Such a case as this has always been looked upon as the height of insult and tyranny. Besides, the Assembly must have all their own creatures in the magistracy; for who, in their estimation, can be so useful and influential at Hustings and other political assemblies, as those in the plenary enjoyment of the magisterial functions? It is no wonder, then, if the measures adopted by the late administration for purifying the commissions of the peace, by dismissing those who had so wantonly and insolently prostituted the dignity and character of the office of justice of the peace, struck the Assembly with dismay. This was a blow which they could not easily recover; and they have not yet recovered it; but as soon as the legislature met, and its stunning effects had somewhat subsided, they lost not a moment in attempting to right themselves. The Bill which they introduced for this purpose, was one of the most absurd, barefaced and unconstitutional things of the kind we have ever heard of. It required all persons appointed to the office of Justice of the peace to swear that they possessed a free unincumbered revenue of £100 *per annum*. This was an attempt to assimilate the qualifications of justices in this province to those in England; though, ignorant as they are, they must have been aware that there exists no analogy whatever in the circumstances of the two countries. It is very true, that in England certain qualifications are in force, with respect to justices of the peace; and, in particular, no one can act as justice unless he have £100 *per annum*, clear of all deductions. But this is not with a view to ensure the services of men of *property* of any denomination whatever; but, on the contrary, men of education, reputation, rank, and learning. Anciently, before the present constitution of justices was invented, there were peculiar officers appointed by the common law for the maintenance of the public peace. The duties of those officers were limited to the mere conservation of the peace. Their ignorance in letters or in law was a matter of no consequence, because a good batton and a well tempered sword were the best promoters of peaceful demeanour; and he who could wield them most dexterously, was considered the best guardian of publick tranquillity. During the reigns of our earlier princes, a "*good Clerk*" was considered but an inferior, being compared to a good "*Archer*," and, in fact, was a less useful member of society, considering the elements and the manners of that society. But as mankind became enlightened, as feudal warfare ceased, as commerce extended, and trade flourished, the laws became numerous and intricate; and no man could administer or enforce them, except he who was either learned in the law, or endowed by education and research with a capacity, equal to the new duties imposed upon him. In fact, as early as the reign of Edward III. justices became Judges in cases of felonies; and it was then that the old conservators of the peace acquired the more honourable appellation of Justices. In progress of time, the criminal laws became still more complicated and voluminous; and, as they now stand and are executed in this province, very few persons can be found in the country of sufficient capacity to administer them as they ought to be administered. Cases wherein the dearest rights of freemen are interested come to be decided before the justices in all their stages from the first rumour of complaint to final conviction. The personal liberty of the subject is discussed before them every day. In their General Quarter Sessions, they are authorized to call Grand Juries before them, who are consequently endowed with the highest powers next to legislative authority. Every subject being entitled, when accused, to a fair and just trial, cases come before these periodical courts of the utmost nicety, demanding the sharpest scrutiny and the most careful discrimination. Are we to be told then that these are duties and functions that can be discharged by *any* man worth £100 per annum of free income? The thing is a palpable absurdity from beginning to end. This is the first time in the annals of mankind, we believe, that intellectual and scientific knowledge has been estimated by acres of land and pounds of money. It is, however, a false estimation; and will never answer in any country whose civilization is such as to render its laws a distinct and professional study. We know a man in a certain city of this province, who is in the receipt of an annual free income of from two to three thousand pounds; but who can neither read nor write his own name! It is enough to disgust and sicken any one who contemplates for a moment the figure which this man and his equals in ignorance would cut on the bench, doling out justice, not according to the rule of law, but the rule of thumb or the ell-wand. For these and other reasons we desire to hear no more upon this subject: it becomes loathsome to us. If we are desirous of keeping our criminal tribunals pure and unsullied, let us have magistrates of adequate education and acquirement. These are only to be found among the respectable English inhabitants of the province, and *such* of the native French ones as really possess sufficient education and information. It is too soon to introduce the English laws of qualification into this province. It will be sufficient to do so when the people become equally well informed, rich, and independent. The Legislative Council, therefore, did right in throwing this bill overboard once more.

As to the discussion which took place in the Assembly on the introduction of this measure, it was truly worthy of the object, and in perfect character with the ends in view. The hue and cry raised against the Governor in Chief for the late dismissions from the commission of the peace is equally *unique*. But who and what are the individuals who were thus dismissed? Why, the very pests and off-scourings of the country; men who, to gratify their own party and seditious views, prostituted their office and station as justices of the peace, and thereby forfeited the confidence reposed in their honour and loyalty by the crown: men who stood in open array against the government of the country, and sounded the alarm-bell of riot and confusion: men who had opened their doors to nocturnal meetings of the most diabolical nature: men who had turned their fire-sides into forums of debating demagogues and mountebanks: men who had sullied the quiet and privacy of domestick life with the impurities of faction and discontent: men who had suffered the unhallowed yells of disloyalty and contempt for the metropolitan state to ring from morning till night in the ears of their wives, children and servants: men who affected to be contaminated by any association with Englishmen: and men who had boarded the highest functionaries in the province with abuse the most degrading and insulting. Did not such men at once despise the law and the authority with which it had clothed them? Did they not from that moment in which their evil deeds commenced forfeit the important trust reposed in them by their sovereign for the preservation of the peace and safety of the country? Who, then, dare throw their poisoned shafts at the head of his Majesty's representative for purifying the commission of the peace of such traitors and incendiaries? Peace is the very end and foundation of civil society. Can it be endured therefore that those who are entrusted with the maintenance of the publick peace, shall be among the foremost ranks in destroying it? The King's Majesty, to use the words of Blackstone, is, by his office and dignity royal, the principal conservator of the peace within *all his dominions*; and may give authority to any other to see the peace kept, and to punish such as *break* it. How were the men—the justices—in question to be punished, except by dismissing them from the commission? As the office of these justices was conferred by the King, so it subsists only during his pleasure. There is a variety of ways for determining and superseding this office; one of which is that which was adopted in the present case; viz: a new commission, which virtually, though silently discharges all the former justices that are not included therein; for two commissions cannot subsist at once.* The powers with which the Governor of this province is invested on this head, are as potent as those of the King himself, as will appear from the

*Vide Blackstone, Vol. 1. p. 359.

following clause in his commission :—" And we empower you, the said Earl of Dalhousie, in case any person or persons, having a commission, or named by us to any charge in our said provinces of Upper or Lower Canada, from which they may be liable to be removed by us, be in *your opinion* incapable of continuing in our service, to suspend or remove such person or persons from their different employments, without giving him or them any reason for such suspension or removal." Wherefore, then the clamour and uproar raised against the Governor in Chief for the discharge of a disagreeable duty for which he was responsible to his King and country? Wherefore this petitioning on the part of the dismissed justices to the present Governor to be replaced in the Commission? Do they not know, that once they have forfeited the esteem and confidence of their sovereign, no governor who has any respect for the civil institutions of the country or the purity of justice, can pardon or reinstate them? Why, then, pester, torture, and torment *Sir James Kempt* with their vile scrawls of complaints and solicitations? Let them desist, and sink again into that nothingness from which they have so prematurely arisen.

With respect to the character of the debates which attended the introduction of the bill in question, we confess that we feel at a loss for language to convey a proper idea of the sentiments which we entertain regarding it. The speech of the Honourable *Speaker*---for *he* must have something to say on all questions—is particularly obnoxious to decency, decorum, good sense, and magnanimity. His abuse of the *Executive Council* is downright blackguardism; and we give it in a note in order to convince the world, that this man is on a level with the dirtiest and most degrading job that can possibly be undertaken by the lowest and meanest of mankind.* It is true, that no one who knows this fellow will be surprised at any thing that proceeds from the *man*. But when we behold the Speaker of the House of Assembly

---

* *Qualification of Justices of the Peace.*—The House in committee entered upon this bill, *Mr. Larriere* in the chair.

The first clause was, that all Justices of the Peace should be appointed by the advice of the Chief Justice, and his Majesty's Executive Council.

The Honourable Speaker held it very improper to entrust the appointment, (or what was the same thing) the recommendation of Justices of the Peace to the Executive Council; that council carried on its delibereticne under the veil of secrecy. They were a secret and invisible body to which past experience had shown we could not entrust this important duty. In the appointment of the Commission of the Pauce, the people of the Province had been extremely ill used. It had been employed to force upon the country the discipline under which it groaned. Dismissions and appointments had been made without respect to character, in

standing up in his place—throwing off the high dignity of his office and the sacred responsibility of his station—and vomiting forth all the bile and corruption of his malignant and cowardly heart upon a respectable and bigly essential body of honourable men, every one of whom is his superior in all relations and capacities, we have no hesitation in concluding that the province is positively dishonoured, and the government ab-

---

fluence, property or ability for the office. Every thing was made subservient to party purposes. The Executive Council was chiefly composed of those who depended entirely on the Administration and who need their office with servility, secrecy and views of advancement. Every thing combined to make their nominations dependent on the caprice of the Governor. In such appointments probity, honour, character, respectability were disregarded or put into the opposite scale. Thus men who were fit for these offices were disgusted with the company they were obliged to keep. No person of merit or standing in the country would consent to hold them. Such offices were degraded. Men who indentified themselves with the suffering cause of the people were expelled and driven into retirement. Upstarts unknown and contemned were substituted in their place. Such were the enormities committed by the Executive under the system which we are now called to support. —*Quebec Star, of January*, 1829.

solutely disgraced by the presence of a being so truly loathsome and disgusting. Were not the Executive Council degraded in their own eyes while such a man mingled amongst them? Were not his Majesty's councils contaminated even by the approbation of such a man? But he is not *now*, thanks to Lord Dalhousie, an Executive Councillor; and the country is indebted to that nobleman for having erased from the Council book the name of a person so little worthy of his majesty's confidence. That nobleman knew too well that the spirit which governed a Pepineau was inconsistent at once with the honour of the crown and the real interests of the province. He dismissed him therefore, under circumstances, which, we are certain, will ensure his absence from the Council board in all time to come, *whoever may be Governor*. Nor is Mr. Papineau a man to be associated with by any one at such a place; especially after the mode, and the tone, in which he has publickly defamed his Majesty's Executive Council. He has neither amity of manners nor generosity of soul to act a proper or dignified part on a stage so important; and of him we may truly and justly say, *Tatus infidus est, et opertæ rupit amicitiæ jura.*

Out of these proceedings with respect to the qualification of justices, arose the more serious and alarming measure of *expelling Mr. Christie*, a member of the House of Assembly, as representative of the county of *Gaspe*. As this is a question which not only involves an interesting constitutional point, but deeply concerns the rights, liberties and franchises of the people, we will consider it in two aspects—*first*, whether the House of Assembly have a right to expel a member in any case, and under what circumstances; and, *secondly*, whether, granting the first proposition, there existed just and sufficient grounds for the expulsion of Mr. Christie? Before doing so, however, we think it proper to state, that we know nothing of Mr. Christie, personally, that we have no partiality or friendship for him, and that whatever we may say with respect to the difficulties in which the proceedings of the Assembly have involved him, shall be solely dictated by the purest regard to the honour of the provincial legislature and the best interests of the country.

I. It must be admitted that no body of men, however or for whatever purpose associated, can exist in an incorporated state for any length of time, unless they are governed by certain laws and customs which not only serve to constitute, organize, and maintain it in being, but which also invest it with a certain authoritative and compulsory jurisdiction over the members that compose it. These are rights inherent and peculiar to all societies, whether barbarous or civil. The wildest race of Cannibals that ever existed have their laws: they have rules, however rude, that cannot be infringed, and usages that cannot be encroached upon, without incurring penalties and punishments the most severe and degrading. Man is, by nature, the member of a community; and when considered in this capacity, the individual appears to be no longer made for himself. He must forego his happiness and his freedom, where these interfere with the good of society. Agreeable to this maxim, every assemblage of men, every order has its own peculiar rules and institutes of government. The army has its orders, regulations, and codes of honour: the church has its canons: the courts of justice have their laws and customs: and the high court of parliament has its own peculiar Law, well known as the *lex et consuetudo parliamenti*. To each of these different laws and customs every member of the community to which they severally apply, is amenable. But such are the imperfections and weaknesses of all human institutions, that even laws founded on the best principles and wisest maxims, may not only be exercised with a total disregard of the rights of those who are principally interested, but carried far beyond the bounds of their legitimate jurisdiction; thus at once affecting the original compact between the members of the particular body to which they apply, and encroaching upon the liberty and independence of another community over which they possess no authority whatever. Every system, as well of law as of every other science, must have its limits. Nature herself has her laws; and the solar-system, infinite as it may appear to us, has its limits and boundaries. In truth, the very aim and object of laws, is to set bounds and landmarks to the follies and passions of mankind. With regard, in particular, to the case before us, it, too, is bounded and circumscribed; and can no more be endowed with extraordinary principles of tension, than the earth can be driven from its orbit. The supreme, sovereign power of this country resides in the *Imperial Parliament* of Great Britain and Ireland. The jurisdiction of this high Court is as extensive as its power is transcendent, and is stretched over every corner, however remote, of the King's dominions. It comprehends Canada as well as Westminister, and New-South Wales as well as Middlesex. Accordingly, it is from this supreme authority that we have derived and accepted our civil and political existence—our judicial and legislative capacity. But the Imperial Parliament has not conferred, and could not confer on a subordinate dependent colony as this is, *all* the sovereign and uncontrolable authority enjoyed by itself. We are therefore bound, as well in duty as allegiance, to exercise the powers actually conferred upon us agreeable to the letter and not beyond the spirit of the deed of conveyance by which we were put in possession of such inestimable rights. We are bound, to look upon ourselves as the executors of a law which we can no more extend nor abridge—alter nor destroy, than a common court of equity can unite legislative to its judicial authority. Neither can we *assume* any right, benefit or privilege further than those expressly conferred upon us. To suppose a Colonial legislature capable of exercising, even if it could inherit, the power and jurisdiction of the Imperial Parliament, would be to suppose a thing which never did, and never can, happen. The mere contemplation of the nature and jurisdiction of parliament will be a convincing proof of this. It has sovereign power and uncontrolable authority in making, confirming, enlarging, restraining, abrogating, repealing, revising and expounding of laws, concerning matters of all possible denominations, ecclesiastical or temporal, civil, military, maritime or criminal; this being the place where that absolute despotick power, which must in all governments reside somewhere, is entrusted by the constitution of these kingdoms. All mischiefs and grievances, operations and remedies, that transcend the ordinary course of the laws, are within the reach of this extraordinary tribunal. It can regulate or new-model the succession to the crown. It can alter the established religion of the land. It can change and even create afresh even the constitution of the kingdom and of parliaments themselves. It can, in short do every thing that is not naturally impossible; and therefore some have not scrupled to call its power, by a figure rather too bold, the omnipotence of parliament.* The laws, customs, and privileges of this great tribunal are equally uncontrolable and extensive! The whole of the

---

*Blackstone, Vol. i. p. 173.

law and custom of parliament, says Blackstone, has its original from this one maxim, "that whatever matter arises concerning either house of parliament, ought to be examined, discussed, and adjudged in that house to which it relates, and not elswhere." As to privileges, the same authority tells us, that they are very large and indefinite." And therefore when in 31 Henry VI. the house of Lords propounded a question to the judges concerning them, the Chief Justice, Sir John Fortescue in the name of his brethren, declared, "that they ought not to make answer to that question; for it hath not been used aforetime that the justices should in any way determine the privileges of the high court of parliament. For it is so high and mighty in its nature, that it may make law; and that which is law, it may make no law; and the determination and knowledge of that privilege belongs to the lords of parliament, and not to the justices." With respect to the jurisdiction of the imperial Parliament, we have already said, that it is as extensive as the empire. It can control, limit, and bind the colonies and their legislatures in any manner most suitable to the welfare and dignity of the nation. And such a government as ours, being of the nature of a civil corporation, has only the power, to use the words of the same author, of making by-laws for their own interior regulation, not contrary to the laws of England; "*and with such rights and authorities as are* Specially *given them in their several Charters of Incorporation.*"

Now, considering the nature, power, and extent of these laws and usages of the imperial Parliament: considering that they are purely incidental to that body; that they are not defined and ascertained by any particolar stated enactment, but "*rest*," to use the words of Blackstone, "*entirely in the breast of the parliament itself*;" and that there exists no code, no statute wherein they may be studied---is it possible to conceive by any stretch of reasoning or analogy, that powers so high and important can either arise of their own accord, or be assumed, *brevi manu*, by the subordinate legislature of any colony whatsoever? This would be usurpation in the highest possible degree, and such an usurpation as no *British* subject could tolerate for a moment. In particular, the laws and privileges of the House of Commons gradually arose with the strength and importance of that body, and were principally created for the purpose of guarding them from the arbitrary power of the throne; and it is a certain fact that the most exceptionable part of the laws and privileges in question, were introduced and asserted by a house of Commons, which abolished both monarchy and peerage together. Are we then, in this province to be subjected to a dark, mysterious, indefinite, arbitrary, and inquisitorial power, merely because the House of Assembly is a body of *similar* parts and functions to those of the house of Commons? Impossible! The commons are a supreme imperial tribunal; but the House of Assembly is a subordinate corporation, subject at all times and in all circumstances to the authority of the imperial Parliament, from which alone it has derived, or can possibly derive its legislative capacity; that capacity, as already observed, being limited and circumscribed by the strictest interpretation that can be put on the charter or constitutional law which creates it. Now we have examined this law—this act of the imperial Parliament—with great minuteness from beginning to end, and the only power which we find it confers on the legislature of this province is, "*to make laws for the* peace, *welfare, and good government thereof, such laws not being* repugnant to *this act*."* It is true, that, when vacancies take place in the Assembly, the Governor or Administrator is empowered to issue writs for new elections; but it is equally true, and the truth is of considerable importance, that these writs can only be issued "*in the case of* any vacancy *which shall happen by the DEATH of the* person chosen, *or by his being summoned* to *the* legislative *council*."† Such a thing as a vacancy caused by the *expulsion of a* member, was never for a moment contemplated. We have seen that the only way in which a seat in the legislative council can be forfeited is by absence, treason or death. So, in the assembly, the only way a vacancy can take place

*Vide Section II. 31 Geo. 3d.
†Vide Section XVIII. 31 Geo. 3d.

is by death or a summons to the Legislative Council. To assume therefore the right of expulsion by a more act of its own, was a stretch of power on the part of the House of Assembly which is at once contrary to the letter, spirit, and intentions of the constitutional act, and destructive of the rights, liberties and franchises of his Majesty's Canadian subjects. It will be in vain to argue, that without privileges and a certain jurisdiction of the nature of a court of judicature, it would be impossible for the Assembly to support its own dignity and authority. But surely no man is so stupid as to conceive that powers and p [illegible] can be *assum*ed by any body of [illegible]out some authority. Surely no *part* of any corporation---and what is the House of Assembly but the part *or branch* of a corporation? can assume any rights that have not been especially given to them without the consent of the *whole*; especially when such assumption of power happens to be prejudicial to the interests of third parties. Can any number of the stockholders of the Montreal and Quebec Banks enact a law excluding any number from a participation in the benefits or profits arising from the operations of the Banks? No! This would not only be punishing the individual, but depriving his relations and creditors of their just rights and demands upon him; and, if it were possible that a law of this kind could exist, it must emanate from the whole, or a majority of the whole, body corporate, under the sanction of the legal tribunals of the country. Here, then, we revert to our original proposition, that, although it be necessary to the preservation of every society to be endowed with powers of self-preservation and a certain jurisdiction over the members of which it is composed, yet it is nevertheless absolutely necessary that such power and jurisdiction should spring and have its origin *from the whole body* of the society, having indubitable right to invest itself with such power and authority. In one word, all we contend for is, that though it is but just and reasonable the assembly should possess some of the powers and privileges which they pretend to, they cannot maintain or exercise them without the sanction of the Imperial Parliament, or an act of the Provincial Legislature.* They cannot take the law into their own hands. They cannot assume this power and waive that one, without the approbation of the whole body politick. As to the laws and privileges of the House of Commons, they cannot usurp them. This would be to suppose themselves possessed of

---

*The Constitution of the United States wisely declares that, "each house may determine the rules of its proceedings, punish its members for disorderly behaviour, *and, with the concurrence of two-thirds, expel a member.*" We do not find any rule of this kind even on the *Journals* of the House of Assembly; far less in the constitutional act. If we did, there could be no dispute on the subject.

the imperial independence of that house, and a branch of the supreme legislature of the state equal in authority, and consequence, instead of a branch of a limited and subordinete corporation. We are therefore firmly and decidedly of opinion, that the House of Assembly have no right to expel a member; and that the expnision of Mr. Christie was arbitrary, illegal and unconstitutional. We know not whether the Governor has signed the writ for a new election for the County of Gaspe; but if he has, we must crave leave to say, that his advisers have misled his Excellency. In similar circumstances his friend, Sir James Henry Craig, acted otherwise; and rather than perform a deed which he conceived to be at once a violation of the constitution and destructive of the rights and franchises of the subject, he *dissolved* the legislature. He could not sign a writ for which there was no provision in the constitutional Charter. His words are memorable: "*Gentlemen, I cannot, dare not render myself a partaker in the violation of an act of the Imperial Parliament; and I know no other way by which I can avoid becoming so, but that which I am pursuing.*" But whether a writ has been issued or not, the people of Gaspe are not bound to proceed to another election. They have been illegally and arbitrarily disfranched by a mere resolution of the House of Assembly, when there was no power on earth that could inflict such a punishment upon them, except an act of the Imperial Parliament, or an act of the provin cial legislature, sanctioned and approved by his Majesty or his Majesty's representative. If, therefore, men of Gaspe! you have a drop of *British* blood beating in your veins —if you have a spark of *British* freedom in your souls—if you detest from your hearts, as I know you do, the idea of being slaves to an usurping and tyrannical house of Assembly—if you wish to secure to your children and their posterity the rights and privileges of Britons, do not proceed to a new election! We warn you of the consequences! If you do, you will extend your sanction and become active participators in one of the most wicked and despotick acts that over disgraced any Legislature. Again, we conjure you to beware of the consequences. Stand by your rights. Petition both the Imperial and Provincial Legislatures. Tell them boldly that you have been illegally disfranchised by an usurping and factious Assembly; and that you wish to be reinstated to the rights and immunities secured to you by the constitution; and that, as that constitutien now stands, you will never acknowledge the authority of any power to deprive you of a voice in the laws of your country. Know you not that the house of Assembly cannot proceed to business without a member from Gaspe? You are of more consequence to the councils of the province than you are perhaps aware of. Use it, therefore, and depend upon it that you will discomfit all your enemics. In 1820, the house of Assembly unanimously resolved, "that the representation of the province being incomplete, no member having as yet been returned for Gaspe, the house was incompetent, and could not proceed to the despatch of business." You can thus suspend the whole legislative business of the country; and you will be cowards and cravens unless you do so until you be placed in the same condition in which you stood previous to the expulsion of your representative. Above all, do not proceed to another election, and you shall have the thanks and gratitude of the country for having settled a constitutional point of the highest importance to yourselves and posterity.

II. But granting, for the sake of argument, that the house of assembly had been fully competent to expel Mr. Christie by a mere vote and resolution of their own, we maintain that there was no good or solid cause for doing so. The delinquency that exposes a man to the contempt and ridicule of the world must be great indeed; that which serves to banish him from a society supposed to be the first in the country for pre-eminence, talent and respectability, ought to be of such a nature as not only to be clearly and satisfactorily proved in the minds of impartial judges, but to be almost next to unpardonable. But what are the facts of the case before us? We have already seen, towards the conclusion of the late administration, how necessary it became to purify the commission of the peace by leaving out the names of those who had characterized them selves as the enemies of the peace and welfare of the province instead of what the laws intended they should be, its best patrons and protectors. On that occasion the chairmen of the Quarter Sessions in the three Districts, the judges, and, we believe, other respectable individuals connected with the government, were directed to give in lists of such individuals as they conceived sufficiently qualified, by rank and conduct, to execute the duties of justices of the peace. On the 2d of June, 1827; Mr. Christie, as Chairman of the Quarter Sessions of the District of Quebec, received written instructions through the Civil Secretary of the Governor to prepare his list. On the 8th of the same month the list was accordingly prepared and given in. On the 5th of July following, the legislature was dissolved by proclamation. On the 14th of August, Mr. Christie, formerly law-clerk to the Assembly, was returned as representative for the County of Gaspe, and, on the 20th of November appeared in the house and voted. On the 15th of February, 1828, the commission of the peace was issued; and the names of certain members of Assembly, formerly justices, were not found recorded therein.* On the 21st of November, 1829, the legislature met again; and the Committee of the house of Assembly appointed to inquire into the qualification of justices of the peace, were instructed to dive

*We are indebted for these facts to the Quebec Mercury of the 21st March, 1829.

deep into the late dismissals, not only because three of their own members, who always voted against government, were amongst them, but because Mr. Christie had become extremely obnoxious to the house, in consequence of having, in the previous session of *two days*, voted with the minority against the legality of Mr. Papineau's election as Speaker. This committee, more fond of tattles which administered to their malice and revenge, than real information, discovered through some week witnesses, who had no more idea of the dignity of conduct or the propriety of manners due to the situation in which they stood than a sucking pig in a canvass sack, that Mr. Christie had a hand in the dismissals in question; and that he even boasted of having been the means of excluding unsound and seditious members from the commission of the peace. This was enough for the committee: they held him "by the hip," they thought, and now let slip the bloody dogs of war upon their devoted victim. The tattles and the *badinage* which were given in evidence before the committee were carried triumphantly to the house in a report. The joy was now universal. Mr. Christie presented a petition, setting forth the injustice that had been done to him as a member of the house by the ex parte nature of the proceedings adopted against him---offering to prove the falsity of the evidence adduced to his prejudice---and craving a fair trial before the house. But tongue had been given; blood had already been tasted, and nothing could stop or quell the eagerness of the sportsmen in pursuit of their game. The petition was declared false, contumelious and vexatious, and an attack "*against*" the honour and privileges of the house. A string of seventeen resolutions were then introduced by *Saint Vallieres*, giving a full and true account of the shocking crimes, delinquencies, and misdemeanours of the said Robert Christie, the cream of which is as follows :

2. That Robert Christie, Esq. a member of this House, being Chairman of the Quarter Sessions for the District of Quebec, was com*man*ded by his Excellency, the Earl of Dalhousie, Governor in Chief of this Province, in the course of the year 1827, to prepare and lay before him a list of those persons whom it should to him appear advisable to appoint to the office of Justice of the Peace, by the new General Commission of the Peace for the said District.

4. That the said Robert Christie, intenti*o*nall*y*, left out of the said list by him made, the names of Francois Quirouet, John Neilson, Francis Blanchet and Jean Bolanger, Esqrs. who had been for many years, and then were Justices of the Peace for the District of Quebec *and members of this House*, for the purpose of causing them to be deprived of the Office of Justice of the Peace, on account of their opinions and the votes they had given in this House.

10. That in consequence of the List prepared by the said Robert Christie, the said

Francois Quirouet, John Neilson, and Francois Blanchet, Members of this House, were dismissed from the office of Justice of the Peace, by the last commission of the Peace, now in force, in and for the District of Quebec, without any other cause than their opinions and votes in the House, and that such is the *public rumour* and notoriety founded *chiefly* on the declaration and language of the said Robert Christie, as well before, as after the said dismissals.

11. That the said Robert Christie, at the time he prepared the said List and advised the Governor in Chief to the said dismissals, was one of the Members of this House, after having been before and up to that time, one of the confidential officers of this House.

15. That the said Robert Christie is guilty of high crimes and misdemeanors, and is unworthy the confidence of His Majesty's Government.

16. That the said Robert Christie, is guilty of a high contempt of this House, and is unworthy to serve or to have a seat as a member thereof.

17. That the said Robert Christie be expelled this House.

Now, all this may sound very well, and may seem very fine to the Assembly, who had evidently no other object than to gratify their revenge by the expulsion of Mr. Christie. But men, especially individuals composing a branch of the legislature, ought to be consistent in their conduct as well as impartial in their judgments. By reference to the second resolution it will be found that Mr. Christie was "*commanded*" to make out the list in question. It was surely therefore, discretionary with him to name *any one* who might appear to him advisable for filling the office of justice of the peace; and will any being, of sense or generosity, say, that a member of the House of Assembly ought to be expelled, and his constituents disfranchised during a whole session of the provincial legislature, *for the mere exercise of an opinion*. Not only Mr. Christie, but every loyal subject in the country, is ready to declare that the individuals dismissed, to say the least of them, were very unfit persons to be entrusted with the King's peace; seeing that they took every opportunity to disturb and encroach upon it in furtherance of their party and political views. But what, in reality, has Mr. Christie or the Assembly to do with these dismissals? Even if Mr. C. had, and we have no doubt he has, positively and pointedly recom*mended* these dismissals, the *act* was not his. It flowed from a higher source, and, if illegal, which we deny, that source alone is responsible for the consequences. But absolutely, this is neither *crime* nor misdemeanour, and is merely an exercise of the judgment, or recom*mendation* at most, over which the most immaculate tribunal can hold no jurisdiction. In the House of Commons, nothing can incapacitate a member but the complaint of a *crime* and proof thereof. Walpole, Sir Richard Steel, and Wilkes, were all accused and proven to have been guilty of *crimes* both at common law and customs of parliament. But by what law either of the province or the legislature, is the charge against Mr. Christie construed or magnified into a *crime?* The Justices of the peace in England are appointed on the recom*mendation* of the Lords Lieutenant of Counties, the Lord Chancellor, and other great officers of the state. It very often happens that in new commissions old justices of the peace are left out and others put in. Has the house of Commons ever expelled a member for any opinion as to who, or who should not be included in the commission of the peace. The king can entrust his peace to whomsoever he pleases; and we maintain, that when the Commons pretend to a voice in the nomination of officers of justice, as has been done in the present case, the rights and prerogatives of the Crown will have been annihilated and the constitution destroyed. But supposing the conduct of Mr. Christie to have been criminal, we maintain with equal pertinacity, that the *present* assembly have no jurisdiction in the case, and that they are incompetent to take cognizance of delinquencies committed by any members of the *last* assembly, there having been a dissolution and a new election. The case of Mr. Christie is still more clear, because when the offence was committed *he was not a member of any Assembly*. It will be observed that is stated in the 11th resolution "*that the said* Robert Christie, *at the time he prepared the said list*, was one of the members of this House." Now, this is a gross and palpable falsehood; for we have seen that the list was prepared and given in on the 8th of June, 1827; whereas the *election* of Mr. Christie did not take place till the 14th of August following! The Assembly have therefore stretched and extended their authority beyond its natural bounds, even if legitimate; and no one can be at a loss to conceive the amount of the injustice which has been done to Mr. Christie and his constituents, in order to gratify that spirit of revenge and vindictiveness which has for some time characterized the proceedings of the Assembly. We warn the province to be on its guard against the assumption of powers and privileges which would prostrate the rights and liberties of the subject at the feet of an arrogant and overbearing Assembly. The fact is, that the Assembly have no privileges or jurisdiction whatever, and can never have, until they are given by the supreme tribunal of the state, or enjoyed in virtue of an act of the three branches of the provincial legislature. Let us not therefore be robbed and chained by mere resolutions of the Assembly, otherwise the time cannot be distant when our lives and property will be entirely at their disposal, to the exclusion of the voice of the other constitutional branches of the legislature. During the last session the Governor declared in a Message to the Assembly, that he was instructed not to sanction the payment of any sum of money for whatever purpose, without an act of the legislature. In the name of Freedom and of Justice, what is a paltry sum of a few hundred, or a few thousand pounds in comparison to the rights and franchises of British Subjects. How is it possible, then, that an act, like the expulsion of Mr. Christie, characterized as it has been by the grossest outrage and violence, and wherein the most sacred deposits of a free constitution are involved, can be enforced without a similar proceeding. If a vote or Resolution of the Assembly be not good for a hundred pounds, surely it cannot be of sufficient authority to expel an innocent individual, and deprive his constituents of his services. This is a point of view in which this subject ought to be seriously considered, and we now call alike upon government and people to withstand any attempts of a similar nature that may be made to ruin and enslave us. As for Mr. Christie, we are surprised that he has submitted in such silence and meekness to the injury that the Constitution has sustained through him. We are surprised that he has at all submitted to the *dictum* of the House of Assembly. We are surprised that he and his constituents have not long before now united in a petition to the supreme tribunal of the empire, and solicited justice in a cause not only clear and just, but in which the whole British nation is interested. We are surprised that he has not made the country ring with his grievances, and introduced the house of Assembly to the world in their true characters of arbitrary and despotic tyrants. If any thing that we have said will lead to such an issue, our reward shall have been perfected, and the object of these observations fully attained.

This seems to be a proper place for introducing all that we have to say, which is only one word on the subject of the resolutions and address of the House of Assembly to the Governor for abolishing the office of Chairman of the Quarter Sessions in the several Districts of the province, merely because their opinions sometimes clash with junior magistrates more subservient to the views and prejects of the house of Assembly than the Chairmen happen to be. We rejoice that the Governor showed no disposition to acquiesce in this fanatick and factions request. The business of the Quarter Sessions, which, except in cases of life and death, is fully as important as the criminal side of the court of King's Bench, could never be carried on with credit to the state or safety to the subject without the aid of Chairmen well versed in the criminal law of the province: We question whether twelve lay justices can be found in the whole country capable of charging a petit jury as to the distinctions between a common and justifiable assault, or between a riot and an affray. While therefore the province is destitute of men of sufficient leisure and independence to take upon themselves the whole duty of the magisterial bench without fee or reward, the Chairmen of the Quarter Sessions must be continued in their situations; and to leave the magistracy of such a country as this with-out head or guide would be like depriving a flock of sheep of their shepherd. But besides being chairmen of the Quarter Sessions, the Magistrates who fill those stations, are also the Police Magistrates of their several Districts, for which they receive no extra remuneration; and no one will say, that *this* is an office which any magistrate would take upon himself without a regular salary, even were the duties of a more agreeable nature than they really are, and the province capable of affording the necessary leisure and talent. We trust therefore that this is a subject which will not be repeated, and that the government is alive to the folly and danger of yielding up to the Assembly an office which they hate because it is useful, and despise because it is filled by men of too much loyalty and integrity to be partizans of the demagogues of the Assembly. The abolition of the situation of Chief Justice of the Court of King's Bench would be attended with far less difficulties and danger, because all the puisne judges are lawyers, and by consequence fully adequate to the duties of their station without the aid or direction of the Chief Justice. We give the Resolutions of the Assembly on this subject in a note, in order to shew the futile and general grounds on which they found charges of the gravest nature against individuals of the highest respectability, and the sweeping nature of all their innovations.

No one who has paid any attention to the

perseverance and pertinacity with which the Assembly have always sought the possession of what has been termed the *Jesuits' Estates*, could doubt for a moment that such a session as the late one could pass without some steps being taken in furtherance of the great object in view. Accordingly a Resolution was passed, as the foundation of an Address to the Governor, setting forth, that the house having during the present session voted considerable sums for the encouragement of learning and learned establishments, nothing could be more just and reasonable on the part of his Majesty than to place at the disposal of "his faithful commons of Lower Canada the estate of the late order of Jesuits, to be applied to the purpose for which it was *originally* destined, in order that the income arising therefrom may be applied to the purposes of encouraging and diffusing education in this province. Really nothing can be more *Jesuitical* than the frequency, character and object of the efforts of the Assembly with respect to the estates in question; for, ever since the commencement of the constitution to the present day, they have not failed to make an *annual* attack upon the rights of the crown to these estams; the first address being voted on the 11th of April, 1793. One would think that the disinclination of his Majesty to listen to these importunate mendicant requests, and his determination not to yield up these estates to the Assembly, confirmed by a positive refusal of nearly forty years' standing, would be sufficient to prevail upon the Assembly to desist from further supplication. But it would appear as a standing maxim of this body, that neither right nor favour can be too great to be solicited, and that, when once asked, no concession can be justly refused. In truth, this seems to be the maxim of all those to whom too much has been conceded. The proverb of the beggar on horseback is well known. The estates of the Jesuits produce some small funds: these funds the Assembly are desirous of having the possession and disposal of, because they have long thought that all the other publick revenue of the province has already been consigned into their hands. This is not the case, however; and as long as the 14th of the King, and the rights of Crown exist, we hope there is not an individual in the country who is so much a villain as to advise a concession that would plunge this province into irretrievable ruin and destruction.

The Assembly have foolishly enough imagined, that, because the Jesuit Missionaries sent to Canada took upon themselves the education of a few Canadian illegitimate children and some young savages, the lands which were given to them were destined to defray the expense of such education. This is a proposition than which nothing can be more preposterous; and if we can shew that the Jesuits did not and could not hold any real property in Canada, we think it will be an easy matter to prove that the "*original destination*" of the estates in question could not be for the purposes of education, and consequently, having become vested in his Majesty by *right of conquest*, his Majesty may dispose of them as he thinks proper. In fact his Majesty has hitherto done so; and although he has deemed it neither wise nor prudent too throw the produce of the lands of the Jesuits into the voracious maw of the Assembly, he has graciously and generously left it in the province to be disposed of, towards the encouragement of education and other charitable establishments, by heads as wise and hearts fully as compassionate as those of a self-sufficient and arrogant popular Assembly.

Our first and best authority on this important question is Sir *James Marriott*, whose able and profound arguments we shall make use of instead of our own; being assured that any one who peruses them will be convinced of the insolence and folly of the claims of the Assembly. These arguments will be found in a letter from this able civilian to the Attorney and Solicitor General* of England in May, 1765, on a reference by the Earl of Halifax, his Majesty's principal secretary of state, of the case of the Jesuits in Canada.

"Besides the Jesuits of the less observance, who are to be found in every part of the world, concealed agents of the society, laymen as well as priests, persons who have been married as well as those who have

*Messrs. Norton and De Grey.

never married, and of all conditions and employments of life, (the whole order amounting to twenty thousand men in the year 1710, and since increased in proportion to the enterprising genius of that society in the course of half a century) the known communities of the Jesuits in Canada were the Missions. The Missions were properly speaking, draughts from the houses of the professed; (agreeably to the plan of this order, founded by a military man upon military principles)—they are engaged by the fourth vow to go to any part of the world where the Pope or his General shall send them, *non petitio viatico*. The missions are so called in their institute in distinction to the houses of the professed, and from the houses of the noviciates and colleges. The missions, like the professed are all under a vow of poverty, and mendicants by institution, and, as the professed hold estates in trust for the noviciates and colleges, and the rest of the society, having nothing for themselves, otherwise than indirectly, (for they never beg notwithstanding their institute) so the missions, who are detached from the professed, hold estates in the same manner. If the estates are donations, then they are held for such uses as the founders, by grant, gift or devise, shall have directed and for such other uses as the father-general shall direct; inasmuch as all donations are constantly accepted by the order, and ratified by the General, with this special salvo, commonly known and supposed to be acquiesced in by the douors or their representatives, *ita tamen ut in omnibus institutii ratio servetur.* And if the estates are acquired by purchase out of the surplus of the funds destined *ad libitum* by the general for the support of the colleges out of the profits arising from commerce or personal industry, then the missions hold these estates for the benefit of the whole society, wheresoever dispersed over the whole world, but united under one sovereign head domiciled at Rome, whose power over his whole order being unlimited he is the sole proprietor, and, as it were the heart of the whole body, into which and from which, all propparty has a constant flux and reflux by a circulation of the system in all its parts. So that the estate of the society must be considered in the possession of *one man*, the general of the order, who is always by birth an Italian, an actual subject ecclesiastical and civil of the Roman pontiff; upon whom he acknowledges a kind of feudal dependence rather than an implicit obedience, (the father-general having sometimes resisted,) and being in some respects independent, even of papal authority being in all other relations an absolute sovereign over his own vassals, who are independent of every civil Government under which they reside; to which they cannot be united in a civil essence by nature of their institute, without ceasing to be what their institute makes them, a distinct nation in the midst of nations, and an empire in the midst of empires. As all other regulars, according to the canon law, are servants of their monastery, so the individuals of the society of Jesuits, according to their institute are the servants or rather slaves of their order and according to the rule of law, by which quid *quid acquiritur servo acquiritur domino, they have no property at all.*

"It is remarkable, that the order, (of which the province of France makes but a very small part) has been only tolerated provisionally in that kingdom, and upon probation of good behaviour, without ever having had any legal complete establishment as a part of the ecclesiastical and civil constitution of the realm. The general of the order has constantly refused the conditions of the original admission made by the acts of the Assembly at Poisey of the Gallican Church, and has also refused the conditions of the re-admission of the society on the same terms after their expulsion, (which te-admission was granted by the royal edict in virtue of a treaty between the crown of France and the papal see) because the terms of re-admission were radically subversive of the whole order. To the original acts of admission all subsequent edicts in their favour have had a retrospect. So that the *arret* of expulsion remained always liable to execution; and the membars of the order were merely as inmates, occupants of houses and lands in France, and in the extent of the dominions of that crown, subject to resumption.

"From all these premises it seems conclusive that the *titles* of the society passed, together with the dominions ceded to Great Britain, (in which dominions these possessions were situated) attended with no better qualification than the titles had by the laws and constitutions of the realm of France, previous to the conquest and cessions of those countries. But it seems further to be clear, that those titles are now in a worse condition since the conquest and cession: for *till* that period they were only in abeyance, and suspended upon a principle of probationary toleration; but by virtue of the natural law of arms and conquest of countries, confirmed by acts of the law of nations, by solemn cession and guaranty, the possessions of the society lost of course all civil protection by the fate of war; but much more so by the only power, whose authority and intervention could have preserved the property of these possessions to their supposed owners, having withdrawn its tolerance and protection, and deserted them, as a derelict at the mercy and entirely free disposition of the Crown of Great Britain, by making no provision in the articles of cession to serve the pretended rights of the community of Jesuits; nor indeed of any other ecclesiastical community, which latter might have been under a more favourable view, having civil being, and each house possessing a separate property, distinct from others of the same order; whereas the order of Jesuits, contrary to all other regulars, is one indivisible order, aggregate indeed by its own institute, but not incorporated by the laws of France;

and the father-general never having been an inhabitant of Canada, nor a subject of the King of France, he could not retire and avail himself of the fourth article of the definitive treaty, nor sell his estates, nor withdraw his effects within the time limited. In a few words the society of Jesuits hàd not and cannot have any estate in Canada, legally and complately vested in them *at any time* and therefore could not and cannot transfer the same before nor after the term of eighteen months, so as to make a good title to purchasers, either with or without the powers or ratification of the father-general, who, as he could not retire, so he cannot retain any possessions in Canada, since the time limited for the sales of estates there, agreeably to the terms of the treaty; because he is as incapable of becoming a British subject as he was of becoming a French subject; nor can the individuals of the communities of the Jesuits in Canada take or transfer what the father general cannot take or transfer; nor can they, having but one common stock with all other communities of their order, in every part of the globe, hold immoveable possessions, to be applied for the joint benefit of those communities which are resident in foreign states; and which may become the enemies of his Majesty and his government.

"Whoever the persons are who occupy the possessions in question, they must be understood to hold the same as trustees for the head and members of the one indivisible society, and political body of Jesuits, of ecclesiastical and temporal union, forming according to their institute, one church and monarchical government, with territorial jurisdiction independent of all civil authorities under which the members of the society are occasionally dispersed, and without stability of domicil; and that such trusts are therefore, from the very nature of this institution, inadmissible by the law of nations and of all civil governments; they are void both in law and in fact, because there is no legal corporate body civilly established to take the use; but an alien sovereign, and aliens his subjects, who were and are utterly incapable, by the very nature of their institute, of any civil existence. The possessions, therefore, of the society of Jesuits in Canada, in every view of the case, are lapsed to his Majesty by right of conquest and acquired sovereignty; by dereliction of the supreme power itself of whose good pleasure the possessions were lately held, no provision having been made by them for it in the act of cession; by the want of an original complete title in a body incapable of legal taking, holding, and transferring; by the nature of defective trusts founded upon such defective titles; and by the non compliance of the order with the provisional terms of their readmission, as probationary occupants, only *pro tempore*, into the dominions of France, domiciled in the person of their father general at Rome, subject to the execution and effect of the *arret* which was passed by the original tribunals for their expulsion in 1594, to which they are still liable, for never having observed, but openly rejected the conditions of their first admission, which are the conditions of the second, and farther are liable, *ipso facto*, whenever they should be hurtful and dangerous to the realm.

"The distinction which the Jesuits have endeavoured to set up, between the Colleges and the order, is neither supported by fact, nor by the institute of the society. For it appears from all the foregoing proofs of their institute, that there is one chain of dependence; that the Colleges are not distinct as communities from the body; that the professed Religious hold in trust for the Colleges; and, therefore, the conclusion is, that if according to their own confession the Religious of the order of Jesuits are not received as persons capable of a civil existence, they are incapable of the Trusts, and then the Colleges are incapable of the uses. Thus every thing built upon the foundation of this anomalous society, falls to the ground together. And it is no wonder, that an institution which seems contrived, with a subtlety more than human, to subvert the laws of every country ecclesiastical and civil, should find in the laws of every country an obstacle to its establishment."

Now, these are arguments which the Assembly will not and cannot comprehend. But education is not the real object of the Assembly, but money and power for party-purposes, as may readily be perceived by any who has paid the least attention to the factions cupidity, with which they have ever pursued every scheme caculated to give force or weight to that exclusive system of government which they have so long aimed at. The refusal of his majesty to renounce all control over the estates of the Jesuits, formed a prominent feature in the petitions of grievance presented last year to the King and parliament; and the petitioners had the singular audacity to draw a parallel between "*la munificence des Rois de* France"—the munificence of the Kings of France—in giving away these estates, and the stuborn parsimony of his Britannick Majesty in withholding them from their original destination." This, we think, was carrying the freedom of petitioning as far as it could decently be carried: and, without waiting to express an opinion of conduct so gross and insulting, we beg leave to ask the Canada Committee, as it has been called, on what grounds they have presumed to recommend the surrender of the Jesuits' estates, while they admitted and "lamented that they had not more full information?" As we do not think that the Canada Committee will be able to give a satisfactory answer to this or any other rational question that may be put to them from this side of the Atlantick, we shall conclude this part of our subject by merely observing, that as the Jesuits could at no period, and under no civil government hold any immoveable property in Canada with any kind of destination, and, at all events, as their lands become vested in the King by right of conquest, so his Majesty and his government will do well never to surrender these lands to the Assembly until, by the cultivation of different sentiments upon this and a variety of other questions, they prove themselves worthy of a trust the value and importance of which they do not at present seem to comprehend.

In the same resolution the Assembly pray "His Excellency to take into his serious consideration the *alarms* excited among the inhabitants by the report spread abroad on subject of the property of the Church of St. Sulpice, at Montreal, which tended to create a belief, that the property which this establishment has quietly enjoyed under his Majesty's government, for more than sixty years, might pass into other hands." This is, indeed, great cause of alarm to such a body as the house of Assembly, who cannot conceive why any establishment supposed subservient to themselves, however bad their title, should be disturbed, even the length of giving offence to prejudices the most rooted and bigoted. We maintain that the Church of St. Sulpice has already remained too long in the undisturbed possession of property which does not, and never did, of right, belong to it; and, if not positively dangerous, nothing can be more blighting so the real happiness and posterity of a state especially a commercial one like ours, than extensive territorial property being held by ecclesiastical communities. Bodies of this description ought never to be allowed to possess property, except for the maintenance of their own sacred institutions; for, to say not a word of its incongruity, nothing can be more detrimental to the rights and energies of an enterprising secular people than the shackles of religious communities. There can be no sympathy between them. The one is grasping the other free and generous: and nothing can possibly reconcile them but a separation bounded by a just distinction of their individual avocations and pursuits. Montreal has suffered much, both in wealth and prosperity from the pretended Seignorial supremecy of the Church of St. Sulpice; and the sooner that supremacy is withdrawn and placed in the legitimate possession of his Majesty, the better for all parties, and the country at large. No clashing is so harsh as that of clerical and secular interests when they relate to matters of this world; and it behooves every good christian and citizen to avoid it. It is this that has brought so much misery on mankind; but we hope the conflict is over. Ancient Rome was destroyed by faction and tyranny: modern Rome by avarice and bigotry. We believe the church of St. Sulpice herself is not unwilling to resign any pretensions that she may have had to secular property in the island of Montreal; at any rate, the candour and liberality with which she has entered into negotiations with his Majesty's government on this subject, do her infinite honour. It would be well for the interests of the province at large if the house of assembly possessed one grain of her meekness christain forbearance and magnanimity. If this were the case we should not be under the necessity of combating, as we are now about to do, the unfounded pretensions gratuitously set up by the Assembly on the part of the church to the property in question. Our arguments we shall draw from the same source as those with respect to the estates of the Jesuits; and, we have no doubt, with equal success as to the result.

"It seems to be pretty clear, says *Marriott*, in his plan of a code of laws for the province of Canada, that any religious communities, who, as principals at the time of the conquest, were not *Inhabitants*, resident in person, do not fall under the privilege of the Capitala*tion*, nor come within what is termed by the civilians, the *casus fœdris*, so as to retain the property of their estates under it; because they were not then the local objects to whom, as a personal consideration for ceasing their resistance and on account of their particular courage or distresses, the conquerors granted terms of special favour; neither could they retire according to the treaty and if they could not retire, they could not take away their persons and estates; therefore, if it is true in fact, that any estates are now held under the grants of foreign religious communities, either in under tenancy, or in trust for them, or by deputation such as the Jesuits and the *Ecclesiastics of the Seminary at St. Sulpice at Paris*, that fact is very important. The community of the latter are the temporal lords of the most fertile part of

Canada, and a city dedicated to the Virgin Mary ; they have an influence there equal to the power of the Italian Clergy in the state of the Church or *campagna di Roma*.

"The parishes in the isle of Montreal and its dependencies, says *Charlevoix*, are still upon the ancient footing of moveable priests, and under directions of the members of St. Sulpice. They possess a fine and improving estate of eight thousand pounds sterling a year at Montreal, and which will in a few years be worth ten thousand pounds. If all the facts are clearly established, as stated, it is a great question of law, whether these estates are not now fallen to your Majesty, of whom the under-tenants and possessors must be intended to hold them *as trustees*, for such uses as your Majesty shall declare.

"It is in proof by several deeds of estates, (it is immaterial whether before or after the conquest) that the religious living in the seminary of Montreal are merely *negotiorum gestores*; they are so described in several instruments of conveyance, which Mr. Mazeres has perused in the course of business. The conveyers are said to be *Fondez de la procuration de Messieurs les Ecclesiastiques du Seminaire de St. Sulpice a Paris*. It appears according to Mr. Lothbiniere's own words, that before the conquest the seminary of St. Sulpice at Paris, was a voluntary partnership among a number of clergy at Paris, who had engaged together in buying and selling ; that the joint house at Monreal had a share in the joint house at Paris, in a sort of mercantile way and an open account. That after the conquest they dissolved the partnership, because the house at Paris could not have any right after the conquest in the effects and estates in Canada; they at Paris (says Mr. L.) transferred (what therefore they could not transfer, having at that period, as he admits, no property in the estate, and only a share) the whole in Montreal to the religious there, who probably were not (vraisemblablement, says Mr. Lethbiniere,) attornies of those at Paris; and this was done by the latter upon paying a compensation, being the difference of the account upon a balance. This, after all, is *oui dire*, as he says he has heard and believes; and it stands against the evidence of Mr. Mazeres, if it were contradictory; but it approves manifestly, that the Religious at Montreal have only a coloured and ostensible title. There is also the evidence of a gentleman of undoubted veracity and knowledge, who having had transactions with father Magnilphi, the person acting in the colony for the community of St. Sulpice at Paris, with a view to some purchase, the real proprietors were forced to come forward, and the uncertainty of the title broke off the negotiation. The evidence of Charlevoix also may be added. In 1657, says he, the Abbe Quelus returned with the deputies of the seminary of St. Sulpice at Paris, to take possession of the island of Montreal, and to found a seminary there. By the French law it is clear, that no persons, aliens not being naturalized can hold lands ; so that by right of conquest, agreeable to Mr. Lotbbiniere's own idea, for want of owners domiciled at the time of the conquest, these estates may be understood in point of law to *be fallen to the Crown in right of* Sovereignty.

We have thus, we think, also made out a clear and strong case against the Assembly so far as respects their pretended right of superintendence over the Church or Seminary of St. Sulpice at Montreal. We have proved, that whatever the "alar*m*," of the Assembly may be in consequence of the "*reports* spread abroad," in relation to this subject the crown has a just right both by conquest and inheritance not only to enter into any negotiations that it may think proper with the present occupiers of the temporal property of the seminary, but to assume the actual possession of that property with as little delay as the forms of legal proceedings can admit of. When this is done, the Assembly will find how vain and weak it is in them to presume to arbitrate gratuitously in every matter and thing in which the rights of the Crown, or the interests of the subject may be concerned. This, perhaps, is one of those claims which Sir George Murray does not conceive ought to be yielded to the Assembly or their adherents. At least, *we* have no doubt it will be found to be so in the long run.

Connected with this subject are the Resolutions* voted by the Assembly with res-

---

*The House in Committee passed the fol-

pect to the waste lands of the crown in the neighbourhood and District of Three-Rivers. These lands, but especially that part

---

lowing resolutions, which were reported to the House and concurred in, and an address voted to His Excellency founded on them.

Resolved, 1. That throughout the greater part of the tract of country on the north side of the River St. Lawrence, extending from about five leagues above, to about five leagues below the town or borough of Three-Rivers, the lands conceded, settled, and partly under cultivation, be within the distance of one league or less from the said river, reckoning from the bank thereof to the rear of the said lands, and that the concessions extend to a somewhat greater distance only in the fiefs and seignores of Tonnancour or Point du Lac, of Cap Magdeleine and Champlain.

2. That the tract of country on the north side of the river lying in the rear of the lands now conceded, settled, and partly cultivated in the vicinity of Three-Rivers and in the seignores aforesaid, there is found immediately adjacent a tract of land of more than sixty square leagues, which would be susceptible of being cleared, cultivated, and settled, if it were conceded to the inhabitants and actual settlers of the vicinity of Three-Rivers, who have for a long time past prayed for grants of land in the said tract, and who have up to the present time vainly endeavoured to obtain them.

3. That the obstacles presented to the set-

of them comprised in the lease of the Forges of St. Maurice, seem a great eyesore to the

---

tlement and cultivation of this tract of land have essentially impeded the progress of industry, and above all that of agriculture in the district of Three Rivers, and of the resources of the town or borough of Three Rivers in particular.

4. That one of the most powerful of these obstacles is the great extent of land, comprised in the lease of the Forges of St. Maurice.

5. That it is necessary to take immediate steps for the removal of the obstacle to the granting and clearing of this tract.

6. That it would be expedient to adopt measures to promote the settlement of that portion of the Province lying north of Quebec, now under the name of the King's posts, now uncultivated, by making grants to actual settlers, and for the purpose of encouraging free trade and industry therein.

Mr. Viger, reported the following answer from His Excellency to the address on the subject of the waste and unconceded lands in the leases of the Forges of St. Maurice and King's Posts:

Gentlemen :—Having every desire to promote the cultivation and improvement of the province, you will assure the House of Assembly that my attention shall be given to the removal (as far as may depend on me,) of any impedimonts that may appear to me to exist to the formation of new settlements

House of Assembly. But the reason is obvious. Perhaps the Assembly conceive that their electioneering influence is not sufficiently extensive in that part of the country. Yet, without having recourse to the *Almanack*, we believe that the Solicitor General is the only Constitutional member returned by *Three Rivers*. But this is enough! The House has often felt the weight of Mr. Ogden's metal: it has too long been writhing under it; and too frequently bleached from the force of his opposition and raillery. We are not, however, sufficiently acquainted with the village politicks of that part of the province to enable us to go into details. It is enough for us to know, that nothing which the art, the intrigue or the perseverance of a faction can effect will be left untried by the Assembly in order to gain possession of all the influence and power vested by the Constitution and the rights of conquest in the crown. The resolutions set forth, that there is a great scarcity of land in the neighbourhood of Three Rivers, and that nothing has tended more to impede the progress of industry and agriculture in the District of Three Rivers than the obstacles presented to the settlement of the crown-lands, but in particular those comprised in the lease of the Forges. Now, nothing can be more absurd and

---

in the tracts of land mentioned in this Address.

Castle of St. Lewis,
March 3d, 1829.

ill-founded than such a statement. Compare for a moment the amount of the population of the District in question with the extent of its territory, and you will see at a glance, that, were the pepulation a hundred times more than it is, there would be bu ndequate and sufficient quantity of lands without any interference with the crown-lands and those belonging to the Forges, which is a mere bagatelle comparitively speaking. Look abroad towards the Townships and behold the vast extent of unconceded territory lying waste and idle there. But the *crowded* population of Three Rivers will not travel so far; the *English* language is spoken there; the roads are too bad, and that Demon of the woods, Judge Fletcher, will immolate on the altar of justice every man who does not properly respect the laws! Oh no! The Canadians must have lands at their doors whenever they want them; they must not—they cannot leave the old seignioral neighbourhood; they must have the *ancient tenure* and *les secours de la Religion*,* and the cures themselves, like true pastrol guardians cannot consent to a separation from their flocks, as any one who peruses their letters to the special committee of the House of Assembly on the crown lands will clearly see. Do any of the labouring classes go and establish themselves in the Townships conceded in free and cemmen soccage, and if they do

*Vide Letters des cures printed by the Assembly in 1823.

not, to what cause do you attribute it?" say the Assembly. "Many of my young men," answers the cure of St. Anne, "go and establish themselves in the seigniories of the Districts of Montreal and Three Rivers; but I know of none who have established themselves in the Townships. This I attribute, in my humble opinion, to two principal reasons, first, because of the distance they would find themselves from religious assistance (*les* secours *de la Religion*;) and, secondly, because of the tenure and conditions of the concessions in free and common soccage!" The cure of St. Joachin, after alluding to the utter privation in the Townships of all religious assistance, says "because, as things are there, they could not have a Catholic establishment; but it would not be so, were these crown lands conceded in *Fiefs*." The Cure of Narville reports, that many are afraid of taking lands in the Townships "*from the dread of expatriating themselves.* The words which a Cure of the name of *Painchaud* puts into the mouth of his people are remarkable: "It is christian prudence thus to expose the *salvation* of our children?—It is notorious that every advantage is for the Protestants, and every disadvantage for us; let us no longer be told that the Government is just and Impartial!" The Cure of St. Roch des Aulents says, "We should have to submit to pass our whole life among Strangers, brought up differently from ourselves, and possessing a different religion from ours." "We would rather see our children chanya *poor*, or at a great distance from us, if only settled in a Seigniorie, than to see them loaded with riches in the midst of such dangers to their *education* and *religion*." "The Canadians will not settle in the Townships," says the Cure of St. Genieve, "until they can be assured of having French Canadians for neighbours, with whom they could freely communicate." The Cure of Boucherville says, "that the Canadians must not be *drowned* among too great a number of *Strangers*." The Cure of St. Leon speaks boldly and without reserve. Alluding to the times previous to the conquest, "he characterizes them as "those happy times--that golden age of Canada." We know not how old this venerable father of the church may be; but we presume, that, like the Apostle Paul, he was born as a man out of due season. "In those happy days," continues he, "the colonists were attached to their king and country; *but now it is quite the contrary!*" We shall only add the words of one more Cure, who says, "the few young men who take new lands, prefer them close to their parents and friends however bad the soil may be!"

What a dreadful system of ignorance, prejudice and bigotry is this! Is there any other country under heaven where such a state of things could be tolerated? Is it possible that this province can prosper while such is the spirit that governs at once the people and their instructors? They will have no lands at a distance, but must be presented with them at the doors of their fathers, and that *en Seigniore!* What apathy—what indolence—what thorough-going indifference to enterprise and independence whilst thousands from other countries cross seas and traverse continents—abandon for ever the country of their birth, the soil of their fathers, their religion, their laws and all the endearing ties of kindred and friendship in search of what the Canadians refuse and despise even in their own native country and at their doors. This has been the bane of this province ever since it has been a province. Afraid to lose sight of the hearth whereon they were born, the people have burrowed together on the margins of the lakes and rivers, like so many rabbits and beavers until the community has at last become so numerous as to leave little more room for a family then the area of the wretched hut which shields them from the inclemency of the weather. Nor will any thing induce them to remove to a distance in order to make room for one another, and establish their families on a new and wilder range of industry and enterprize. Nothing ministers more to this unfortunate state of things than that hideous and destructive law of *partition* which prevails in the country—a law which at once annihilates the moderate laudable ambition natural to man and that spirit of honesty, freedom, and independence of seigniorial and ecclesiastical rule which should ever characterize an agricultural people—and a law which, we sincerely regret, has not been more particularly referred to by the true friends of Canada in the late discussion of our affairs in parliament. All writers agree in deprecating this law ; and nothing has been more detrimental to the French Colonies, as an obstacle to the clearing and cultivation of more lands, than the law of partition, as it now exists in this province. Its injurious effects are so strongly painted by the *Abbe Raynal*, that we cannot refrain from citing his opinion and observations at large as conclusive on this subject.

"It is scarce credible, that a law, seemingly dictated by nature ; a law which occurs instantly to every just and good man ; which leaves no doubt on the mind as to its rectitude and utility ; it is scarce credible, that such a law should sometimes be prejudicial to the preservation of society, stop the progress of colonies, divert them from the end of their destination, and gradually pave the way to their ruin. Strange as it may seem, this law is no other than the equal division of estates among children or co-heirs. This law, so consonant to nature, ought to be abolished in America.

"This division was necessary at the first formation of colonies. Immense tracts of land were to be cleared. This could not be done without people ; nor could men who had quitted their own country for want be any otherwise fixed in those distant and desert regions, than by assigning them a property. Had the government refused to grant them lands, they would have wandered about from one place to another; they would have begun to establish various settlements, and have had the disappointment to find, that none of them would attain to that degree of prosperity as to become useful to the Mother Country.

"But since inheritances, too extensive at first, have in process of time been reduced by a series of successions, and by the subdivisions of shares to such a compass as renders them fit to facilitate cultivation; since they have been so limited as not to lie fallow for want of hands proportionable to their extent, a further division of lands would again reduce them to nothing. In Europe, an obscure man who has but a few acres of land, will make that little estate more advantageous to him in proportion, than an opulent man will the immense property he is possessed of, either by inheritance or chance. In America, the nature of the productions, which were very valuable, the uncertainty of the crops, which are but few in their kind; the quantity of slaves, of cattle, of utensils necessary for plantation; all this requires a large stock, which they have not in some, and will soon want in all the colonies, if the lands are parcelled out and divided more and more by hereditary successions.

"If a father leaves an estate of thirty thousand livres, or £1312 10s. sterling, a year, and this estate is equally divided between three children, they will be ruined if they make three distinct plantations; the one, because he has been made to pay too much for the buildings, and because he has too few negroes, and too little land in proportion; the other two, because they must build before they can begin upon the culture of their land. They will all be equally ruinad if the whole plantation remains in the hands of one of the three. In a country where a creditor is in a worse state than any other man, estates have risen to an immoderate value. The possessor of the whole will be very fortunate if he is obliged to pay no more for interest than the net produce of the plantation. Now, as the primary law of our nature is the procuring of subsistence, he will begin by procuring that without paying his debts. These will accumulate, and he will soon become insolvent; and the confusion consequent upon such a situation, will end in the ruin of the whole family.

"The only way to remedy these disorders, is to abolish the equality of the division of land. In this enlightened age, government should see the necessity of letting the colonies be more stocked with things than with men. The wisdom of the legislature will, doubtless, find out some compensation for those it has injured, and in some measure sacrificed the welfare of the community. *They ought to be placed on fresh lands, and to subsist by their own* labour. This is the only way to maintain this sort of men; and their industry would open a fresh source of wealth to the state."

This is true philosophy; yet the system it

deprecates is that which obtains throughout the whole of the seigniorial lands in this province; and, however desirable, no attempt has hitherto ever been made, by the introduction of primogenial laws, or otherwise, to get rid of an incubus which retards industry and presses the people to the very dust. But besides the evil effects of this law in respect of industry and cultivation, its demoralizing consequences are doubly alarming. There are many parishes and seigniories in this province, which, twenty or thirty years ago, were occupied by a sober, industrious, and moral yeomanry, who are now in consequence of the partition laws, infested with a rabble peasantry the most dissolute, dissipated and indolent—a brood of young rascals who are too lazy to work and too proud to beg—who destroy the peace of society by the evil effects of idle habits, and break the hearts of their very parents by claims the most wanton and unjust upon their lands and other property. We appeal to every lawyer in the province, whether it is not a common thing, and almost a matter of every day's occurrence, to see father and son, mother and daughter, in hostile and opposing attitudes on either side of the bar? If this system continue, by the young men of the country being either prevented or discouraged from establishing themselves at a distance from their fathers on free and common soccage lands, this province from being the most peaceful and moral in the British empire, will become the most wretched, riotous and mendicant. In truth, the partition laws, is a school of immorality and mendicity. Neither Ireland nor Italy can be compared with us. We shall outstrip them both in all the vices peculiar to an over crowded and poverty-stricken population.

Wherefore, then, all this noise and clamour on the part of the Assembly for new lands in districts already over-peopled, and really where there are no lands to be given away on the part of the crown, whatever may be said of the seigniories. But even if there had been such waste land, we ask, would the Canadians accept of grants in free and common soccage? By no means. They must have them *en seigneurie*, or not have them at all. But, we trust, that when the crown comes to dispose of its lands, it will never do so by this barbarous and ruinous tenure. It cannot have a better warning in this respect than in the disinclination of the seigniors themselves to concede new lands; knowing, when a vassal deserts his farm, the difficulty and expense of re-investing themselves in their property; the latter, almost in every case, amounting to ten or twelve pounds. We repeat that we hope the crown will never expose itself to such a destructive system as this; and that, instead of doing so, every possible means will be pursued for the purpose of establishing a system of laws more conducive to the settlement of the province, and more consonant to the views of an enlightened and enterprizing people.

With regard, in particular, to the lands, comprized in the lease of the Forges of St. Maurice, nothing can be more idle and wanton than to claim them for general and indiscriminate distribution, even were the soil as fertile as that of Eden. Works of this kind cannot be carried on without a great extent of territory containing both ore and fuel; and as the Forges of St. Maurice are the only permanent and respectable manufactory of the kind in these provinces on an extensive scale, every facility and encouragement ought to be afforded to an undertaking so stupendous. Supposing, then, the lands around the Forges to be settled, how are the proprietors to find ore and firewood to make their charcoal and carry on all their necessary operations on a given lot of ground, on which, perhaps, neither ore nor timber is to be found? *Prometheus* and *Vulcan* might indeed carry on the business without such necessary materials; but we do not think that the honourable *Matthew Bell* has as yet made any pretensions to equal the gods in power and invention. It is enough for him to keep the works in operation by human means alone, without aiming at impossibilities. It is very true, that in all concessions of land the crown reserves to itself any mines or minerals that may be found thereon; but, in the event of the lands in question, being settled who is to secure to the owner of the Forges the peaceable possession and uninterrupted enjoyment of those mines and minerals, as well as ready access to them? The

Crown, in all the might of its power and prerogative, could not do this, without having recourse to a process so tedious, and measures so dilatory as at once to ruin the works and destroy their acknowledged utility in the country. But, fortunately, the sentiments of the crown are no more in unison with those of the Assembly with respect to this subject than many others; and the integrity of the lands around St. Maurice has ever been an object of care and attention on the part of government. Every governor who comes to the country is instructed to this effect. This the Assembly are well aware of, for their own journals bear witness of the fact; and, therefore, no one can be at a loss to discover at once the insolence and impudence of their beggarly addresses with respect to these lands. The following are the Instructions to Lord Dorchester; and though we have no access to the archives at Quebec, yet we believe we are correct in asserting that the present instructions are in the same terms: "And whereas it appears from the representations of our late Governor of the District of Three-Rivers, that the Iron Works of Saint Maurice, in that District, are of great consequence to our service; it is, therefore, our will and pleasure, that *no* part of the lands upon which the said Iron Works were carried on, or from which the ore used in such works are procured, or which shall appear to be necessary and convenient for that establishment, or for producing a necessary supply of wood, corn and hay, or for pasture for cattle, be granted to any private person whatever; and also, that as large a District of land as conveniently may be adjacent to any lying round the said Iron Works over and above what may be necessary for the above purposes, be reserved for our use, to be disposed of in such manner as we shall hereafter direct and appoint."* We think it would be quite superfluous to say more on this topick.

We have already said somewhat on the subject of the *education*; and were about to treat of it more at large in this place in defence of the Royal Institution from the calumnies of the House of Assembly; but at the moment the *Quebec Gazette* of the 16th of April, containing a most able and excellent document on this subject, was put into our hands, which we make no apology for presenting entire to our readers. They will learn from it, that there is no institution, however pure and respectable—no characters, however sacred and unimpeachable, that can escape the malice and derision of the Assembly. Will the country never learn the extent and danger of the pretensions of this faction? The following is the substance of the document alluded to, as addressed by the Board of the Royal Institution to *His Excellency Sir James Kempt.*

It commences by stating, that the Board of the Royal Institution for the advance-

---

*Vide Journals of the Assembly for 1823; Appendix T.

ment of Learning in this province, sensible of the importance of their not being allowed unjustly to seffer in public estimation, and aware, at the same time, that injurious and unfounded impressions have been propagated abroad respecting their principles and proceedings, and have found admission within the halls of Legislation—feel it incumbent upon them to approach His Excellency, in the desire to lay before him a simple statement ef fects, and in the consciousness that such a statement is all the advantage which they can wish for, when appealing to a judge whose impartiality and candour are so well known to the public at large and so fully appreciated by themselves.

The animadversions which have been passed upon the Board, amount in brief to this—that their proceedings have been characterized by an exclusive spirit as it regards differences of Religious belief; that they are themselves in a great measure persons in charge of the interests of the Church of England, and that it has been their aim and study to render the interests of Education which constituted the direct and proper object of their duties, an engine to subserve their party views.

These are reflections of grave description; —but they have been often cast and as often convincingly disproved, and as an answer to them in a general way, the Board have submitted to His Excellency the following extract from a Petition addressed to His Majesty in the year 1825.

EXTRACT.

"That however deeply your Majesty's Petitioners may deplore the alienation of feelings which is here," (i. e. in public documents to which the allusion is made,) shewn to subsist, they have the full consolation of reflecting that in all the proceedings connected with their Institution from first to last, they have never once either individually or collectively, afforded the slightest ground for any suspicion or distrust of their designs.

"That if it so happens that that part of the corporation of the Royal Institution which consists of Ecclesiastics, is exclusively Protestant, the failure of your Majesty's gracious intentions in this point, is in no way whatever, ascribable to your Majesty's Petitioners,—the Bishop of the Roman Catholic Church in Canada, having, in the first instance, assigned as impediments to his acceptance of the trust, some scruples of conscience which your Majesty's Petitioners are perfectly ready to respect, but the effects of which they esteem it some hardship to find visited by any other party upon *themselves*.

"That if it also happen that amongst the Parish Schools which are under the control of the Royal Institution in this Province, and supported by the annual bounty of the Legislature, those in the Roman Catholic Parishes are reduced to a small number, which is still diminishing, and are falling off from a flourishing condition,—the cause is to be found in the operation of similar scruples in the minds of the Cures, who are known to be unfriendly to a connexion with the Institution, and who have, one by one declined the office of *visitors* of the schools, which they have been invariable requested, in due form, to accept, and which would have placed in their hands the immediate controul and surveillance of the schools in their respective parishes.

"That, nevertheless, in this Institution which is affirmed *to* be so constituted as to create jealousy and alarm among the great body of your Majesty's subjects in this Province, there were, before the recent death of the Hon. A. J. L. Duchesnay, whose successor has not yet been appointed, no less than *seven* Roman Catholic Members, among whom is the Speaker of the House of Assembly itself *ex officio*, and the late Speaker, who is still a Member of that House, and that, so far from having afforded room for any suspicion of projected interference with Religion or indirect influence upon it, your Majesty's Petitioners have uniformly felt it to be their duty to guard, in the most scrupulous manner against the shadow of such a suspicion and they challenge the most rigorous scrutiny that can be instituted upon the subject; that they have refused the appointment to a school in one of the Roman Catholic Parishes to a master whose native tongue was French, upon the sole ground of his being a Protestant, and that they committed exclusively to the Members who belong to the Roman Catholic Church, the framing of the Regulations for the Schools of that communion.

"That under all these circumstances, Your Majesty's Petitioners humbly conceive it to be desirable that they should be exonerated from all charge or control of the Roman Catholic Schools—a charge which has exposed them only to unmerited odium and afforded to them no opportunity of usefulness: a charge, however in the execution of which they have faithfully done all that was in their power.

"That they therefore pray your Majesty to provide in such other manner as to your Royal Wisdom shall seem best, for the general superintendance of the Education of your Majesty's Roman Catholic Subjects in the country parishes of this Province, and to extend your bounty for the extrication of Your Majesty's Petitioners from the state of embarrassment and destitution in which they are placed."

To these statements which were laid before the Throne, the Board beg permission, with reference in particular, to a letter addressed by a private Clergyman in the country, then recently from Europe, to a Schoolmaster in the year 1823, and very lately produced as evidence of their disposition to render Education instrumental to Proselytism,—to add their assurance to His Excellency that this very letter was at the time proved to have been written without authority and under erroneous information wholly contrary to the facts of the case, and that means of satisfaction were furnished upon this point, in the very quarter from which the charge has now proceeded. The proof that such a charge was unfounded had been lodged in the hands, which brought the document forward to support it—and the Board can only express their surprise and regret, that the author of the charge could have retained his original impressions upon the subject.

An opportunity is here taken by those Members of the Board who happen to be Ecclesiastics of the Church of England, to declare that they are far from wishing it to be understood that they can for one moment be indifferent to the rights and interests of the Protestant Religion or to those of their own immediate Communion, but they have uniformly felt that, as Members of the Royal Institution they act in a distinct capacity, and in the discharge of a trust imposing obligations with which their own particular views should no otherwise mix themselves than as it is imperative upon them to provide for regulating the religious part of Education, among those who profess an adherence to their own Church. And they call upon those who are suspicious of their designs to produce a single example in which they have deviated from those principles, or endeavoured to exert the smallest indirect or improper influence in the fulfilment of their public duty.

That His Excellency may better judge of the correctness and candour which have characterized the representations respecting their proceedings, the Board crave leave, in the first place, to refer to a paper annexed to their representations, (which is also here subjoined,) in which they state each specific accusation that has been pubicly brought against them, (as far as they are informed,) with distinct and specific answers on each point ; and they farther proceed to lay before His Excellency, a few particular instances which may serve, among other proofs, to refute the principal charge against them,— that in the discharge of their public trust, they have shewn an exclusive spirit and an undue preference for the Established Church.

In the year 1824, they recommended to His Excellency's predecessor in the Government the appointment of Mr. Norman McLeod, a Catechist of the Church of Scotland, to the charge of a School at Williamstown in the Seigniory of Beauharnois,—a charge which he still holds: and in the year 1827, they procured in a similar way Mr. G. W. Bruce, a Minister of the Scotch Seceding Church to be appointed to the School at New Longueil, and Mr. Gardener Bartlett, a preacher of the Baptist Persuasion, to a School in the Township of Potton. In adverting to this part of the subject, the Board have mentioned the fact, as worthy of remark, that no less than 16 Petitions to the Legislature praying that provision should be made for the continuance of the operations conducted by the Board, were recently sent down from the Eastern Townships, signed by 337 persons of all Religious Denominations who concur in stating their entire satisfaction with the management of the Schools and their earnest desire that it may not pass into other hands.

The Board declare themselves to have felt these reflections the more,—*first*, because they are publicly stated to have proceeded from persons holding seats at the Board, and thence possessing the means of acquiring a correct knowledge of the facts, from whom, consequently, it might rather have been hoped that they would prevent or correct erroneous impressions, than suffer themselves to become instrumental in diffusing them; and, secondly, because the Board are prepared to shew that through a series of difficulties and discouragements they have succeeded in effecting great and undeniable good, in the promotion of Education, chiefly among the inhabitants of the more newly established parts of the Province, who commanded the smallest means for effecting that important object themselves. They conclude by saying that "Through evil report and good report" they have held their even course—correcting many abuses,—supplying many destitute settlements,—rendering as diffusive as was practicable the resources placed at their disposal,—and progressively advancing in the confidence and respect of the people where their endeavours have been suffered to take effect.—And in this course, so long as they are enabled by the countenance of His Majesty's Government and the Provincial Legislature to proceed at all—they assure His Excellency that, with the blessing of Providence, they will persevere to the last.

ALLEGATIONS AGAINST THE ROYAL INSTITUTION.

I. "That for the purposes of Proselytism "the Royal Institution have attempted to "force Protestant Schoolmasters on the Ro-"man Catholic Parishes."

Answer.—The Royal Institution have never sent Protestant schoolmasters to the Schools in the Canadian parishes, or where the majority of the children to be taught were of the Roman Catholic persuasion: but they have felt themselves perfectly justified in sending Protestant schoolmasters to teach in places where there were a sufficient number of Protestant children to form a school, although there might also be Roman Catholic children in these places: such instances however have been very rare; and there are perhaps an equal number of cases where they have sent Roman Catholic masters to schools where there was an intermixture of Protestant children. Of the twelve schools in the Canadian and Roman Catholic parishes which fell under their superintendence, there is not one to which they have appointed a Protestant master; if it be alleged, that they have sent Schoolmasters of the Church of England to schools where there were many children of dissenters, the Royal Institution aver that they have indifferently appointed Protestant masters to schools of this description, without considering of what particular persuasion they might be, and without regard to any other qualification or recommendation than their moral fitness and their attainments, and that in some instances they have actually appointed Dissenting Ministers as masters of these schools.

2. That the Royal Institution have not allowed the inhabitants of the country any influence in the appointment of Masters or of Trustees, or in the management of schools."

Answer.—The Royal Institution have always nominated as Trustees such persons as the inhabitants recommended, or where there was no such particular recommendation, the most respectable and influential among those who have applied for the establishment of schools. In the nomination of Schoolmasters, it has been their rule to give a preference among candidates, to such as were recommended by the people, if otherwise well qualified; they have even in some cases appointed persons upon such recommendation alone, whom they did not consider as in all respects the fittest; and they have cancelled appointments of Schoolmasters, for no other reason than that they were not acceptable to the inhabitants.

3. "That they have required the Masters appointed by them to use in their schools the religious formularies of the Church of England."

Answer.—By one of the Standing Rules established by the Board, Schoolmasters are required, where there is no Church in the place, to read on Sundays to Protestant children only such portions of the Service of the Church of England as should be prescribed by the Board: it will be admitted, that in such remote situations as this rule has in view, some provision for the religious observance of the Sabbath is desirable; that for this purpose the use of some formulary is better than to leave it to the discretion of the Schoolmaster, to pray or to preach what he pleases; and that it is only in the Church of England that such a formulary is to be found, containing prayers in which all christians may join, and a selection of parts and passages of Scripture suitable to all places and all understandings; but the Board have never rigidly acted upon this rule, nor have the masters generally conformed to it, and the rule itself did not contemplate a compulsory attendance even of Protestant children, whose parents should on conscientious grounds object to it.

4. "That they have mismanaged the funds entrusted to them, that education has been retarded by them, and that they have done more harm than good."

Answer.—In 1819, when the Royal Institution was incorporated thirty-three schools which had been previously established by Government, under the act of 1801, fell under their superintendence. It appears by returns laid before the House of Assembly in 1821, that the number of scholars in those schools did not exceed 1200, and that the salaries paid by the Province to the Schoolmasters amounted to more than £2000, curreacy. Under the management of the Royal Institution, the number of schools has increased to 84, the number of scholars to upwards of 3700, and yet by the economy which the Board have practised, no larger sum is drawn from the public chest for the support of these schools, than before.

5. "That the Board feeling at last their total inefficiency, have now sought the co-operation of the Roman Catholic Clergy, and Laity, after long struggles on the part of the Roman Catholics to obtain a share of influence in the education of their children."

Answer.—This allegation is attributed to a member of the Board, who knows that the Board sought the co-operation of the Roman Catholic Bishop and Clergy, from the very commencement of their labors; but that having failed in obtaining it, they long ago manifested their desire to be relieved from the charge of Roman Catholic Schools; that, in consequence of this desire, he himself in 1823, with the privity of several members of the Board, and of the Roman Catholic Bishop drew a Bill for establishing a separate corporation, consisting of the Roman Catholic Bishop and other members of the Roman Catholic Clergy and Laity, for the exclusive superintendence of Roman Catholic Schools; that this Bill was submitted by the late Governor in Chief to His Majesty with a strong recommendation, that it should be adopted, which recommendation was rejected; that in 1826, as soon as this rejection was known to the Board, they again sought the co-operation of the Roman Catholic Bishop and Clergy, by proposing to the Provincial Government an arrangement for the formation of a separate Roman Catholic Committee of the Board, and in promoting that arrangement, they have made every concession that has been asked on the part of the Roman Catholics.

6. "It is further alleged, that the Royal Institution has lost the confidence of the country."

Answer.—As long as the Roman Catholic Clergy shall continue their opposition to the labours of the Board, or withhold their support, the Royal Institution must feel and admit that they cannot have the confidence of the Roman Catholic population, but that they have enjoyed the confidence and have secured the gratitude of the rest of the population of the country, is abundantly proved not only by the rapid increase of the number of schools under their superintendence and by the applications for new schools which they are constantly receiving from all parts of the country; but the direct and unequivocal expression of that confidence and gratitude, in numerous Petitions which have been recently addressed to the Assembly, signed for the most part by Dissenters in the Townships expressing their entire satisfaction with the measures of the Board, and deprecating as a public injury any attempt to abridge their resources or labours.

In the name of heaven, let these brawling Roman Catholics have a Royal Institution of their own, and teach their brats according to their own notions and tenets. It is in vain to imagine that they will ever join the present Institution whilst they have the House of Assembly to advocate their cause. Any Institution, whether Royal or Plebeian, having the Bible and the English language for its object, they lay its account to persecution in this province; and may be assured of having every obstacle thrown in its way that an ignorant people, and a jealous factious House of Assembly can array against it. But are we British subjects and Englishmen, inhabiting a British colony, having the *Habeas Corpus* as the guardian of our persons, and the British Constitution as the sheet-anchor of our liberty, to be told, that, in all Institutions of learning, the language of Frenchmen and an Alien nation is to have co-equal, if not paramount importance attached to it? We scout the degrading idea with scorn and contempt; and therefore trust, that whether the Canadians get a Royal Institution of their own or not, there will ever be in this province an establishment having for its primary objects the instruction of the *English Language, Loyalty to the King, Attachment to the Constitution, and the Dissemination of the* Scriptures *of God!*

The conduct of the Assembly with regard to the Militia Bill, was no less assumptive of judicial authority than destructive of the just prerogative of the Crown. The Militia force of this Province was first organized in virtue of Ordinances passed in 1787 and

1789, by the Governor and Council of Quebec. These Ordinances continued to be the law of the country upon this important subject until 1793, when, during the second session of the first Provincial Parliament, an Act was passed repealing the Ordinances, and making such further provision on the subject as the situation of the Province rendered necessary; but this act was a *temporary* one, and ceased on the first day of July, 1796. This Provincial Statute was renewed from time to time till 1802, when by a new act passed, the Ordinances of 1787 and 1789 were *again repealed*. This is proof positive that these Ordinances were always considered as permanent laws by the Legislature, and would ever continue to be so in the absence of any subsecutive law depriving them expressly of their force, vigour and existence. Therefore, as no statute was ever passed subsequent to this second repealing act having any tendency to disturb the principle established by it, nothing can be more clear, than that the instant any future Militia law should expire, the Ordinances were naturally, and as a matter of course, resuscitated. In fact, all the succeeding acts were temporary acts, founded on the second repealing act of 1802. In 1827, the Militia Bill sent up by the Assembly to the Legislative Council, contained a clause foreign to the Bill, [illegible] a separate act containing an appropriation of money for payment of the Militia Staff was declared to be null and void though not repealed. A Bill so fraught with danger, and contrary to the King's Instructions, could not constitutionally be sanctioned by the Legislative Council; and it was accordingly amended and returned to the Assembly, who refused to proceed on it. The consequence was, that when the temporary Militia acts expired, the Ordinances revived: and had the Governor-in-Chief, Lord Dalhousie, not given due notification of this event to the publick, and, in his official capacity, called the attention of the Province to these Ordinances, the country would have been wholly deprived of the most necessary and constitutional safe-guard known under our Constitution of Government. Nothing can be more demonstrative of the true character of a people than their obedience to the laws. Nothing reflects greater honour on the character of the people of this Province than the readiness with which they submitted to the duties imposed upon them by laws framed at a very unsettled period of our history, and at a time when the Government of Canada had scarcely emerged from the ordeal of its military and feudal origin, notwithstanding the factions and seditious opinions circulated amongst them by the newspapers and other emissaries of the leaders.

Towards the conclusion of the late Session, a new Militia Bill was sent up to the Legislative Council by the Assembly; but strange to tell, this bill also contained a clause so monstrous, and so sweepingly destructive of the prerogatives of the Crown and the most elementary principles of constitutional legislation, that the Legislative Council struck it out at once. This clause need only be perused to be condemned :

"Provided always, and be it further enacted by the authority aforesaid, that nothing in this Act contained shall extend or be construed to extend to revoke or annul all or any of the commissions of the different Officers of Militia appointed in this Province prior to the first day of May which was in the year of our Lord 1827, the said Commissions being conformable to the provisions of the said Acts, hereby revived and continued in respect to the qualification and residence; and provided always, and it is hereby declared and enacted by the authority aforesaid, that all Commissions or changes of Officers of Militia, issued or made subsequently to the said first day of May, be and the same are hereby revoked and annulled, till such time as further provision be made therein by the Governor, Lieutenant Governor, or person administering the Government for the time being."

Let it be remembered, that shortly after the Ordinances of 1787 and 1789 came into force in 1827, a great deal of insubordination and refractoriness took place among the Officers of the Militia; a set of men bound by every tie of civil and military law to exhibit a pattern of peace and obedience to those placed under their immediate command. No country could be safe—no service could be either effective or honourable with the participation of such men. They were, therefore, very properly dismissed; and others more loyal and obedient appointed in their place. These dismissals were made a subject of complaint in the *Petitions of Grievance*; and are to this day a subject of irksome reflection to the Leaders and their dismissed patrons. There is no principia of our Constitution better established, than that the King may call into and dismiss from his service, either civil or military, at pleasure, whom he will. Yet, the Canada Committee and the Assembly presume to think otherwise; the latter, by the clause above cited, attempting not only to re-appoint the dismissed officers, but to revoke and annul "all commissions or changes of Officers of Militia, issued or made subsequently to the said first day of May." "When an army is established,' says Montesque, in his Treatise ou the British Constitution, "it ought not to depend immediately on the legislative, but on the executive power; and this, from the very nature of the thing; its business consisting more in action than in deliberation." On what principles of Constitutional justice, then, the Assembly could assume the right of passing such a law as the one above alluded to, we are totally at a loss to comprehend or to conceive. They perhaps thought this a fair and fit opportunity to ingratiate themselves with their constituents by a mere attempt to legislate for popular clamour, as well as to reinstate the cashiered Officers. But they forgot that the people had all along paid the most implicit obedience to the revived Militia Ordinances, and that His Majesty's Government had entirely approved of the dismissals in question; an approval founded on the opinion of the Law Officers of the Crown, as well as on that of every sound lawyer in Canada; many of the latter continuing to do duty both as Officers and Privates under the existing laws! In what other light, then, can we look to the Assembly than as barefaced usurpers of the just authority of the executive government. Thanks to the Legislative Council, they have in this instance at least failed in their unjust and inglorious pretensions; but the country cannot watch too narrowly the proceedings of a set of men so bent on the destruction of every thing sacred in our system of government.

But this is not all. When the Bill, in its amended form, reached the Assembly, our friend Mr. Viger proposed a series of Resolutions, which, to convince the doubtful reader, if there be such, we shall give, at full length, as exhibiting in stronger colours than any language of ours could do, that nothing can stop the progress of the Assembly in their attempts to clothe themselves with judicial authority.

"M. Viger proposed to resolve seconded by Mr. [illegible].

"That it is the opinion of this committee, that an humble address ought to be presented to His Excellency the administrator of the government, expressing that the act of the Imperial Parliament of the 14th year of the reign of his late Majesty George Third, chap. 83 which established for the Province of Quebec a Legislative Council, had limited its jurisdiction within certain bounds it overstepped in passing the ordinances of the 27th and 29th of the some reign for the government of the militia of this Province, of which several provisions are moreover repugnant to the principles of law and of the constitutional rights of England, which are the law of this country.

"That when a temporary abrogates a perpetual law, and substitutes on the same subject, provisions only established for a certain time, the repealed law does not revive, when the time for which the new law had been made is expired, without the intention of the Legislature has been expressed on the subject.

"That nothing in the clauses of the two laws of the Legislature of this Province of the 34th and 43d years of his Majesty's Reign, respecting the Militia, by the words of which the ordinances of the Council are abrogated, expresses any intention to allow them to revive after the expiration of the temporary laws, which substituted new provisions in the place of these old ordinances.

"That the aforesaid ordinances of the Council of the 27th and 29th years of his late Majsety Geo. III, cannot revive by the expiration of these temporary laws, which abrogated them, and can only be put into force by a law of the Provincial Parliament without the authority of which the citizens of this province could not be obliged to submit to the exercise of martial law."

Now, without waiting to express our sentiments on the contemptible opinion and subterfuge here recorded with respect to want of due authority on the part of the Governor and Council of Quebec, which we affirm to have been as extensive as that of the present Governor and Legislature,* what can be more insolent and insane than their drivelling about the revival of the ordinances, and the want of authority to oblige the "*citizens*" of this province to submit to the exercise of *martial law?* But this trash will appear still more strange and ridiculous when we inform the reader, that so far back as the mouth of June, 1828, the only legal tribunal in the province capable of prononncing judgment in a case involving alike the proroga-tive of the crown and the rights of the subject, declared, by an unanimous decision, that the Militia Ordinances of 1787 and 1789 were then, still are, and ever will be in force while they remain unrepealed or unsuspended by any subsequent existing act of the legislature! This judgment will be found on the margin,† and does honour to the learned individuals who pronounced it. Yet, in the face of this solemn judgment,

*The only inferiority on the part of the former was in the want of authority to levy taxes.

†Vide Appendix.

which not only ought to be venerated, but treasured up as the rule of conduct of every man in the province, whatever his profession or pursuits may be, the Assembly, by their Resolutions, attempt to pronounce a judgment diametrically opposite both as to fact and principle! Can this be endured? Can it be endured that the House of Assembly may wage eternal war with every power and tribunal in the state? Are his Majesty's courts of law to be brought into contempt by a pack of arrogant demagogues, whose constant object—as we have said a hundred times over—is to paralyze and destroy the King's Government in this province? Are the people to be taught to recognize no other authority but that of the Assembly? And is the bar to fly for refuge to the forum? These proceedings must be stopped. They have gone too far already; but if the Assembly be not checked—and that speedily—in its wilful and headlong career, England will ere long curse the day in which *Wolfe*, the greatest and the bravest of her generals, won his glories!

If any further proof be necessary to confirm the opinion which we entertain on this subject, we have only to refer to the proroguing speech of His Excellency the Administrator, and the "circular" of the Adjutant General of the Militia of the 10th of April. In the former of these documents the absolute existence of the Militia Laws is averted and maintained by the following sentence :—

"I had entertained a hope, that the inhabitants of the Province would have been relieved from any inconvenience to which they may be subjected under the Ordinances *now in force*, by the passing of a Militia Bill, and I cannot but express my regret that it has not taken place."

In the latter, which is addressed "to Commanding Officers of Militia Battalions," by this introductory clause:—

CIRCULAR.

Office of the Adjutant General *of Militia*,
Quebec, 10*th April*, 1829.

SIR:—His Excellency the Commander-in-Chief, being desirous of relieving the Militia of the Province from the inconvenience to which they might be subjected in the course of the present year, by attending the Five Monthly Reviews, ordered and required by the Ordinances now in force. I have received His Excellency's Commands to acquaint you that he is pleased to dispense with Three of the said Reviews."

Thus we find the House of Assembly as much at variance with his present Excellency, on *this subject at least*, as with Lord Dalhousie. Why, then, are the Assembly and the "Canada Committee" silent on a matter so important? Whatever tribunal will now decide the case, must do so with as much reference to Sir James Kempt as Lord Dalhousie; for the one is as guilty of the crime of declaring these ordinances "now in force" as the other. We have therefore no hesitation to say, that the Defender of Peltier* himself, with all his erudition and legal acquirements, could not have made out a stronger case than we have thus done with respect to the Militia Laws. The Assembly and its friends have indeed abused and vilified even Sir James Kempt for his opinions on this subject; but Sir James knows how to despise such abuse; and cares as little about it as his noble predecessor did.

We come now to the last and most important question of the whole. We allude to the Supplies. We have already, in a preceding number, entered so fully upon this subject, that at present, we deem it neither necessary nor desirable to discuss it at much greater length. We should, however, consider it as a cowardly desertion of our post, were we to pass over the proceedings of the late Session, in relation to this matter without recording our sentiments on a question which has so long and so fearfully agitated the Country.

It will be observed, that this Session was characterized by two appropriation acts: one to defray the expenses of the civil government incurred in 1828, there being no session in that year; and another to make provision towards defraying the civil expenditure during the current year. But we will not consider these acts separately. They are the same in principle: equally destructive of the Constitution, equally at variance

---

*Sir James Mackintosh.

with the King's instructions, and equally insulting to the feelings and good sense of the country! The Message upon which they are founded, claims "provision in aid of the Crown Revenues." It has been asserted, that the Bills, as passed, have reference to this principle, and are couched accordingly. This we shall never admit. The Bill making provision for 1829, instead of making "provision in aid of the Crown Revenues," appropriates the whole publick revenue of the province in "such sum or sums of money as together with the monies already appropriated by law for the said purposes, shall amount to a sum not exceeding £54,542 2 6, Sterling."* There is no word of an "*aid*" in this enactment. The Assembly knew better; and were aware, that if that term were once made use of, their pretensions over all the revenues of the province, would instantly fall to the ground. The term "*Together*" was substituted, which they blindly imagine to be tantamount to a full recognition of their claims. But had the act been worded otherwise, and expressed in the identical terms of the Message, it would, in our opinion, be equally unconstitutional; because, in voting the supplies, the Assembly did not confine themselves to the unappropriated revenue, over which alone they hold control, and which alone they have a right to dispose of; but spread their authority over the whole of the "Crown

*Vide Appendix, No. III.

Revenues;" appropriating, disposing, deducting, controlling, and adding each Civil Officer's allowance according to a rule of benovolence of their own: thus entirely abrogating the appropriations already made by his Majesty and the Lords of the Treasury, and cutting them off from all intervention with the "Crown Revenues" created and appropriated by the 14th Geo. III. with the disposal of which they are entirely and exclusively invested. Now, if the Crown submit to this usurpation on the part of the Assembly—if it tamely submit to be stripped of a power with which it is clothed by an act of the Imperial Parliament—if it submit to be told, that its judges and other civil officers, who, in virtue of this act, have been permanently provided for according to a scale long in use and yearly submitted to the inspection and guidance of the Assembly, are henceforward to become annual pensioners on the bounty of that Assembly, in that case, we humbly submit, the Crown is bound to give due notice to the province of its having relinquished its claims to the appropriation of the "Crown Revenues," in order to prevent us from quarrelling with the Assembly, for assuming an authority acquiesced in by his Majesty's government. But fortunately for us, the Crown has not, will not, cannot, dare not commit a deed so atrocious, whilst the 14th of the late king remains in the statute book. The Crown may, indeed, solicit and obtain the repeal of this act; but while it remains in force the Crown is bound to pay it as implicit obedience as the meanest subject, and can no more avoid submission to the law of the land than it can suspend the habeas corpus without the consent of parliament. The law has invested the crown with no discretionary powers; and it can no more transfer the performance of its own duties to the subject, than the subject can usurp the regal functions. We know not what the Crown may do with respect to the subject under consideration; but hitherto, so far as has come to our knowledge, we are not aware that it has betrayed any symptoms of compromise. We owe it a debt of gratitude for this. Even that infamously popular term conciliation would, in this instance, be dangerous; but compromise would be ruinous. The government of England is not a democracy, nor a party-government that veers with the political vane of every man who comes into office. It is a government founded on principle, consistency, and uniformity of conduct; and it is to this that we owe the war that has so long been waged against these characteristicks of the House of Assembly. But is this social warfare to be continued for ever? If the government of England have the inclination, they have surely the power of putting a stop to it. The past attempts to do so, have proved ineffectual; but if England be truly desirous to entail peace and prosperity on this province, where have those wonderful and much-boasted Arcana of her strength been hid for the last ten years. Have not the

House of Assembly, like the Philistines on another occasion, defied and made sport of them! The supply Bill passed during the administration of Sir Francis Burton was considered so unconstitutional, and at such variance with the rights of the Crown, that his Majesty's Representative in the province was instructed, not to sanction any measure of a similar nature. Yet, let any one who can read, compare the Bill of 1825 with those of the present Session, and we defy him to pronounce them otherwise, than identically the same both in principle and in terms!* This is a defiance which we certainly did expect, but which we never for a single instant, dreamed would have proved successful. So far as regards the Assembly, the only remark we shall make is, that led and actuated, as they have ever been, by a spirit of opposition to British supremacy, it would at once be impossible and inconsistent with themselves to have acted otherwise. Their language to Britain has always been;—

"She is my bane, I cannot bear her;
One heaven and earth can never hold us both;
Still shall we hate, and with defiance deadly
Keep rage alive till one be lost forever."

But what shall we say of the Legislative Council? In what terms can we express our shame and grief at the conduct of that

---

*Vide Appendix, No. IV.

body, who have hitherto stood in the breach between us and anarchy, and who have hitherto exercised their authority in such a constitutional way, as at once to incur the displeasure of the Assembly, and the approbation of their Country? We lament, we grieve to say, that the public character of the Legislative Council, for honour and consistency, has been forfeited for ever! But when we pronounce a sentence so repugnant to our feelings, we do not mean to say that that body is individually infamous. No; we thank God, that there are individuals in that Assembly who are an ornament to society, and an honour to the country, individuals whom the king may trust and the province be proud of—individuals who will neither bend the knee to power, nor worship at the shrine of avarice—individuals who will be consistent while others are abject—individuals who will defend their country and their birthrights, when others desert them to tyrants and enemies.

We believe that the Legislative Council never presented a more interesting scene than during the discussion of the Supply Bills. Of the speeches and efforts which were made in favour of those infamous Bills, we refrain from speaking: because, to our mind, nothing degrades human nature more than to behold it free to-day and a slave to-morrow—then to see it, lion-like, braving the dangers and the scorn of popular obloquy in the cause of justice and truth, and anon prostrate, licking the dust from the foot of heartless avarice and proud authority. Far otherwise are we disposed to speak of those who resisted them. Would that we could write the names of Kerr, Bell, Coffin, Felton, Grant, Bowen, and John Stewart in letters of gold! The resistance of these men was stern, manful and patriotick. It has endeared them to every loyal person in the Country, and, when they are gone, will embalm their memories in the grateful remembrance of all who love that Country and venerate the Constitution. Let their tombs bear the record *Here lies a defender of the Constitution!* Of course, it cannot be expected ei' ns te enter into a detail of the arguments made use of by these honourable individuals in opposition to the Supplies as voted by the Assembly. It will be merely sufficient to say that they were unanswerable. Being founded on the principles of the Constitution they could not be rebutted: being in accordance with the laws of the country, they could not be refuted. The only reasoning urged against them was expediency and conciliation. But what can be more expedient than an adherence to the letter and the spirit of the Constitution; and what can be more conciliating than the due execution of the laws? As to the arguments of their opponents, we must admit they were of the most solid and weighty kind; and because they were so, they prevailed. Let us attend for a moment to the manner in which this took place and to the individuals by whom it was effected.

As the same circumstances characterized

and disgraced the passage of both Bills, we apprehend that the history of one will be quite sufficient. When the Bill for the civil expenditure of the current year came under discussion, there were fifteen members in the House, exclusive of the Speaker; and the votes were as follows:

For *the Bill*.—1. Cuthbert, 2. De Lery, 3. The Bishop, 4. Ryland, 5. Tachereau, 6. Caldwell, 7. Hale.

Against the Bill.—1. Coffin, 2. Bell, 3. Grant, 4. Felton, 5. Stewart, 6. Bowen, 7. Kerr, 8. Percival.

Now, there being Eight votes against the passing of the Bill, and only Seven in its favour, it will naturally excite surprise how the measure could pass at all, consistently with the rules of voting, there being a fair and legal majority of One on the side of the *Nays*. But let it be remembered, that there was a being called *the Speaker* in the house, who as such, like his brother of the Assembly, had a stake of three thousand pounds in the game! It was hard therefore to be deprived of a sum so considerable by the vote of a single individual, when a remedy lay within his reach. It was no difficult matter, in the first place, to vote as a member on the side of the yeas, the numbers being by that means rendered equal, and then, as Speaker, give the casting vote on the same side. This was done! The Speaker of the Legislative council, who is also Chief Justice of this province, has long been esteemed as a man of some virtue and talent. There may be talent; but surely there is no virtue in an act of this kind. As a lawyer and a judge Mr. Sewell must know, that he had no right to act in this way; and that by doing so, he has forever blasted his own character as a man of candour and impartiality. If otherwise, God help those who, by the laws of the country, are bound to seek justice at his hands. There is no rule better established by our laws, than that a president or chairman of any publick body cannot vote but once; and that one vote can only be, a casting vote in case of their being what is termed a *tie*. By the laws of the Imperial Parliament the act of the majority binds the whole. But what constitutes this majority? Not, surely, two votes given by the Speaker of either house, as has been done in the case before us. By no means; but tho bona fide majority of votes, fairly put and fairly given; and a majority, it is well known, may be constituted by one as well as a thousand. Neither the Speaker of the House of Lords, nor of the House of Commons has ever been known to give more than one vote, and that vote only when there is an equality of votes.* It is true that the Speaker of the House of

*On the question for the impeachment of Lord Melville, the division of the House of Commons being *equal*, the motion for the prosecution was carried by the casting vote of Mr. Abbott, then Speaker. By the Constitution of the United States, it is declared that "The Vice President of the United

Lords, if he be a Lord of parliament. may, contrary to the privileges of the Speaker of the Lower House, give his opinion or argue any question in the House; but he never votes, except when the numbers on a division happen to be equal. This is a point clearly established by parliamentary usage; and upon what grounds the Speaker of the Legislative Council could lay claim to two voices, is to us incomprehensible. But let us consult our constitutional Act on a subject so important. By the twenty eighth section, it is enacted "That all questions which shall arise in the said Legislative Councils or Assemblies respectively, shall be decided by the Majority of voices of such members as shall be present; and that in all cases where the voices shall be equal, the Speaker of such Council or Assembly, as the case shall be, shall have a casting voice." There is no authority for a double vote here. It is not to be found in the customs of parliament, nor is it sanctioned by any law or usage known within the realm. We will thank the Honourable Speaker of the Legislative Council, then to point out the authority whence he has derived this new law, which gives him, what no other man can enjoy, a double capacity, and renders him of double importance to which ever side of the house he may be disposed to lend his assistance. But, with all his cleverness we think we are

---

States shall be president of the Senate, but shall have no vote unless they be equally divided."

safe in bidding him defiance. We know where he found all the authority that can be produced on the subject. He found it in a timid, wavering, vacilating disposition—in a heart more prone to court present favours than to entertain gratitude for the past—and in a passion of personal avarice and family aggrandizement, which reflect as little honour on the judge as on the patriot—on the man as the confidential friend.

Of the companions and tools of the Honourable Speaker, in this work of publick infamy, we are disposed to speak with as much decency and decorum as their deeds of atrocity will admit of. The Bishop we have always admired as a man of piety, learning and humanity. But he cannot serve God and mammon; and it is our fervent prayer, that the Church may never again be put to shame and confusion on account of his political subserviency and delinquency. We have said, that we admire the piety of this good and evangelical man; we will only add, from his politicks, Good Lord, Deliver us. The real views of Mr. Cuthbert will be disappointed; and when that happens, he will remember that we told him so. Of Mr. De Lery we say nothing, as he is a man totally unknown to fame of any kind. Mr. Ryland we believe to be the personal enemy of the late representative of his Majesty in this province. Any man who could be so, is totally unworthy of publick, or private respect. At all events, he shall never have ours. We understand, that at the time Mr.

Taschereau was thus voting away the publick money into the pockets of the two Honourable Speakers, he ought to have been attending to his duties as a Judge in another district of the province; and that, in consequence of his absence it was with great difficulty the term was commenced at all; a loss had it taken place, of more serious consequence to the country than the whole civil list together. When questioned as to his absence, he answered that "The Chief Justice laid his commands upon him!" Of this we have no doubt; but we can assure Mr. Taschereau, that had his vote been on the other side, he should next session have been impeached by the Assembly for neglect of duty as a Judge. As it is, we hope some independent member will take up the business; for the Judge ought to know, that, whatever becomes of politicks, nothing is more injurious to a state than a faithless and time serving judicatory. Mr. Caldwell is a public defaulter, and has been so declared by the House of Assembly and the Canada committee. Mr. Hale is an honest man, we believe; but what Receiver General can be an honest politician! Such are the men who have aided the House of Assembly in their attempts to destroy the constitution. Such are the men who have compromised the character of the Legislative Council. Such are the men whom Mr. Felton stated in his place to have been every way deserving the character given of them by Mr. Neilson in his evidence before the Canada committee, as well as in the Report of that committee itself. With these brief observations we leave them in the hands of the country and posterity. But the list would not be complete without the name of the Attorney General, who probably, from a motive similar to that of the two Speakers, gave ex officio, a favourable opinion of the supply bills. Were Mr. Attorney now member for William Henry, we ask him whether his opinion would be the same? If so, the vote of a dissecter of bodies is at any time as good as that of a dissecter of briefs and indictments, for destroying the constitution. But Mr. Stuart was never either a good or consistent politician; and we fear it is now too late to teach him. We may, perhaps, try our hands on him by and by. He has been said to intimidate and overawe the Bench; but he will not do either with us. Should he be tempted to indict us for a libel; we shall take refuge under the late instructions transmitted to him from England with respect to meaner libellers, and so escape his malevolence. Upon the whole Mr. Attorney will understand us, when we say:

> De Summo planus: sed non ego planus in
> uno
> Versor utrinque manu, diverso et munere
> fungor;
> Altera pars revocat, quicquid pars altera
> fecit.

With respect to the part which His Excellency the Administrator of the Government took in this business; we are disposed to say as little as we can, consistently with our duty to the publick. We entertain the most unqualified esteem for His Excellency as a man, a gentleman and a soldier. In each of these capacities he deserves, and we believe, universally receives the respect and gratitude of his country. As the representative of Geo. IV. he shall ever receive from us the homage and obedience of free and loyal subjects; ready to serve him for the benefit of our beloved country in any capacity or on any mission. But our loyalty to the King, and respect for his representative, will never deter us from giving the freest expression to our sentiments on questions of public importance. We have therefore neither fear nor hesitation in saying, that, considering the nature and character of the Bills of supply of this session; considering the manner in which the supply bill passed the Assembly; considering the circumstances under which the bills were passed in both houses; considering the illegality of the double vote of the Speaker of the Legislative Council; but, above all, considering the Despatch of the Colonial Minister of the 4th of June, 1825, wherein, with respect to the last Bill of Supply sanctioned by the legislature, instructions were conveyed "Not to sanction any measure of a similar nature," His Excellency ought to have withheld the Royal sanction from the Bills in question, at least until His Majesty's approbation should have been obtained. The instructions alluded to are as binding upon the present Governor as upon any of His Excellency's predecessors, unless formally and expressly recalled: a circumstance which there is no authority to conclude, has ever taken place. It is said that Sir James Kempt is in possession of conciliatory despatches. We are far from disbelieving this, because it is very likely, considering the spirit which at present rules his Majesty's government in England. But, why should His Exellency's instructions be different from those of his brother Governor in Upper Canada? There Sir James Colborne expressly tells the Legislature, that he does not want supplies, because the revenue arising from the 14th Geo. III. of which the crown has the entire disposal and control, is sufficient for the exigencies of the government.* Have the Assem-

---

*Gentlemen of the House of Assembly.—I thank you for your offer of making a provision for the support of the civil Government, which I should have gladly accepted in His Majesty's name had not the Revenue arising from the Statute of the 14th Geo. III, chap. 88, the appropriation of which, for the public service, is under the control of the Crown, appeared quite sufficient to defray the expenses of the current year. An intimation to this effect, was conveyed to you in my reply to one of your Addresses early in the present month.

Sir John Colborne's Speech, 20th March, 1829.

bly of Upper Canada set up a claim to the distribution and appropriation of these Crown revenues? They have not, and dare not. Why should the Assembly of Lower Canada be permitted to pursue a different line of conduct, having the same Constitution to guide them? It will be vain to say, that it was because supplies had been demanded in Lower Canada, and that the legislature in such a case, have a right to interfere with the appropriation of the Crown revenues, in order to limit or extend those at their own disposal. Can a claim of supplies in aid of the Crown revenues alter the laws and constitution of the country? If they can, why should not the interpretation apply in Upper Canada as well as in this province; and why should not the point in dispute be freely and candidly given up to the assemblies of both provinces. But there is another point of view in which His Excellency's acceptance of supplies in the mode voted by the assembly, ought to be considered; and it seems to us the only mode of disposing of the question so far as respects *him*. At an early period of the session, his Excellency, by the "King's commands," sent a Message to the legislature explanatory of His Majesty's views with regard to the difficulties which agitate this province. In that message, after the nature and amount of the "Crown Revenues" are described and summed up, it is positively and pointedly declared, that these revenues "constitute the whole estimated revenue arising in the province, which the Law has placed at the disposal of the Crown;" and "His Majesty has been pleased to direct that from this collective Revenue of £38,000, the salary of the Officers administering the Government of the province and the salaries of the Judges shall be defrayed." It is added "His Majesty fully relies upon the liberality of his faithful provincial parliament to make such further provision as the exigencies of the public service of the province (for which the amount of the Crown Revenues above mentioned may prove inadequate) may require."* Now, if His Majesty has been pleased to declare that the "Law" has put the revenue in question at his "disposal:" and if His Majesty has been pleased to "direct" the expenditure of this revenue to the Judges and the other officers of the government, how can His Majesty's Representative submit to be told by the legislature that they have an equal right in the disposal of this revenue, and will therefore dole it out, as they have done this session, in such portions as they think proper? Is not the insult as well as the illegality of the thing clear to every mind? His Excellency has therefore suffered both his Royal Master and himself to be imposed upon by the legislature; and has allowed his own Message of the 29th of November, not only to be neglected and spurned, but absolutely trampled under foot. Why is it so then? If contrary, or contradictory instructions

*Vide Appendix, No. V.

have been received, why have they not been published to the world, that the country might have been made aware of its true situation—that the province might know whether it is to his Excellency or to His Majesty's government in England, that it owes measures so full of danger, contradiction and inconsistency? Having said this, we have said all that was necessary, and all we intended on the present occasion. The Protests of the dissentient Legislative Councillors will bear us out in all we have said against them* we appeal for a full and complete confirmation of all our statements on this question.

Having discussed at such length, the unconstitutional measures of this eventful session, it may perhaps, be expected that we should touch upon those that were useful and in real unision with the principles of the constitution. We do not deny that there were such measures. But we leave them, in their free course, for the benefit of our country, and the example of posterity.

In conclusion, we feel that we have discharged a most invidious but important duty. We feel that we have stood alone on the Watch-tower of our country's salvation, exposed to all the weapons that faction, malice and revenge can bring against us. But, as we write neither for fame, patronage nor profit, being equally independent of them all, we have honestly and fearlessly—no

---

*Vide Appendix, No. VI.

matter how feebly—discharged a debt due by every British subject who loves his country—loves his king—and venerates the constitution. If we have spoken boldly, we feel and know that our language has been that of truth. What have we to fear then ! Thank God ! one free press still exists in the country ; and while that is the case, the Constitution cannot be destroyed. He who will attempt to put it down is an enemy to the Palladium of British Liberty and the basest criminal known to our laws.

APPENDIX.

NO. I.

(*Vide p.* 12.)

Tuesday 18th November 1806.

" A message was delivered from his Ex-
" cellency the Lieutenant Governor, by Mr.
" Gautier, Deputy Secretary, to acquaint
" the Members, that it was His Excellency's
" pleasure, they should proceed to choose a
" fit person to be their Speaker ; and to pre-
" sent the Member chosen for His Excellen
" cy's approbation.

" Mr. Northup then proposed to the House,
" William Cottnam Tonge, Esquire, His
" Majesty's Naval Officer, and Member for
" the County of Hants, and Mr. Pyke pro-
" posed Lewis Morris Wilkins, Esquire,
" Member for the County of Lunenburg, for
" their Speaker; and the choice of the House
" having fallen upon William Cottnam
" Tonge, Esquire, he stood up in his place,
" and expressing the honour proposed to be
" conferred on him by the House, submitted
" himself to the choice, and he was taken out
" of his place by Jeremiah Northup and
" Shubael Dimock, Esquires, and conducted
" to, and placed in the Chair, accordingly ;
" and thereupon Mr. Speaker, elect, ad-
" dressed the Members, as follows, &c. &c."

" A Message was delivered from His Ex-
" cellency the Lieutenant Governor, by Mr.
" Gautier, Deputy Secretary of the Prov-
" ince, commanding the attendance of the
" House in the Council Chamber.

"Accordingly, Mr. Speaker elect, with
" the House, went up to attend His Escal-
" loncy in the Council Chamber, where Mr.
" Speaker elect, was presented to His Ex-
" cellency by Mr. Northup, when His Ex-
" cellency was pleased to say that he did
" not approve of the choice the House had
" made, and desired them to return, and
" make another choice, and present the
" Member whom they should elect for His
" Excellency's approbation to-morrow, at
" one o'clock.

" The Members being returned,

" Mr. Northup reported that the Members
" had been in the Council Chamber, when
" His Excellency had not been pleased to
" approve of the choice they had made of
" Willium Cottuam Tonge, Esquire, to be
" their Speaker; and had directed they
" would make another choice, and present
" the Member whom they should elect for
" His Excellency's approbation at one o'-
" clock to-morrow.

" And thereupon, the Clerk, by direction
" of the Members present, adjourned the
" House until to-morrow, at eleven of the
" clock.

" *Wednesday*, 19*th November*, 1806:

" The Members met agreeably to the ad-
" journment of yesterday; and the Clerk by

"order, adjourned the House till To-morrow "at ten of the clock.

"*Thursday, 20th November*, 1806.

"The Members met agreeably to the ad-"journment of yesterday; and, in obedi-"ence to the commands of His Excellency "the Lieutenant Governor, proceeded to "the choice of a Speaker, in the place of "William Cottnam Tonge, Esquire, who "had not been approved of by His Excel-"lency; and, thereupon, Mr. Mortimer pro-"posed Foster Hutchinson, Esquire, Mem-"ber for the Town of Halifax, and Mr. Pyke "proposed Lewis M. Wilkins, Esquire, for "their Speaker; and the choice of the House "having fallen upon the latter Gentleman, "he stood up in his place, and expressing the "honour proposed to be conferred on him by "the House, submitted himself to their "choice, and he was taken out of his place "by John George Pyke and Jeremiah North-"up, Esquires, and conducted to, and placed "in, the Chair, accordingly; and, there-"upon, Mr. Speaker elect, addressed the "Members as follows: &c. &c."

"A massage was delivered from His Ex-"cellency the Lieut. Governor, by Mr. Gah-"tier, Deputy Secretary, commanding the "attendance of the House in the Council "Chamber.

"Accordingly, Mr. Speaker elect, with "the House, went up to attend His Excel-"lency in the Council Chamber, where Mr "Speaker elect, was presented to His Ex-

"cellency by Mr. Northup, upon which His "Excellency approved of the choice the "House had made.

"The House being returned, and Mr. "Speaker having taken the chair.

"Mr. Speaker reported that the House "had been in the Council Chamber, where "His Excellency had been pleased to ap- "prove of the choice the House had made "of him to be their Speaker, and that he "had spoken to the following effect :

"May it please your Excellency,

"The House of Assembly having chosen "me their Speaker, and your Excellency "having approved of their choice, I have to "observe to your Excellency, that I feel "very sensibly the weight and importance "of the duties incident to that office, and "my inability to perform them. I trust "however, that an honest and fervent zeal "to promote the ease and comfort of your "Excellency's Administration, the peace "and harmony of the different Branches of "the Legislature, and the general good of "the Province, will, in some measure, com- "pensate for all other deficiencies ; I beg "leave to require of your Excellency, on "the part of the House of Assembly, that "their words and actions may receive the "most favourable consideration : and that "the Members may from time to time have "access to your Excellency, and that they "may enjoy their usual privileges."

Saturday, 22 *November*, 1826.

[Extract from the Address of the House of

Assembly in answer to the Speech, in which, however, the refusal of the Speaker had not been noticed :]

" While we lament that Your Excellency
" has been pleased to exercise a branch of
" His Majesty's Prerogative, long unused in
" Great Britain, and without precedent in
" this Province, we beg leave to assure Your
" Excellency, that we shall not fail to culti-
" vate assiduously a good understanding be-
" tween the different branches of the Legis-
" latore, and to prosecute with diligence the
" business of the Session."

NO. II.

(*See p. 24.*)

Coke in his Institutes, 4. p. 8. in substance says, that after the choice is made the King may assent him, and that it is usual to recommend a discreet man that will be received. Blackstone, in his Commentaries, says, "the Speaker of the House of Commons is chosen by the House, but must be approved of by the King," (I. p. 181.) Comyn in the 4th volume of his Digest of the laws of England, (6,297) says "that none can be Speaker without elections of the Commons, and their claction is free, but the King may recommend or refuse him. If the Speaker be approved by the King, he prays, 1st, Freedom of Speech" &c. Jacobs in his Law Dictionary, in continuance of what has been already cited says, " the commons are commanded to choose a Speaker, which done, two or three days afterwards, he is presented to the King and after some speeches is allowed and sent down to the House of Commons when the business of Parliament proceeds." Custance in his treatise on the British Constitution (p. 104.) says "the House of Commons always elect their own Speaker, who must be presented to the King for approbation." Chitty in his late work on the Royal Prerogative also says, "The Speaker of the House of Commons is chosen by the House, but must, it seems, be approved by the King." (p. 74.) Hammond, one of the latest writers on Parliamentary proceedings, in his treatise on Precedents, says, "that the Speaker of the House of Commons is chosen by the House but must be approved by the King, who though he cannot nominate, may nevertheless recommend, nor is he till confirmed, called Speaker (p. 64.) The work on the British Constitution by a Doctor of the Laws already cited, states "the commons being returned to their House in obedience to the Royal command, choose their Speaker, who is generally one recommended by the Sovereign, for though they have a right to choose a Speaker, who is their mouth and trusted by them and so necessary that the House of Commons cannot sit without him, the king has a right to disallow or to refuse him, after he is so chosen (2. p. 62.) Whitelocke says, "then the commons repair to their house, and usually some of the members before acquainted with the King's mind doth nominate one among them to be chosen for their Speaker, wherein there is seldom contradiction. Coke saith that after their choice the King may refuse him, and that the course is for avoiding expense of time and contest (as in the conge d'elire of a bishop) that the King doth name a discreet and learned man whom the Commons elect, but without their election (saith he truly) no Speaker can be appointed." This practice of disapproval does not apply only to a British House of Commons, for in Neal's History of New England (2 p. 24.) it is said of the General Assembly of that Province, "as soon as the House is called over and the several members have taken the oaths, repeated and subscribed the Declaration and took and subscribed the oath of abjuration, they proceed to the choice of their Speaker, whom they present to the Governor for his approbation." A striking authority will be found in a work published by the House of Assembly themselves as a guide to young beginners in parliamentary warfare the "Lex Parliamentaria" where at p. 263, it is said "It is true, the Commons are to choose their Speaker, but seeing that after their choice, the King may refuse him," and then proceeds to mention the conge' d'elire which may be issued by the Sovereign. The numerous and unvarying authorities from the most authentic sources cannot fail to demonstrate with sufficient clearness the existence of the prerogative.

But that the prerogative exists may be further demonstrated by shewing the actual exercise of it in various British and Colonial Assemblies either by the Sovereign himself, or by his representatives. It is well known that on the election of a Speaker, the individual chosen generally excuses himself to the house on account of disability or want of sufficient talents to maintain the situation with dignity. But the House refuse his request and he then excuses himself before the King and with all humility prays that he may be disallowed. This excuse has been made more or less since the 5th Richard II. (1381) when Sir Richard Waldegrave made that suit to the King. Thus in 1450 Sir John Popham was chosen Speaker, his excuse was admitted by the King and he was discharged from his office. On the same day the Commons presented William Tresham for the same purpose who was allowed. The words of the record which mentions the disallowance are "Rex ipsam suam éxcusationem admisit et ipsum de occupatione predicts exoneravit." At the commencement of the new Parliament in 1678-79—Edward Seymour (afterwards Sir Edward) who had become very popular in the house for the violent stand he had taken against Popery, was chosen Speaker. In the address of excuse which he made to the House, he said "But since you are pleased to sequester your judgments, in his choice, give me leave to present my excuse to the King, and I hope the King will have no cause to disagree with you in any thing but your choice of me," and prayed for leave to intercede with His Majesty to discharge him of his duty. When brought before the King for approbation he addressed His Majcaty "I am coma hither for your Majesty's approbation which if your Majesty please to grant I shall do them and you the best service I can." From his having several disagreements with Lord Danby then high in favour, it had been determined to disallow him, but Mr. Seymour being aware of this intention avoided making his excuses in the usual form, but the Lord Chancellor addressing Mr. Seymour said "the approbation which is given by His Majesty to the choice of a Speaker would not be thought such a favour as it is and ought to be received, if His Majesty were not at liberty to deny, as wall as to grant it. It is an essential prerogative of the King to refuse as well as to approve of a Speaker. This is a matter which by mistake may be liabla to misrepresentation, as if the King did dislike the persons that chose or the person chosen. As to the first there can be no doubt. They are old representatives of his people whom he hath a desire to meet and there can be no doubt of the latter, nor has his Majesty any reason to dislike you, having had great experience of our ability and service. But the King is the best judge of men and things. He knows when and where to employ.

He thinks fit to reserve you for other service and to ease you of this. It is His Majesty's pleasure to discharge this choice and accordingly by his Majesty's commands I do discharge you of the place you are chosen for and in His Majesty's name command the House of Commons to make another choice and command them to attend here to-morrow at 11 o'clock." The popularity of Seymour made this disallowance very disagreeable to the Members, who in the debate which ensued spoke in strong terms against those who had counselled the measure, but seemed little disposed to assail the prerogative. During the debate Mr. Sacheverell said "I would not lose a hair's breadth of the King's right" and he moved an adjournment that in the interim the records might be searched for precedents in this matter. Mr. Garraway said, "I would not give the King offence but not part with one hair of our right." "I am satisfied we could not fix upon a fitter person for Speaker than Mr. Seymour, he is a Privy Counsellor, treasurer of the navy and has done the King very good service here which makes me wonder he should not be approved of by the king. I thought we could not have obliged the king more." Notwithstanding that the adjournment took place, the house addressed the king for a longer time to consider the question as being one of "such great importance." The king granted them the delay required, at the same time observing "as I would not have my prerogative encroached upon, so I would not encroach upon your privilege." At the continued debate Mr. Hampden said the choice they had made they had reason to think "would have been acceptable to the king." Sir John Ernly remarked that "tha choice is in the Commons and it is undoubted that the refusal of a Speaker when chosen is of right in the king." In the address which the House made to the king they deciated that they had a tender regard "for the rights of your Majesty and your royal prerogative which we shall always acknowledge to be vested in the Crown for the benefit and protection of the people." During the many days to which this debate was continued, the opinions of the members, however much in favour of Mr. Seymour were nevertheless favourable to the choice of a third person in preference to the one nominated by the Crown. The king having prorogued the House for a few days, on its again meeting it unanimously chose Sergeant Gregory, thus succumbing to the right of the crown. Throughout this transaction we find the House pertinacious of their own right but at the same time showing a great respect to the privileges of the Crown, thereby affording a striking contrast to the conduct of our Commons, who in all their proceedings and debates affected a total neglect of the wishes and directions of the Crown as expressed by its representative. These are certainly the only instances on record in English Parliamentary History where the disallowance took place; but Sir Fletcher Norton, having displeased his late Majesty in 1773 in a speech on presenting a Bill of Supply, the determination of the Sovereign to exercise the Royal prerogative against that individual should he be again chosen was urged by Lord North as a reason against his election, and the House notwithstanding the popularity of Sir Fletcher rather than dispute the wishes of the Crown chose Charles W. Cornwall Esq. who was accepted of.—There are however several instances to be found in Colonial History where Speakers of the Representative Body have been disallowed. In the late Province of Massachusetts Bay, in 1704, Mr. Oakes being chosen, was disallowed and the House persisted in their choice. On account of the affairs of the war being so pressing, the Governor waived the prerogative, "saving to her Majesty her just rights at all times." This disapproval was sanctioned by the approbation of the then Commissioners of trade and plantations. In 1720, the Speaker chosen in the same colony was disallowed by the Governor, who had to dissolve the Assembly. On the meeting of the new one, though composed of nearly the same members, they chose one who was acceptable to the Governor. These disallowances caused ill will between the Governor and the House, and the disputes were referred to England. Through the means of Governor Dummer, the Assembly in 1726 passed an act, whereby the doubts which, they said, might have existed, were set at rest by a positive enactment, that the administrator of the Government should have a negative in the election of their Speaker. The House of Assembly of South Carolina on the 12th Jan. 1773 having presented the Hon. R. Lowndes to be their Speaker the Governor disapproved and disallowed their choice, and directed them to proceed anew, but the House, persisted in their views and it was thereupon prorogued. About the year 1810 James Tucker was elected Speaker of the House of Assembly of Bermuda, but being disapproved of by the Lieutenant Governor, John Noble Manley, was subsequently elected and approved of by His Excellency.

The first notice or mention made of the approbation of the Speaker by the monarch being formally announced, was in 1399, when Henry IV, approved the choice made in the person of Sir John Cheney, who next day was obliged to resign his charge from sudden disease, and the Commons elected Sir John Doreward in his place, who was then approved of. On the election of the Speaker, it has been already mentioned as being usual to excuse himself on presentation to the king, and this practice has been almost hitherto invariable.

In 1592, Sir Edward Coke, an individual whose knowledge of law and the constitution under which he lived, cannot be doubted, in his speech to the throne said: "This is only as yet a nomination and no Election, until your Majesty giveth allowance and approbation." In 1660 Sir Harbottle Grimstone was chosen, but on account of the absence of the king, was not presented for approbation. The Speech of Sir Edward Turner who was chosen the succeeding year, is not recorded in the Journals of the Commons, but in substance as given in the Lords' Journals, is as follows: "From this their judgment, if I must so call it, I do most humbly appeal to your Sovereign justice, beseeching your Majesty for the errors that are too visible and apparent in their proceedings, that you will review and reverse the same." The Lord Chancellor replied "you have not discredited yourself enough to persuade the king to dissent from the House of Commons in the election they have made." In 1672, Sir Job Charlton was chosen, who addressed the king as follows: "I therefore with a plain humble heart prostrate at your Royal feet, beseech, that you will command them to review what they have done, and to proceed to a new election." The king in reply said; "He cannot disapprove the election of this House of Commons, especially when they have expressed so much duty in choosing one worthy and acceptable to him." This individual became unwell and desired to retire to the country and vacate the Speaker's chair. In his address to the king, he said; "I humbly beseech your Majesty's leave that I may move your most dutiful and loyal House of Commons, to permit me to retire to the country, and to give them leave to choose another Speaker." This leave was granted, and the House on the 18th Feb. 1672, elected Edward (afterwards Sir Edward) Seymour, who was approved. On the 20th May 1689, Sir John Trevor was re-elected, and on being presented to the king, humbly beseeched his Majesty "to command the Commons to make a better choice." On the election of Paul Foley in 1694, the Lord Keeper in addressing him after he had made his excuses said: "He (the king) does well allow of the choice which the House of Commons have made, and does approve of you for their Speaker." When Sir Thomas Littleton was chosen in 1695, he said to his Majesty: "I need enumerate no more particulars wherein I am wanting to your Majesty, to whom my insufficiencies in business are not unknown, hoping I have said enough already to induce your Majesty to disapprove me." Having been approved, he replied; "Since your Majesty has been pleased to approve the choice which your Commons have made, it becomes me not to contend longer with your Majesty." When Robert Harley was chosen in 1701, he addressed the king in the usual strain of excuse, but it was not allowed by his Majesty. Harley in reply said; "Since your Majesty hath not been pleased to admit of my excuse, it is my duty to submit, and I do in the first place with the utmost thankfulness acknowledge the undeserved honour your Majesty is pleased to confer upon me, and that I may the better discharge that great trust which your Majesty and the Commons have committed to me, I am an humble suitor to your Majesty," and then prayed the usual liberties. In 1708, Sir Richard Onslow addressed the Lords Commissioners; "May my most humble intercession to your Lordships to disapprove this choice obtain pardon." In 1710, William Bromely being chosen, he addressed the Queen, that in obedience to her commends he had been chosen, and that he was a humble suitor to her Majesty, that she would be pleased to excuse his undertaking it, and to command the Commons to make a better choice. In 1713, Sir Thomas Hanmer being chosen, he thus addressed the Queen: "That for her own service and satisfaction, for the better success of those arduous and urgent affairs which have induced her to call this Parliament, and for the honour of the House of Commons, she will be pleased to order them to re-consider this their resolution and to come again prepared to present some other person to her Majesty, more worthy of their choice, and of her royal acceptance and approbation." To this the Lord Chancellor answered that the Queen expected nothing else from that House, "than the choice of a person for their Speaker equally qualified for that important trust, by a just regard for her prerogative, and an hearty zeal for the welfare of her people;" and the Queen further stated that their choice was acceptable to her and therefore approved and confirmed it. In 1714, Mr. Spencer Compton was chosen. He stated his incapacity to act, and professed the most unshaken fidelity to the protestant succession. He said, "This your Commons hope may be some excuse for their presuming to present to your Majesty a person whose insufficiency rendered him so improper for them to elect or your Majesty to approve." The same individual in 1722, besought His Majesty, "to command your Commons to present to your Majesty, some other person more worthy of your Royal approbation." Mr. Arthur Onslow in 1727 craved leave to implore His Majesty's goodness "to command your commons to do, what they can easily perform to make choice of another person,-more proper for them to present to your Majesty on this great occasion." Mr. Onslow in 1734, hoped the king would send back the Commons to reconsider their choice and choose one "more proper than I am for their service and your royal approbation." The same gentleman in 1741 stated that he had been elected Speaker, "how properly for me, for themselves, and for the public is now with your Majesty to judge, and to your Royal judgment, Sir, I do with all humbleness and resignation submit myself, being well assured that should your Majesty think fit to disapprove of this present choice your commons will have no difficulty to find some other person among them to be presented to your Majesty on this occasion, to whom none of these objections can be made which I fear may too justly, from my imperfection, arise in your Royal breast, upon being again the subject of your Majesty's consideration for this important charge." In 1747 the same gentleman begged with silence and submission to resign himself to the Royal determination. In 1754 the same gentleman in addressing the Lord Commissioners, stated that he resigned himself "entirely to His Majesty's pleasure, well knowing his own Royal wisdom can have best determined his own choice either to approve or disapprove what his commons have now done. Sir John Cust in 1761, said, "I have this satisfaction that I can now be an humble suitor to your Majesty that you would give your faithful commons an opportunity of rectifying this, the only inadvertent step which they can ever take and be graciously pleased to direct them to present some other to your Majesty whom they may not hereafter be sorry to have chosen, nor your Majesty to have approved." The same person in 1768 addressed the Lord Commissioners. "His Majesty must, I am assured have observed so many imperfections in my conduct during the last Parliament that I need urge no other reasons to induce His Majesty to give his faithful Commons an opportunity of presenting one worthier of their choice and His Majesty's loyal approbation." The addresses of Sir Fletcher Norton in 1770 and 1774, and of Mr. Cornwall in 1780, and 1784, are all in the same strain. In 1789, 1790, 1796 and 1807, Mr. Addington implored the king to direct the commons to proceed to a new choice and to present one more worthy of the royal approbation Mr. Abbott in 1807 said "in humbly submitting myself at this bar to his Majesty's judgment, I have the satisfaction to reflect, that if it should be His Majesty's Royal pleasure to disallow this choice." Again in 1812, he said "whatever considerations may have weighed with the House of Commons in forming this determination, they well know that their choice must nevertheless await the Royal pleasure, and I now with all humbleness do in their behalf present myself in this place in order that His Majesty's faithful Commons may learn whether it be His Majesty's Royal will that they shall proceed to a consideration of the choice which they have made." In 1820 Mr. Sutton addressed the Lord Commissioners, "should, however, it be His Majesty's pleasure to reject the choice thus made by His faithful Commons, it is consolatory to me to know, that there are many members of the house much better qualified than myself to fulfil the office of Speaker, upon one of whom their choice may most advantageously devolve." These numerous declarations of Speaker in various years, speaking for and in the names of the Commons of England are heavy arguments against the pretensions of our Assembly. It is not very likely that a British House of Commons would permit their Speaker for them, to use such language, did they not acknowledge the Royal Prerogative, and that in the language thus used, there is something more than mere matter of form, or mere courtesy. If any of the Members of the late Assembly will consult the Journals of the Irish House of Commons, he will find the same strain made use of throughout. There, in 1639, Maurice Eustace appealed to the Lord Lieutenant to direct the Commons of that House to make choice of another Speaker, but His Lordship by the Chancellor declared his "approbation and good liking and allowance of the said election." In 1771, Mr. E. S. Perry addressed the Vice Roy, "I confess it is the highest point of my ambition, and if I have the honour of your Excellency's approbation &c." and in 1776, the same individual said it was his "duty as well as inclination to submit if their choice shall be confirmed by your Excellency's approbation." At the commencement of the House of Assembly of Jamaica in 1671, it appears that the Governor nominated the Speaker who was then elected by the House and afterwards presented for His Excellency's approbation, and during the whole period from the time already alluded to, the Speakers of that House have invariably been presented for approbation and have invariably used the same language as the representative branch of England. The Journals of that Island afford a denial of the assertion that the presentment of the Speaker and the demand and grant of the usual privileges are mere matter of form and courtesy. In 1765, the Speaker did not demand the usual privileges when approved of, and the next day, the Governor (W. H. Littleton Esq.) addressed the Speaker, (C. Price Esq.) in the following terms. " Mr. Speaker, as you omitted at the time when I approved of the choice which the House of Assembly made of you to be their Speaker, to apply to me for the usual privileges. I have sent for you to ask, whether you will now make application for them or not. The Speaker replied " Sir, I do not intend to make any." The Governor replied " Sir I once more ask you whether you will now make applicatien for them or not" to which Mr. Price shortly said " Sir, I shall not." The Governer then replied, as it is my duty to see that the just order of the proceedings of the House of Assembly is preserved, and their privileges maintained as well as that His Majesty's prerogative suffers no violation, I do in His Majesty's name dissolve the General Assembly and it is dissolved accordingly. " In Nova Scotia in 1806 both Mr. Tonge, who was disallowed, and Mr. Wilkins who was confirmed, after election but before presentation, expressed their thanks for the honour proposed to be conferred upon them, thereby publicly declaring that as yet they were but inchoate Speakers whose existence had not yet perfectly taken place.

But it can be shown also by the Journals of the House of Assembly of this Province, that they have tacitly acknowledged this right. Upon every new Parliament they have invariably been directed and commanded to present their Speaker for the approbation of the King's representative. They never denied this right, but always did as they were directed, and their Journals invariably say in such terms as the following, " that the house being returned, the Speaker stated that the Governor in Chief had been pleased to approve of their choice." Mr. Panet in 1793, 1797, 1801, 1806, 1809, 1810, and 1811, made use of nearly the same language whether front a paucity of words or not, it is difficult to imagine. He generally stated that the choice of the house had fallen on him and he implored " the excuse and commands" of His Excellency. Mr. Belohiniere, elected on the appointment of Mr. Panet to the Bench, said " that you will be pleased to order the Assembly of Lower Canada to do that which may be easily done, that is to choose another person better qualified than I am to fill that office, and fitter to be presented to you on this present occasion." Mr. Papineau the Ex-Speaker in 1815, 1817, 1820, 1821, and 1825, generally made use of the same language, by imploring the " excuse and commands" of His Excellency, and after approbation has replied " the manner in which your Excellency has been pleased to signify your ASSENT to the choice of the Assembly, demands my warmest gratitude." When Mr. Papineau, in 1823, resigned the Speaker's chair, in order that he might proceed to England in aid of the Anti-Union Petitions, he addressed a letter to the Clerk of the House of Assembly wherein he made use of the following terms, "It is not therefore to avoid fulfilling the duties of that honourable station with which it has pleased His Excellency the Governor in Chief and the House of Assembly to honour me."

Mr. Vallieres when elected in 1823, in Mr. Papineau's stead, implored the excuse and commands of His Excellency, and after approbation, in his reply he returned thanks "since the choice of the House of Assembly has been sanctioned by your Excellency's approbation." At that time he had not the slightest idea that the approbation was "a mere matter of form or of courtesy."

NO. III.

(*See* p. 46.)

PROVINCIAL PARLIAMENT OF LOWER CANADA.—House of Assembly.

Tuesday, Nov. 20th, 1827.

The following gentlemen took the usual oath and subscribed the Roll, viz:

Messrs. Christie, Robitaile, Borgia, Fortin, Letourneau, Blanchet, Boissonnault, Lagueux, Samson, Bourdages, Proulx, Nelson of Sorel, Dessaules, De St. Ours, De Rouville, Amiot, L. J. Papineau, Viger, Quesnel, Cuvillier, Raymond, Heney, Leslie, Nelson of Montreal, Perrault, Valois, Labria, Lefebre, Turgeon, A. Papineau, Leroux, Poirier, Deligny, Mousseau, Bureau, Caron, Dumoulin, Ogden, Cannon, Neilson, Clouet, Vallieres de St. Real, Stuart, Young, Lagueux. Quirouet, 46; absent Messrs. Laterriere and Larue, 2; elected for 2 places, 1; dead, 1;—total, 50.

At two o'clock the presence of the Members was required on the part of His Excellency in the Legislative Council Chamber, when the Speaker of the Council informed them that his Excellency did not think fit to declare the causes of summoning this Parliament until there be a Speaker of the Assembly, and requiring them to choose a fit and proper person to be their Speaker, to be presented for his approbation to-morrow at two o'clock.

On the Members being returned, Louis Bourdages, Esq. Member for the County of Buckinghamshire, seconded by J. C. Letourneau, Member for Devon, moved that Louis Joseph Papineau, Esq. Member for the West Ward of Montreal, be Speaker.

C. R. Ogden, Esq. Solicitor General, Member for the Borough of Three-Rivers, seconded by N. Boissonnault, Member for Hertford; moved that J. R. Vallieres De St. Real, be Speaker.

There being no debate, the question was called for, and a divison being asked, the names were required to be taken down, and are as follows:

Yeas, (*For Mr. Papineau as* Speaker,) Messrs, Robitaille, Borgia, Fortin, Letourneau, Blanchet, L. Lagueux, Samson, Bourdages, Proulx, Nelson of Sorel, Dessaules,

De St. Ours, De Rouville, Amiot, Viger, Quesnel, Cuvillier, Raymond, Heney, Leslie, Nelson of Montreal, Perrault, Valois, Labrie, Lefebre, Turgeon, A. Papineau, Leroux, Poirier, Deligny, Mousseau, Bureau, Caron Dumoulin, Cannon, Neilson, Clouet, E. C. Lagueux, Quirouet, (39.)

Nays, Messrs. Ogden, (Solicitor General) Christie, Boissonault, Stuart and Young. (5.)

Mr. Papineau was accordingly conducted to the Chair, where he thanked the House for the renewal of their confidence, requested a continuance of their support in maintaining the Rules of the House and preserving order and decorum in its proceedings.

The House then adjourned, till to-morrow at one o'clock, and most of the Members with a number of the Citizens, conducted the Speaker elect to his lodgings.

Wednesday, 21st Nov. 1827.

The House met at one o'clock, and their presence being required on the part of His Excellency, in the Legislative Council Chamber, Mr. Speaker elect, and the Members, proceeded thither, when Mr. Speaker addressed His Excellency in the usual form, acquainting His Excellency with the choice of the Assembly.

His Excellency then said, in substance, that in His Majesty's name he disallowed the nomination of Mr. Papineau, and required the House to make another choice, to be presented for his approbation on Friday, when he would inform them of certain instructions relative to the affairs of this Province received from His Majesty's Government.

On returning to the House Mr. Papineau took the Chair, upon which Mr. Neilson observed that the Chair was still occupied by Mr. Papineau, as the Speaker of the House, and they were perfectly competent to proceed to business.

Mr. Ogden asked by what authority Mr. Papineau entered into that seat. His election as Speaker had been disallowed by the Crown, and he was now no higher in rank or authority than any other member of the House. He was nothing more than Member for the West Ward of Montreal. They had no Speaker and could not be looked upon as a House, till a Speaker had been chosen with the approbation of the Crown. It would be the duty of the Clerk of the House, to report such proceedings as had taken place, in the Upper-Branch of the Legislature.

Mr. Stuart stated that Mr. Papineau should be cautious in taking the Chair.

Dr. Blanchet insisted on the propriety of Mr. Papineau entering into the Chair of that House. He had been chosen their Speaker and until the new one was nominated, he only could preside at their deliberations. The Clerk of the Assembly did not belong to their body, and was not a competent person to act on this occasion. The House was perfectly competent to proceed to business, it had its Speaker and the allowance of the Crown was perfectly unnecessary.

Mr. Papineau reported that during the time the Members had been in the Legislative Council Chamber, he had addressed His Excellency the Governor in chief in the usual form. To which His Excellency, through the Honorable the Speaker of the Legislative Council, had addressed him as follows:

Mr. Papineau, and Gentlemen of the Assembly,

I am commanded by His Excellency the Governor in Chief to inform you that his His Excellency doth not approve the choice which the Assembly have made of a Speaker; in His Majesty's name His Excellency doth accordingly now disallow and discharge the said choice.

And it is His Excellency's pleasure that you, Gentlemen of the Assembly, do forthwith again repair to the place where the sittings of the Assembly are usually held, and there make choice of another person to be your Speaker—and that you present the person who shall be so chosen, to His Excellency, in this House, on Friday next, at two o'clock, for his approbation.

And I am further directed by His Excellency to inform you, that as soon as a Speaker of the House of Assembly has been chosen, with the approbation of the Crown, His Excellency will lay before the Provincial Parliament certain communications upon the present state of this Province, which, by his Majesty's express command, he has been directed to make known to them.

Mr. Ogden said he could not find any precedema in the History of the English Parliament, to permit such an assumption of authority as the present—Mr. Papineau, the Hon. Member for the West Ward of Montreal, and who had also the honour of serving for the County of Surrey, had assumed the Chair of that House though not its Speaker. The instances in English History which he had been able to find, went directly to the contrary. He ought to leave the Chair.

Mr. Bourdages called on the honorable member to cite his authorities.

Mr. Vallieres then read from Hatsell's Precedents the case of Sir Edward Seymour, who on being disallowed in 1678, did not return to the House, it seeming doubtful whether he could act either as a member or as Speaker. The proceedings in that case had been erased from the Lord's Journals, though the discussions of the subject were found in Grey's Debates.

Mr. Baurdages stated that the erasure of the proceedings would seem to point out the illegality of what the House of Commons had done, and that they did not wish them to act as precedents to future Parliaments. The case Mr. Vallieres had cited was directly in favour of his (Mr. B's.) opinion, since erasures had followed its entry.

Mr. Ogden was astonished at what had fallen from the honourable member who had just sat down. The precedent which had been cited was directly in favour of the prerogative of the Crown—It was astonishing also, to hear some honourable members stating that the Crown had not the prerogative of disallowing their Speaker—a prerogative which was tacitly allowed by their own acts, did not positive law declare it. For what purpose did the House go up that morning to the Council Chamber, but to present their Speaker elect, for His Excellency's approbation? Why should they do so if he had not the prerogative to grant that approbation?'

Mr. Cuvillier stated that the present case was almost unprecedented. There were only two cases on record in the English History of the disallowance of a Speaker by the King, and these instances were in 1450, when Sir John Popham, and in 1678 when Sir Edward Seymour, was disallowed. These instances were looked upon with shame by the English people, and no instance could be found of a disallowance of a Speaker since the revolution in 1688, when the Constitution was re-modelled. Though the House of Commons went up to the King, for his approbation of their Speaker, this was done as a matter of course, by politeness only, and the King could not disallow him. But allowing the king in England to have such authority, no instance in the Colonies could be pointed out to sanction such an assumption. The whole proceeding of disallowance was an encroachment upon the free choice of the House of their Speaker, and he would therefore submit a series of resolutions, which he hoped would express the sense of the members. He then read the following resolutions, tending to dispute the authority of the Crown to disallow a Speaker.

Resolved, 1. That it is necessary for the discharge of the duties imposed upon this House, viz to give its advice to his Majesty, in the enactment of Laws for the peace, welfare and good government of the Province, conformably to the Act of the British Parliament, under which it constituted and assembled, that its Speaker be a person of its free choice, independently of the will and pleasure of the person entrusted by his Majesty, with the administration of the local government for the time being.

2. That Louis Joseph Papineau, Esquire, one of the Members of this House, who has served as Speaker in six successive Parliaments, has been duly chosen by this House to be its Speaker in the present Parliament.

3. That the Act of the British Parliament under which this House is constituted and assembled, does not require the approval of such person so chosen as Speaker, by the person administering the government of this Province in the name of his Majesty.

4. That the presenting of the person so elected as Speaker, to the King's Representative for approval is founded on usage only, and that such approval is and hath always been a matter of course.

5. That this House doth persist in its choice, and that the said Louis Joseph Papineau, Esquire, ought to be and is its Speaker.

Mr. Ogden stated no motion could be received till a Speaker was nominated, and the mace on the table, which was not now the case.

Mr. vallieres stated that the members, who had taken the side of the crown, argued that the House tacitly admitted the authority of the crown to disallow, when they asked for approbation. Did not the House at the same time ask for freedom of debate, for their ancient privileges and rights, and would they not be astonished if his Excellency were to deny their requests. No instance could be produced since the revolution of 1688, of such allowance, and in every respect the address to the King's representative was but an act of politeness on the part of the House.

Mr. Ogden was happy in having it in his power to answer the Honorable member for Huntingdon (Mr. Cuvillier.) On many occasions he had heard the Colonies cited as favourable to the views of the former houses—when they were asked to vote a civil list after the example of England—the answer was that the Colonies did not do so. He would now cite an instance from Nova Scotia in 1806 when the Speaker elect was disallowed, and a new one chosen in his place by the Lower House of that province. He hoped the House would now follow the act of the Colony, they were so fond of referring to for example.

Mr. Quesnel stated Mr. Papineau was the Speaker of the House and the mace ought to be on the table.

Mr. A. Stuart stated though his opinion might differ from that of the majority of the members he would not shrink from addressing them. He could not deal in the same roundness of assertion or boldness of asseveration as the Honourable member for Huntingdon, (Cuvillier) but he would make some remarks on what the gentlemen had advanced—The mace could not be on the table till a Speaker was chosen—they had no Speaker and no motions could be mooted now. He would not refer to the qualifications or the personal character of the individual who had been yesterday chosen by the members—but he would briefly remark that their Speaker ought not to be a leader of any party in that house—he ought to be an individual who was not hostile to the Executive part of the Government, or in any way unfriendly to the representative of the Sovereign. His duty is to carry the flag of truce between the contending parties in the body over which he presides—it becomes him to carry the white flag of peace—not the bloody flag of war. Would the House of Commons of England elect an individual to the Speaker's chair who had rendered himself obnoxious to the Government by his gross inconsistency of conduct?—certainly not. No Speaker would there be chosen who had placed himself in personal collision with the Government, and such a choice if made would never be acquiesced in by the people. The duty of the Speaker is well defined. He is a mediator—he is to preside over a popular body from its very nature equally liable to storms as the ocean. The election of an individual the known head of a party would in England be considered a disgrace if such an election ever should take place, but the good sense of the people of that country rendered such a supposition improbable.—They elect the Speaker for purposes of public good (a duty not to be expected from the avowed head of a party) and for the purpose of allaying the difficulties which arise in a popular body. That the Crown has a right of refusing the Speaker named by the House has never till this moment been denied. It is absolutely necessary that a person should be chosen whose character and disposition were such as to be agreeable to that branch with which he was to be continually in communication. It is also absolutely necessary that the power should exist in the Executive to give or refuse its approbation of the choice made by the House—As far as authority and law go, they had no right to proceed to any business till the Speaker was named, and he could not be named till the approbation of the Governor was attained—If the law was such how could the mem-

of the Speaker be placed on the table without flying directly in the face of that authority which had declared its disapprobation of their choice—how could they proceed to the consideration of any business, without the approbation of the Government. The Clerk of the House is the individual to whom all the addresses of the members ought to be spoken: he is then chairman—he acts as such ex necessitate rei—there is no necessity that the Speaker elect, should on this occasion have taken the chair to report what had occurred this day in the Upper House—for any one of the members was competent to declare such proceeding as they were to state the order of yesterday to elect a Speaker. The Speaker chosen by the House takes the Chair subject to the approbation of the Governor in Chief—he has only a quasi possession of it, till the period when he goes up to the Upper House—for his appointment is subject to a defeisanee or a further confirmation by the Executive. He is nothing more than an inchoate Speaker—a Speaker yet in embryo or he may be considered as an absolute Speaker whose title is absolute, should the conditions to which it is subject not be enforced. The approbation of the Executive not being given, he ceases to be a Speaker. He is the organ of that House only till the choice is finally determined and who is the competent authority to determine that choice? The Government only. The Governor acting for the King had disapproved of their Speaker elect and he is a competent authority. To what tribunal could they appeal but to themselves—They must in all particulars elect according to the law of the land.

Mr. Neilson said the House were called on to elect a Speaker, but it since appeared they were not to elect.

Mr. A. Stuart.—By law we have proceeded in our choice and have done what we could—but the work is not finished. We have the free choice and power to choose whom we like, and now that we have been sent back to re-consider our choice we can again elect Mr. Papineau and again present him for approbation.—If again disapproved of we must proceed de novo. The present incumbent ought only to have made the communication he had received, and nothing more. His assuming the chair at the present time is an usurped authority, and could not be countenanced. The mace must not be put on the table.

Mr. Papineau stated his intention to have been, only to have made the communication of proceedings and then retire, because he looked upon the Clerk as not a competent organ of communication. He then left the Chair.

Mr. Cuvillier movad his first resolution.

Mr. Ogden opposed it on the ground that the Clerk could not listen to any motion that did not relate to the election of a new Speaker. They had no reasons to offer for their choice, and at the same time that they so strenously insisted on their own privileges, they ought not to forget that the other branches had theirs.

Dr. Labrie stated, they had all an account yet to render to their constituents.—The Doctor moved an adjournment till to-morrow at 10 of the clock, which was seconded by Mr. Ogden, and carried.

THURSDAY, 22d November, 1827.

The house met at 10, pursuant to adjournment. The Clerk stated that at the adjournment they were considering Mr. Cuviller's 1st Resolution which had been seconded by Mr. Leslie. Mr. Ogden stated, he had opposed the motion yesterday, as tending to destroy the privileges and the prerogatives of the Crown. They had no right to have any motion before them, but elect a Speaker. He was sorry that so much time had been lost, but it had given him an opportunity to search for presedents. He had found that the House of Commons in 1672, acted differently to what the House of Assembly were now doing. Then, a member had made a complaint of privilege previous to the confirmation of the Speaker by the Crown, and it was decided that no proceedings could be had till a Speaker was approved. Let the motion before the House be for the re-election of Mr. Papineau, and he could not object to their hearing it, but to bring forward a string of Resolutions was contrary to what he conceived right. He therefore, entered his protest against such an illegal, unprecedented and unwarrantable proceeding. The members who had urged these Resolutions ought to cite precedents to satisfy the new members of that house. He had shewn a precedent of the rule to be adopted. Upon what grounds were they proceeding? By what rules were they to be bound? By their own; which said that reference was to be had to the Commons of England, where their own rules were deficient.

Mr. Cuvillier said, they could only proceed to the election of a Speaker. Did not the Resolutions before the House, by declaring Mr. Papineau the Speaker, relate to that subject? The House claimed a right, viz. that Louis Joseph Papineau was the Speaker, that the act of the 14 Geo. III. gave no power to the Governor to disallow the motion of the House. If the motions were foreign to the object of the Speaker's election, the Clerk could refuse them, but they were perfectly in order.

Mr. Neilson.—Many examples might be found in the Journals when motions were received before the ratification of the Speaker, concerning writs of election.

Mr. Ogden.—They have all since been expunged.

Mr. Viger said, that the Hon. member for Three-Rivers (Ogden) was correct in saying, that if they employed themselves in debating any subject foreign to the election of the Speaker, it should be laid aside,—for the House must have a Speaker, before we could proceed to business. It was a principle well established, that a motion, not pertinent to the subject, could not be received. But the present Resolutions were relative to matters of debate. They were logical deductions from matters of fact, and established principles from which consequences were to be drawn.

Mr. A. Smart would keep himself to the point in question. He had yesterday endeavoured to prove the Governor had the prerogative of disallowance, and he had heard nothing advanced to the contrary. How can the House send these Resolutions to the Governor? By what organ is —They should act in accordance with that respect and kindness that ought to exist between the two branches. The members ought to keep up the forms. The only way was by an address. The House must go on Friday with their new Speaker. He never heard of Resolutions being sent to the King or his representative in the manner proposed, and he knew not how the Resolutions could be sent to the Governor. The House of Commons, in Sir E. Seymour's case persisted in their choice, and voted an address to the King stating their reasons for persisting. The King replied in the negative, upon which debates took place. The example might here be followed—this was a form, though some members despised form, and thought more of their own understandings than the wisdom of ages. If the House was determined to inform the Governor of their purpose, they must do so by address.

Mr. Quesnel.—If by following the House of Commons, they did it suaviter in modo—they ought to act fortiter in re. The representatives of this country knew their rights and had two methods of sending the Government notice to their intentions—and that was by address or by message.

The reason of Mr. Seymour's disallowance, had been the King's promoting him to a more elevated rank, but the House wished to retain him. If the Governor had stated his intention to make Mr. Papineau Chief Justice, they might still think he was going to serve his country, and act accordingly. But no such offers had been made, and the House must persist in their choice and adopt the Resolutions.

Mr. Christie said, the 1st Resolution was ambiguous and wished Mr. Cuvillier to state whether he would pretend to say the Crown could elect independently of the Sovereign. He hoped he would be precise and explain his views.

Mr. Cuvillier.—The resolution explains itself.

Mr. Borgia addressed the Clerk, but in a voice too low to afford us an opportunity to report. He said, the precedents quoted were during the Reign of Chas. 2d, when liberty was but feeble—during a most stormy period. To the honour of the House of Commons, the proceedings were expunged.

Mr. Ogden moved the previous question, whether the Resolutions would be heard.

Mr. Stuart seconded the motion.

For motion, 4 Against, 30.

The Resolutions were then carried.

Mr. Papineau then took the Chair, and the Mace was put on the table.

Mr. Ogden asked, by what authority Mr. Papineau took the Chair and the Mace was on the table--whether by a new election, or by a perseverance in their former choice.

Several voices, "by former choice."

Mr. Ogden, Stuart, Young, and Christie, immediately left the House.

Mr. vallieres moved an address to the Governor which he said was nearly the same as in Seymour's case, explaining their reasons for persisting.

His Excellency could not refuse accepting the address, as the King had done so in Seymour's case. The King had made certainly a short answer, but still he noticed. Mr. V. moved, that messengers be appointed to carry the address. Messrs. Vallieres, Cuvillier, Bourdages, Letourneau and Papineau, were appointed.

The House adjourned till to-morrow, Friday, at 1. But the House never met again, being prorogued by Proclamation.

NO. IV.

(p. 97.)

Extracts from the Resolutions passed at a General Meeting of the inhabitants of Montreal, 5th December, 1827.

"Resolved,—That among other unconstitutional powers which the House of Assembly has arrogated to itself—the claim set up on a recent occasion to appoint its own Speaker, independently of the allowance, and approval of the King or of His Majesty's Representative, is in the opinion of this Meeting without precedent in the practice of the British Parliament and Colonial Assemblies, and highly dangerous, and subversive of the undoubted and hitherto undisputed rights and prerogatives of the Crown in this Province.

"Resolved,—That in the opinion of this Meeting, His Excellency the Governor in Chief, under such trying and unprecedented circumstances acted with a wisdom and firmness becoming his high character, and with a proper regard to the rights and dignity of His Majesty's Crown, and the welfare of the inhabitants of this Province, in asserting His Majesty's prerogative, and in proroguing the Provincial Parliament, a measure which whatever temporary inconvenience may arise from it, was the only one which his Excellency could consistently adopt without compromising those recognized Rights,—in the maintenance of which the inhabitants of this Province are very deeply interested."

Extract from the Address founded on the above Resolations. presented to His Excellency the Governor id Chief.

"But although we had observed with melancholy presentiments the tendency of the course adopted, which from the defective state of our representation, derived only from the Seignories, was unalterable except by some interposition of the Parent Country (such as occurred to repress the injustice attempted towards Upper Canada,) we were nevertheless not prepared for so sudden an exhibition of the spirit of domination, so haughty a disregard of the Prerogatives of the Crown, and so wanton a violation of the Constitution under which alone they exist, as has been manifested by the Assembly, immediately before the recent prorogation.

"We feel deeply that it has been to the power and prerogatives of the Crown that under Providence we must chiefly ascribe the preservation of those characteristics by which this province can be distinguished as an English Colony. We feel that these prerogatives and power, necessary to good government throughout the British dominions, must be to us in this Province more essential, as constituting our chief refuge in danger, our strong tower of defence against feudal ascendancy, and our sole reliance against anarchy and confusion."

Extract from the Resolutions passed at a similar meeting, held at Three Rivers, December, 1827.

"X. That it is both with sincere and extreme regret this meeting witnessed, shortly after the prorogation of the said twelfth Provincial Parliament, the conduct of several leading members of that Parliament, headed by the Speaker of the House of Assembly, *L. J. Papineau*, Esquire; conduct deserving the highest censure of a free people knowing the bounds of their constitutional rights and privileges, in as much as, by publications and other inflammatory means, addressed to the passions and prejudices of a simple but honest and loyal peasantry, they endeavoured to destroy the wonted respect entertained by the people of the King's Representative in this province, by defaming his personal and parliamentary conduct; being in his latter character alone responsible to parliamentary check and inquiry, and in the former to himself and the laws of his Country.

"XI. That it is with equally deep and sin-vere regret this meeting have witnessed a party, by no means inimical to the views of the same individual, during the late elections and at various other times, endeavouring to establish national and religious distinctions in a Province where it is the interest of all to be united under one King and Government, and where every individual is protected in the worship of his God in the way most approved by his conscience; and where, in one word, priest and people are equally protected in their secular as well as sacerdotal rights and immunities.

"XII. That, therefore, the thanks of this Meeting are in a peculiar menaor due to His Excellency the Governor in Chief for having, at the late Meeting of the first Session of the thirteenth Provincial Parliament, exercised that branch of the royal prorogative, which in common with every other negative power, is so essentially the legislative capacity of the Crown, allows a negative, upon the House of Assembly's choice of Speaker, with respect to the said L. J. Papineau, Esq. an individual who has identified himself with the most unwarrantable breaches upon our Constitution, and the most unjustifiable insults to His Majesty's Crown and dignity, through the person of his noble representative in this Province.

"XIII. That it is with abhorrence and alarm this meeting have heard of the unprecedented assurance of the House of Assembly, last above referred to, in violating the Constitution and the King's just and legal prerogative, in presisting to declare their choice of Speaker absolute, without the approbation of His Majesty's representative, according to the ancient customs of both Imperial and Provincial Parliaments.

XIV. That the thanks and gratitude of this Meeting are also due to His Excellency the Governor in Chief for his constitutional firmness in withstanding so violent an attack upon His Majesty's lawful prerogative."

Extract from the Address, to his Excellency the Governor in Chief, founded on the foregoing resolutions.

"We also complain, that they have refused to admit your Excellency's negative upon their choice of Speaker, and persisted in declaring that choice absolute without the approbation of your Excellency; thus denying an undoubted Prerogative of the Crown and an inherent principle in the Constitution; and that their uniform disregard and contempt of your Excellency's recommendations, even when accompanied by instructions and despatches from his Majesty's Paternal Government, betray a spirit no less destructive of the supremacy of the Mother Country, than hurtful and prejudicial to the true interests of his Majesty's loyal subjects in this Province. We complain, moreover, that a leading and influential party amongst them, untrue to their duty as representatives of a free people, and disregarding that generous spirit of conciliation which should ever characterize the people of this Province, and permanently unite them in one bond of national feeling and sentiment, avail themselves of every means and opportunity to institute civil and religious distinctions for purposes, as unworthy of true partriotism as detrimental to the happiness and prosperity of this part of the British Empire."

Extract *from the Resolutions of the like meeting held at Quebec, 24th December*, 1827.

1. Resolved—That in the opinion of this meeting, it is the well-established prerogative of His Majesty to disallow or confirm the Election of the Speaker of the Assembly of this Province.

2. That, in the opinion of this meeting, the public conduct of the person elected to be the speaker of the Assembly, at the late meeting of the Provincial Parliament afforded sufficient grounds for the disallowance of his Election, and that the exercise of that office by him was incompatible with the good understanding which ought to subsist between the Assembly and the other Branches of the Legislature.

3. That, in the opinion of this meeting, the Assembly by pertinaciously persevering in an election, which, in the exercise of the Royal Prerogative, had been disallowed, rendered the proregation of the Legislature matter of indispensable necessity, and is chargeable with all the public inconvenience and injury consequent on an interruption of the proceedings of the Legislature."

Extract from the Address founded on the above Resolutions.

"We, His Majesty's dutiful and loyal subjects, Inhabitants of the City and vicinity of Quebec, beg leave most respectfully to approach your Excellency for the purpose of expressing the entire satisfaction we have derived from the firm and dignified conduct evinced by your Excellency, on the recent meeting of the Legislature of this Province, in the judicious exercise of the Royal Prerogative, by the disallowance of the Speaker, chosen by the House of Assembly, and in the Prorogation of the House on their subsequent proceedings.

"The Prerogative of His Majesty, to disallow the Election of a Speaker of the House, we maintain to be incontestible and co-ordinate with the right of approval of that choice.

"We deeply regret in common with other of His Majesty's subjects, solicitous for the welfare, peace and Constitutional Government of this part of His Majesty's Dominions, that a sufficient regard for established authority and for the Public Interest was not found in the Majority of the House of Assembly, to have restrained them from their pertinacious perseverance in the Election of the person disallowed by your Lordship; and while we view the interruption of Public Business by the Prorogation of the Legislature as a most serious evil to the Province, we are at the same time fully satisfied that under circumstances, there was no alternative left for your Lordship, on this uncommon and trying occasion."

NO. V.

COURT OF KING'S BENCH.—Quebec.

Chasseur vs. Hamel.

This important case came regularly before the Court on Wednesday last when it was ably argued by the Attorney General, on behalf of the Defendant, the Counsel for the Plaintiff not appearing to support his demurrer:—and on the last day of the Term the Judges proceeded to give judgment as follows:

Chief Justice.—This is an action for a trespass, or voide de fait. The declaration of the plaintiff sets forth that the defendant entered into the plaintiff's house, and seized and sold certain articles of moveable property, belonging to the plaintiff, without any lawful authority so to do; and therefore he prays compensation in damages. The defendant, by an exception peromptoire en droit, justifies the entry, seizure and sale of the property in question, under the authority of a judgment awarded by a Militia Court Martial against the defendant, for a fine of ten shillings incurred under and by virtue of the provisions of the ordinances of the 27th Geo. III. cap. 2, and 29th Geo. III. cap. 4, for a breach of duty. This justification the plaintiff has traversed by a general denegation of the fact and of the law. The cause has been heard upon the pleadings, and the question submitted to us is, whether the justification be a sufficient bar to the action? if the matters of fact stated in the plea be true, and this question turns entirely upon the inquiry whether the Militia Ordinance passed in the 27th and 29th Geo. III. be or be not now in force.

These ordinances were passed by the Governor and Legislative Council, under the Quebec act, before the establishment of the present constitution, and were permanent acts. But by the Provincial Statute 34 Geo. III. cap. 4, they were repealed in these words :—"And be it further en-"acted, that from and after the passing of this "act, an ordinance of the late Province of Quebec, "passed in the 27th year of his Majesty's reign, "intituled, &c. and also an ordinance passed in "the 29th year of his Majesty's reign, intituled, "&c. shall be, and they are hereby repealed," The Provincial Statute 34 Geo. III. c. 4, was not, however, a permanent act : it was a temporary act in consequence of the 35th section which is in these words : "And be it further enacted, by the au-"thority aforesaid, that this act shall be and con-"tinue in force from the passing thereof, until the "first day of July, which will be in the year of our "Lord 1796, and no longer." And from hence has arisen the doubt whether the ordinances repealed by this statute were repealed permanently, or temporarily.

I admit the principle that a temporary act may repeal a permanent statute ; but to effect such a repeal, the intention of the legislature to be so should, in my opinion, be manifest ; for, prima facie, an act which is declared by the legislature generally to be temporary, ought to have no other than a temporary effect. "If," says Mr. Justice Bayley, speaking of the usual clause of continuance in temporary acts, in the case of the King vs. Rogers, (10 East. p. 575) "this act mean the "whole of the act, then there is an end of the "question.—And I consider it as relating to the "whole act ; and after the time limited by the act "for it to have effect, I consider the question the "same as if that act were no longer to be found in "the statute book."

If the present case had stood upon this ground, I should have thought it to be a case in which the intention of the legislature to repeal permanently, was particularly required to be manifest upon the face of the statute; the consequence of a permanent repeal of the ordinances would have been to leave the province, its government, and its inhabitants, without the protection of a Militia, and so far in a defenceless state, in the immediate vicinity of a foreign dominion; and to presume such an intention in the legislature by mere construction, is that which, in my opinion, could not be done.

But the case stands upon batter ground, namely, the construction of the Legislature itself as to the effect of the 34th of Geo. the III. cap. 4. upon the ordinances which is expressed in the subsequent statute of the 43d Geo. III. c. 1. sec. 53. To explain this, I must observe that the 34th Geo. III. c. 4. was continued by the 36th Geo. III. c. 1. sec. 53, to the first of July 1802, and from thence to the end of the then next Session of the Provincial Parliament; both these Statutes, however, were repealed by the 53d section of the 43d Geo. III. and to prevent the operation of the Ordinances of the 27th and 29th Geo. III. which, in consequence of this repeal of the Statutes, would have revived, if their repeal was temporary. They (the ordinances) by the same 53d section, were again repealed during the continuance of the 43d of Geo. III.; and this clearly shews that the previous Statutes and the suspension of the ordinances which they contained, were considered by the Legislature to be co-equal in their duration, and consequently that the original intention of the Legislature was to effect a temporary repeal of the Ordinances and no more. Had it been otherwise, and their original intention had been to effect a permanent repeal, there would have been no necessity for a second repeal.

"It will be admitted that the Legislature is the best interpretor of its own intentions and of its own acts;" and as no alteration has been made in any

Statute subsequent to the 43d Geo. III. which bears upon the question now before us, and the original repeal of the O dinances was temporary and not permanent, we are of opinion that upon the the expiration of the last Statute 5 Geo. III. cap. 21. on the first of May 1827, the Ordinances revived and have since continued to be and still are in force.

KERR, J.—Since this question first came to be mooted, I never entertained the least doubt upon the subject. It is entirely a question of construction that is, whether the probationary statute 34, Geo. III. cap. 4. and the subsequent experimental acts did, or did not, operate a permanent repeal of the Provincial Militia Ordinances? The very preamble of the 34th of the late King shews the anxiety of the Legislature to provide for the protection and security of the Province, and that it is considered a well organized Militia as the best means towards these objects. The words in the preamble are "whereas a respectable Militia, established under proper regulations, is essential to the protection and defence of this Province." The same words are to be found in the next, and, I believe, in every succeeding temporary act relating to the Militia; and are we in the absence of any express enactment to presume that the Legislature intended, by the clause of repeal in these temporary statutes, to withdraw from the Province that protection and security which a Militia is calculated to afford? There is not only an absence of a plain and clear declaration of the intention of the Legislature that these ordinances should be for ever repealed: but a presumption of the strongest kind, derived from the words of the temporary acts to the contrary. There is another circumstance which has very great weight on my mind, derived from the Civil Law of the country. Here the Militia are, in some respects, ministers of justice, adding strength to the civil arm, as well as a military force for its defence; and can we presume that the Legislature should be so wanting to the interest of their fellow-citizens, as to meditate the depriving the civil magistrates of their support! The authority of the King vs. Rogers, is to my mind conclusive, and I am of opinion that judgment should be entered for the Defendants.

BOWEN, J.—I also heartily concur in the result of the opinion just delivered by the learned Judges who have preceded me, although when the revival or non-revival of the Militia Ordinances, first came outlet consideration in another place, where I have the honour to hold a seat, the opinion which I then entertained was different.—This however proceeded from my having over-looked the second repeal of these Ordinances contained in the 53d sec. of the statute 43 Geo. III. c. 1. and having considered the question solely upon the words of repeal as contained in the first statute 34 Geo. III. c. 4. The latter is entitled "An act to provide for "the greater security of this Province by the "better regulation of the Militia thereof, and "for repealing certain Acts or Ordinances "relating to the same." The preamble recites that "a respectable Militia under proper regulations is essential to the protection and defence of this Province and the "laws now in force are inadequate to the "purposes intended." The 31st section then enacts "that from and after the pas-

"sing of this Act—(March 1793.) an Ord-
"inance of the late Province of Quebec,
"passed in the 27th year of his Majesty's
"Reign, entitled "An Ordinance,"* &c.
"and also an Ordinance passed in the 29th
"year of his Majesty's Reign, entitled "An
"Act or Ordinance,† &c. shall be, and
"they are hereby repealed."—And by the 35th section, it is enacted "that this Act "shall be and continue in force from the "passing thereof, until the 1st of July, 1796, "and no longer, provided always that if at "the time above fixed for the expiration of "this Act, the Province shall be in a state "of war, invasion or insurrection, the said "Act shall continue and be in force until the "end of such war, invasion or insurrection." What was the intention of the Legislature in any case, can only be collected from the language used by it in its enactments, and in every such case it becomes a question of construction as to what the Legislature really intended.

It is a clear rule that by the repeal of a repealing Statute, the original Statute is revived, for by so doing the Legislature declares that the repeal shall no longer exist, and it is the same thing if the repealing law itself provide that the repeal shall be only temporary. But it is not true, as has been asserted, that a perpetual law can in one instance be repealed by a temporary one; for it is an undoubted principle in law, that a

*27th Geo. 3. c. 2. †29th Geo. 3. c. 6.

Statute, though temporary in some of its provisions, may have a permanent operation in other respects. This point came under discussion in the Court of King's Bench in England, in 1803,* when the question was whether the Statute 26, Geo. III. c. 108, sec. 27, which repealed the Stat. 19 Geo. II. c. 35, having itself expired at the end of the Session of Parliament, after June 1795, the Stat. 19 Geo. II. did not revive; and Lord Ellenborough in delivering the opinion of the Court expresses himself thus, "that "would not necessarily follow, for a law "though temporary in some of its provisions "may have a permanent operation in other "respects. The Stat. 26 Geo. III. c. 108, "professes to repeal the Stat. 19. Geo. II. "c. 35, absolutely, though its own provis-"ions which it substituted in the place of it "were to be only temporary."

With a view to the construction for which I formerly contended, it may not be altogather unprofitable to compare the words of repeal as contained in the 26th George III. cap. 108, with the words of repeal in our Provincial Statute to which I have already referred,—"and be it further enacted by the "authority aforesaid, that this Act shall "commence and take place upon Monday "the 24th of June 1795, and from thence "to the end of the then next Session of Par-"liament, and that from and after the said "24th July 1786, the said recited Acts of the

*3, East, p. 206, Warren vs. Windle.

" 19th. 23rd. 24th, 31st, 32d Geo. II. and of " the 6th and 21st years of the Reign of " his present Majesty, shall be, and is, and " are hereby repealed." Words of repeal, which according to my construction of them, are in nowise more absolute than those contained in the Provincial Statute 34 Geo. c. 4. The use of the words " this Act" in the foregoing clause, affords an answer to much of the argument founded upon the case of the King vs. Rogers,* which has been relied on as decisive of the question under consideration. That case so far, in my opinion, from over-turning the principle for which I contended, goes directly to strengthen and confirm it. Lord Ellenborough there said " It is a question of construction on every act professing to repeal or interfere with the provisions of a former law, whether it operates as a total or a partial and temporary repeal. Here the question is whether the provisions of the Stat. 42 Geo. III. which was originally perpetual be entirely repealed by the 46th of the King, or only repealed for a limited time. The last Act recites indeed that certain provisions of the former Act should be repealed; but this word is not to be taken in an absolute, if it appear upon the whole Act to be used in a limited sense only." I trust enough has been shewn, were it any longer an open question of construction, or were it necessary to justify the opinion formerly entertain-

*10, East, p. 569.

ed by me of the subject, that the repeal in the Statute of 1793, (34th George III.) was then contemplated as an absolute repeal. But the same Legislature having subsequently in 1803, (and it is upon this ground alone that I yield my former opinion to which I must still have adhered whatever might have been the consequences) taken from me the right to inquire at present what might have been its true intention in 1793 by again repealing the Ordinances in question ; this Legislative interpretation of the clause of repeal in the Statute of 1793, must therefore have the effect to preclude me from putting any other or different interpretation upon the like words of repeal contained in the Statute of 1803 which after being continued by various Statutes was suffered to expire on the 1st May, 1827. The supposed trespass for which the Plaintiff seeks to recover damages from the defendant in the present instance, being acts done in pursuance of the revived Ordinances, I am of opinion with the other Judges that it proved they do, in law, amount to a justification of the Defendant.

Taschereau, J.—This case falls within the principle of the cases cited by the Defendant. It is evident that there was no intention in the Legislature to repeal permanently the Militia Ordinances and that the words and good sense of the several Statutes referred to require that construction. Therefore judgment must be for the Defendant.

NO. VI.

Bill to make further provision towards defraying the Civil Expenditure of the Provincial Government.

Most Gracious Sovereign—WHEREAS, by Message of His Excellency, Sir James Kempt, Knight Grand Cross of the most Honourable Military Order of the Bath, and Administrator of the Government of Lower Canada, bearing date the twenty-eighth day of January, one thousand eight hundred and twenty-nine, laid before both Houses of the Legislature, it appears that the funds already appropriated by law are not adequate to defray the whole expenses of His Majesty's Civil Government of this Province, and of the Administration of Justice and other expenses mentioned in the said Message; and whereas it is expedient to make further provision towards defraying the same for the year commencing one thousand eight hundred and twenty-nine, and ending on the 31st day of December in the same year:—We, your Majesty's most faithful and loyal subjects, the Commons of Lower Canada, in Provincial Parliament assembled, most humbly beseech your Majesty that it may be enacted, and be it therefore enacted, &c; And it is hereby enacted by the authority of the same, that from and out of the unappropriated monies which now are or hereafter shall come into the hands of the Receiver General of the Province for the time being, there shall be supplied and paid towards defraying the expenses of the Administration of Justice and of the support of the Civil Government in this Province, for the year commencing on the 1st day of January, 1829, and ending on the 31st day of December in the same year, such sum or sums of money as together with the monies already appropriated by law for the said purpose, shall amount to a sum not exceeding £54,542. 2s. 6d. sterling.

II. And be it further enacted by the authority aforesaid, that the due application of the monies by this act appropriated, shall be accounted for to his Majesty, his Heirs and Successors, through the Lords Commissioners of his Majesty's treasury for the time being, in such manner and form as his Majesty, his Heirs and Successors shall be pleased to direct.

III. And be it further enacted by the authority aforesaid, that a detailed account of the monies expended under the authority of this act, shall be laid before the Assembly of this Province, during the first fifteen days of the next Session of the Provincial Parliament.

NO. VII.

An Act to make further provision towards defraying the Civil Expenditure of the Provincial Government.

22d March, 1825.

Most Gracious Sovereign,—Whereas by Message of his Excellency the Lieutenant

Governor, bearing date the eighteenth day of February, one thousand eight hundred and twenty five, laid before both Houses of the Legislature, it appears that the funds already appropriated by law are not adequate to defray the whole of the expenses of your Majesty's Civil Government in this Province, and of the administration of Justice, and other expenses mentioned in the said Message; and whereas it is expedient to make further provision towards defraying the same for the year commencing the first day of November, one thousand eight hundred and twenty-four, and ending the thirty-first day of October, one thousand eight hundred and twenty-five; We, your Majesty's most dutiful and loyal subjects, the Commons of Lower-Canada in Provincial Parliament assembled, most humbly beseech your Majesty, that it may be enacted, and be it enacted by the King's most Excellent Majesty, by and with the advice and consent of the Legislative Council and Assembly of the Province of Lower-Canada, constituted and assembled by virtue of and under the authority of an Act passed in the Parliament of Great-Britain, intitled, "An Act to repeal certain parts of an Act passed in the fourteenth year of his Majesty's Reign, entitled, "An Act for making more effectual provision for the Government of the Province of Quebec, in North America, and to make further provision for the Government of the said Province;" And it is hereby enacted by the authority of the same, that in addition to the revenues appropriated for defraying the expenses of the administration of Justice, and for the support of the Civil Government of the Province, there shall be supplied and paid from and out of the unappropriated monies which now are, or hereafter may come into the hands of the Receiver General of the Province for the time being, such sum or sums as may be necessary to make up and complete a sum not exceeding fifty eight thousand and seventy-four pounds, two shillings and eleven pence, sterling, for the purpose of defraying the said expenses of the civil Government of this Province, and of the administration of justice therein, and the other expenses of the said year commencing the first day of November, one thousand eight hundred and twenty-four, and ending the thirty-first day of October, one thousand eight hundred and twenty-five, not including the sum or sums by Law provided for the support of wounded or disabled Militia-men, nor the appropriations made by the Acts passed in the third year of his Majesty's reign, chapters third and thirty-ninth.

II. And be it further enacted by the authority aforesaid, that the due application of the monies by this Act appropriated, shall be accounted for to his Majesty, his Heirs and Successors, through the Lords Commissioners of his Majesty's Treasury for the time being, in such manner and form, as his Majesty, his Heirs and Successors shall be pleased to direct.

III. And be it further enacted by the authority aforesaid that a detailed account of the monies expended under the authority of this act, shall be laid before the Legislature during the first fifteen days of the nest session.

NO. VIII.

House of Assembly, November 28, 1828.

F C. Yorke, Esq. Secretary to the Administrator of the Government, presented a Message from his Excellency, which was read by Mr. Speaker.

James Kempt,—His Excellency the Administrator of the Government avails himself of the earliest opportunity of conveying to the House of Assembly, the following Communication, which he has received the King's Commands to make, to the Provincial Parliament.

In laying the same before the House of Assembly, his Excellency is commanded by his Majesty to state, that, his Majesty has received too many proofs of the loyalty and attachment of his Canadian Subjects, to doubt their cheerful acquiescence in every effort which his Majesty's Government shall make to reconcile past differences, and he looks forward with hope to a period, when, by the return of hermony, all branches of the Legislature will be able to bestow their undivided attention on the best methods of advancing the prosperity and developing the resources of the extensive and valuable Territories comprised within his Majesty's Canadian Provinces.

With a view to the adjustment of the questions in controversy, his Majesty's Government has communicated to his Excellency Sir James Kempt, its views on different branches of this important subject; but as the complete settlement of the affairs of the Province cannot be effected but with the aid of the Imperial Parliament, the Instructions of his Excellency are at present confined to the discussion of those points alone, which can no longer be left undecided without extreme disadvantage to the interests of the Province.

Among the most material of those points, the first to be adverted to, is, the proper disposal of the Financial Resources of the country; and with the view of obviating all future misunderstanding on this matter, his Majesty's Government have prescribed to his Excellency, the limits within which his communications to the Legislature on this matter, are to be confined.

His Excellency is commanded by his Majesty, to acquaint the House of Assembly that the discussions which have occurred for some years past, between the different branches of the Legislature of this Province, respecting the appropriation of the Revenue, have engaged his Majesty's serious attention, and that he has directed careful inquiry to be made, in what manner these questions may be finally adjusted with a due regard to the Prerogative of the Crown, as well as to their Constitutional Privileges, and to the general welfare of his faithful subjects, in Lower Canada.

£25,500 5,000 4,200 ——— £34,700 ———	His Excellency is further commanded to state, that the Statutes passed in the 14th and 31st years of the Reign of his late Majesty, have imposed upon the Lords Commissioners of his Majesty's Treasury, the duty of appropriating the

produce of the Revenue granted to his Majesty by the first of these Statutes; and that, whilst the law shall continue unaltered by the same authority by which it was framed, his Majesty is not authorised to place the Revenue under the control of the Legislature of this Province.

14th Geo. III. 35th Geo. III. 41st Geo. III.	The proceeds of the Revenue arising from the Act of the Imperial Parliament 14th Geo. III. to-

gether with the sum appropriated by the Provincial Statute 35th Geo. III. and the duties levied under the Provincial Statutes 41st Geo. III. cap. 13 and 14, may be estimated for the current year, at the sum of *l*.34,700.

Casual Revenue, *l*.3,000		The produce of the Casual and Territorial Revenue of the Crown, and of Fines and Forfeitures, may be estimated for the same period, at the sum of *l*.3,400.
Fines, &c. - - - - -	400	
	l.3,400	

These several sums making together the sum of *l*.38,100, constitute the whole estimated Revenue, arising in this Province which the Law has placed at the disposal of the Crown.

His Majesty has been pleased to direct that from this Collective Revenue of *l*.38,100, the salary of the Officers administering the Government of the Province, and the salaries of the Judges shall be defrayed. But his Majesty being graciously disposed to mark, in the strongest manner, the confidence which he reposes in the liberality and affection of his faithful Provincial Parliament, has been pleased to command his Excellency to announce to the House of Assembly that no farther appropriation of any part of this Revenue will be made until his Excellency shall have been enabled to become acquainted with their sentiments, as to the most advantageous mode in which it can be applied to the public service; and it will be gratifying to his Majesty, if the recommendation made to the Executive Government of the Province on this subject shall be such as it may be able with propriety, and with due attention to the interest and the efficiency of his Majesty's Government to adopt.

His Majesty fully relies upon the liberality of his faithful Provincial Parliament to make such further provision as the exigencies of the Public

Service of the Province (for which the amount of the Crown Revenues above mentioned may prove inadequate) may require.

The balance of money in the hands of the Receiver General, which is not placed by law at the disposal of the Crown, must await the appropriation which it may be the pleasure of the Provincial Legislature to make.

His Excellency is further commanded by his Majesty to recommend to the House of Assembly, the enactment of a law, for the indemnity of any Persons who have heretofore, without authority, signed or acted in obedience to warrants for the appropriation to the public service of any unappropriated monies of this Province. And his Majesty anticipates that they will, by an acquiescence in this recommendation, show that they cheerfully concur with him in the efforts which he is now making for the establishment of a permanent good understanding, between the different branches of the Executive and Legislative Government.

The proposals which his Excellency has been thus instructed to make for the adjustment of the pecuniary affairs of the Province, are intended to meet the difficulties of the ensuing year, and he trusts they may be found effectual for that purpose.

His Majesty has, however, further commanded his Excellency to acquaint the House of Assembly, that a scheme for the permanent settlement of the Financial concerns of Lower Canada, is in contemplation, and his Majesty entertains no doubt of such a result being attainable as will prove conducive to the general welfare of the Province, and satisfactory to his faithful Canadian Subjects.

The complaints which have reached his Majesty's Government respecting the inadequate security heretofore given by the Receiver General and by the Sheriffs, for the due application of the Public Monies in their hands have not escaped the very serious attention of the Ministers of the Crown.

It has appeared to his Majesty's Government, that the most effectual security against abuses in these departments, would be found in enforcing in this Province, a strict adherence to a system established under his Majesty's instructions, in other Colonies, for preventing the accumulation of balances in the hands of Public Accountants, by obliging them to exhibit their accounts to a competent authority at short intervals, and immediately to pay over the ascertained balance into a safe place of deposit;—and in order to obviate the difficulty arising from the want of such place of deposit in Lower Canada, his Excellency is authorised to state that the Lords Commissioners of his Majesty's Treasury will hold themselves responsible to the Province for any sums which the Receiver General or Sheriffs may pay over to the Commissary General, and his Excellency is instructed to propose to the House of Assembly, the enactment of a law, binding those officers to pay over to the Commissary General such balances as, upon rendering their accounts to the competent authority, shall appear to be remaining in their hands, over and above what may be required for the current demands upon their respective offices;—such payments being made on condition that the Commissary General shall be bound on demand to deliver Bills on his Majesty's Treasury for the amount of his receipts.

His Excellency is further instructed to acquaint the House of Assembly, that although it was found necessary by an Act passed in the last session of the Imperial Parliament, 9th Geo. IV. cap. 76, sec. 26, to set at rest doubts which had arisen whether the statute for regulating the distribution between the Provinces of Upper and Lower Canada, of the duties of customs collected at Quebec, had not been inadvertently repealed by the general terms of a late date: his Majesty's Government have no desire that the interference of Parliament in this matter should be perpetuated, if the Provincial Legislatures can themselves agree upon any thing for a division of these duties which may appear to be more convenient and more equitable; and on the whole of this subject, his Majesty's Government will be happy to receive such information and assistance as the Legislative Council and Assembly of this Province may be able to supply.

The appointment of an Agent in England to indicate the wishes of the Inhabitants of Lower Canada, appearing to be an object of great solicitude with the Assembly, his Majesty's Government will cheerfully accede to the desire expressed by the House of Assembly upon this head; provided, that such Agent be appointed, as in other British Colonies, by name in an Act to be passed by the Legislative Council and Assembly, and approved by the Executive Government of the Province; And his Majesty's Government are pursued-ed that the Legislature will not make such a selection, as to impose on the Government, the painful and invidious duty of rejecting the Bill on the ground of any personal objection to the proposed Agent.

His Majesty's Government is further willing to consent to the abolition of the Office of Agent as it is at present constituted, but it is trusted that the liberality of the House of Assembly will indamnify the present holder of this Office, to whose conduct in that capacity no objection appears ever to have been made. Indeed, without some adequate indemnity being provided for him, it would not be compatible with justice, to consent to the immediate abolition of his Office.

His Majesty's Government being very sensible of the great inconvenience which had been sustained, owing to the large tracts of lands which have been suffered to remain in a waste and unimproved condition, in consequence of the neglect or the poverty of the grantees, it has appeered to his Majesty's Government to be desirable that the laws in force in Upper Canada, for levying a Tax upon wild land, on which the settlement Duties had not been performed, should be adopted in this Province, and his Excellency is instructed to press this subject on the attention of the House of Assembly with that view.

The attention of his Majesty's Government has also been drawn to several other important Topics; among which may be enumerated, the mischiefs which are said to result from the system of tacit mortages effected by general acknowledgment of a debt before a Notary; the objectionable and expensive forms of conveyancing said to be in use in the Townships; the necessity of a Registration of Deeds; and the want of proper Courts for the decision of causes arising in the Townships.—Regulations affecting matters of this nature can obviously be most effectually made by the Provincial Legislature; and his Excellency is commanded to draw the attention of the House of Assembly to these subjects, as matters requiring their early and most serious attention.

In conclusion, his Excellency has been commanded to state, that his Majesty relies for an amicable adjustment of the variaus questions which have been so long in dispute, upon the loyalty and attachment hitherto evinced by his Majesty's Canadian subjects, and on that of the Provincial Parliament; and that his Majesty entertains no doubts of the cordial concurrence of the House of Assembly in all measures calculated to promote the common good, in whatever quarter such measures may happen to originate.

NO. IX.

Protests against the passing of the Supply Bill, for 1829.

Dissentient.—1. Because His Excellency the Administrator has asked of the Assembly a sum not exceeding £24,028 10 9 in aid of the Revenue at the disposal of the Crown, and that body had passed a Bill of aid and supply, whereby the whole permanent Revenue is mixed and blended with unappropriated monies and though ostensibly a much larger sum than £24028 is thereby given, yet in point of fact the Assembly has granted for the limited space of one year no larger sum than £16,342 2 6 in aid of the permanent Revenue at the disposal of his Majesty.

2. Because, whatever may appear to be the obvious construction of the trends of this Bill, the Assembly having used the same words in an Act which passed the Legislature in the year 1825, which received an exposition, according to what was conceived to be the intention of the Assembly, and whereby some of the Public Servants, who had been long paid from the permanent Revenues were deprived of their salaries, it cannot now be presumed that any other interpretation will be put on this Bill than that which was given to the Act of the year 1825.

3. Because, by this Bill the Assembly assumes to itself a right of disposing of a revenue exceeding £38,000 per annum, arising as well from the Britishp Statute, 14 Geo. III. as the Provincial Statutes 35 Geo. III.

and 41 Geo. III. as the hereditary Revenues of the Crown, which are at the exclusive disposal of his Majesty for the maintenance of his Government and the due administration of the law.

4. Because, the Assembly in its frequent attempts to obtain the disposal and management of these Revenues, is deeply impressed with an opinion that its authority and influence will be increased in the same proportion as the authority of the Crown in this Province will be thereby circumscribed.

5. Because, the Assembly has thus in part achieved its plan of wresting from the Crown the means to carry into effect its agreements with tile Public Servants, who are engaged to serve during their lives or good behaviour.

6. Because if the practice now attempted to pass annual Bills of a similar nature should prevail, all the officers of Government will thereby become dependents on the Assembly, subject at the end of twelve months to be deprived of their salaries, as the pleasure or caprice of that body may dictate.

7. Because by the operation of this Bill the incomes of twenty-eight Public Servants who are not, considering the labour and responsibility attached to their offices, adequately paid, will be diminished and some of whom, after years of Public Service be deprived of a livelihood.

8. Because it has been quaintly said that "certainty is the mother of quiet and repose." and, persisting to grant the salaries of all the officers of the Civil Government in

an Annual Act, the Assembly will perpetuate that disquietude, which this Province has unhappily laboured under for many years.

9. Because if the entire disposal of the permanent Revenue of the Crown should be resigned to the Assembly, the Legislative Power will thereby obtain means to obstruct the operations of the Executive Government at the conclusion of every succeeding year.

Lastly, Because the words of the third clause namely, "a detailed account of the monies expended under the authority of this Act shall be laid before the Assembly" are a departure from the ancient and accustomed similar clause, which has heretofore invariably provided that such account should be rendered to both Houses of the Provincial Legislature, and a clause so conceived is therefore an infringement on the rights and privileges of this House.

T. Coffin, Edwd. Bowen, J. Kerr, J. Stewart, W. B. Felton, Matthew Bell.

Dissentient.—For the above reasons and also because in our opinions this House ought not to concur in a Bill to which the King's Representative cannot assent without sacrificing the rights of his Majesty, to distribute the Revenue at the disposal of the Crown, and this House has no assurance that his Majesty has consented to waive the exercise of that right, but on the contrary there exists on the Journals of this House sufficient evidence to prove that his Majesty's instructions to his representative in this Province probibit him from giving the Royal assent to a similar Act.

Because the Bill contains a clause which is unusual, unconstitutional and destructive of the rights of this House.

W. B. Felton, Matthew Bell, Edwd. Bowen.

Dissentient.—1. Because this Bill contains a clause which is unusual, unconstitutional, and destructive of the rights of this House.

2. Because the decision of the House as shewn by the division on the question, was against the passing of the Bill; the non-contents being eight in number and the contents seven, exclusive of the Speaker, and the questions having been carried in the affirmative only by the Speaker in the chair giving a vote as a member and then as his casting vote, a practice which is at variance with the usage of the Imperial Parliament, and in our opinion is not authorised by the Act 31 Geo. III. cap. 31, which gives the Speaker of the Legislative Council and Assembly, only a casting vote.

W. B. Felton, J. Kerr, Matthew Bell, Thos. Coffin, Edwd. Bowen, John Stewart.

Lightning Source UK Ltd.
Milton Keynes UK
UKHW012246110219
337137UK00006B/945/P

9 780331 213799